FabJob Guide to

Become an Interior Decorator

TAG GOULET AND CATHERINE GOULET

FABJOB® GUIDE TO BECOME AN INTERIOR DECORATOR
by Tag Goulet and Catherine Goulet

ISBN: 978-1-897286-74-6

Library and Archives Canada Cataloguing in Publication

Goulet, Therese, 1959-
FabJob Guide to become an interior decorator /
Tag Goulet and Catherine Goulet.

Accompanied by a CD-ROM.
Includes bibliographical references.
ISBN: 978-1-897286-74-6

1. Interior decoration—Vocational guidance. 2. Interior decoration.
I. Goulet, Catherine, 1961- II. Title.

NK2116.G69 2010   747.023   C2010-906211-6

Important Disclaimer: Although every effort has been made to ensure this guide is free from errors, this publication is sold with the understanding that the authors, editors, and publisher are not responsible for the results of any action taken on the basis of information in this work, nor for any errors or omissions. The publishers, and the authors and editors, expressly disclaim all and any liability to any person, whether a purchaser of this publication or not, in respect of anything and of the consequences of anything done or omitted to be done by any such person in reliance, whether whole or partial, upon the whole or any part of the contents of this publication. If expert advice is required, services of a competent professional person should be sought.

About the Websites Mentioned in this Guide: Although we aim to provide the information you need within the guide, we have also included a number of websites because readers have told us they appreciate knowing about sources of additional information. (TIP: Don't include a period at the end of a web address when you type it into your browser.) Due to the constant development of the Internet, websites can change. Any websites mentioned in this guide are included for the convenience of readers only. We are not responsible for the content of any sites except FabJob.com.

FabJob Inc.
19 Horizon View Court
Calgary, Alberta, Canada T3Z 3M5

FabJob Inc.
4616 25th Avenue NE, #224
Seattle, Washington, USA 98105

To order books in bulk phone 403-949-2039
To arrange a media interview phone 403-949-4980

www.FabJob.com

PRINTED IN CANADA

Contents

About the Authors

Sisters Tag (seated in photo) and Catherine Goulet are the founders of FabJob Inc., an award-winning publisher of career books. As leading experts on how to break into a dream career, Tag and Catherine's career articles have been published at top sites including AOL, CNN and Microsoft's MSN, and have appeared in newspapers in the United States, Canada, and Europe. Their own website, FabJob.com, has been visited by more than 50 million people.

Tag and Catherine have written and contributed to more than a dozen books, including a *USA Today* bestseller, and are authors of the bestseller *Dream Careers*. The sisters have been featured in many media including ABC, Oprah.com, *Woman's Day*, *Female Entrepreneur*, and news stories at the *Wall Street Journal* and *Entrepreneur Magazine* sites.

For the *FabJob Guide to Become an Interior Decorator*, they interviewed successful interior decorators and interior design experts who share their insider advice for getting started and succeeding as a professional interior decorator.

Acknowledgements

Thank you to the many interior decorating and design experts who have generously shared their knowledge in the creation of this FabJob guide including the following professionals who are listed alphabetically: Lynn Donaldson, Kennedy Lightle, Susan Mielke, Jan L. Riddell, Sallie M. Ritchey, Debbie Travis, and Frederick Udey. Thanks also to Homestore, Inc. and Erin K. Campbell, for allowing us to reprint some of their decorating tips.

Thank you to the following interior decorators and interior designers for generously sharing some of their fabulous work in the color section of this book:

- *Barbara Green*
  Sensibly Chic Interior Design
  Cornelius, North Carolina
  www.sensiblychic.biz

- *William Green*
  William Green & Associates
  New York, New York
  www.wgaarchitects.net

- *Keith Lichtman*
  KL Interiors
  New York, New York
  www.KL-Interiors.com

- *Bobbie Lyons*
  Affordable Elegance
  Room Design, LLC
  Stamford, Connecticut
  www.affordableelegance roomdesign.com

- *Gail Mayhugh*
  GMJ Interiors, LLC and
  author of *A Decorating 10!*
  Las Vegas, Nevada
  www.GMJinteriors.com

- *Jeanine Naviaux*
  On The Inside Design
  La Jolla, California
  www.ontheinsidedesign.com

- *Sallie M. Ritchey, D.I.D.*
  A Decorative Touch
  at the Centre for
  Decorators & Designs
  Calgary, Alberta

- *Judson Rothschild*
  Rothschild Interiors
  Beverly Hills, California
  www.Rothschild Interiors.com

- *Marlaina Teich*
  Marlaina Teich Designs
  Merrick, New York
  www.MTDNY.com

Thank you also to the photographers whose work appears in this book, including Everett Fenton Gidley (**www.efg3.com**), Oleg March (**www. marchphoto.com**) and David Watt (**www.davidwattphotography.com**).

Thank you to Dave Brandt, Emily Courtney, Peter Cyngot, Jennifer James, John McDougall, Wendy McDonald, Brenna Pearce, and Kimberly M. Stone for their assistance in the production of this book.

Opinions expressed in this guide are those of the authors and not necessarily those of individuals interviewed for the guide.

1. Introduction

"A great decorator doesn't just 'decorate.' A great decorator has to be a true Artist of Life. They must create a home for the client that is a place they feel they can go to retreat from the world, a place they can live comfortably, and safely, a haven closest to heaven."

> − Susan Mielke,
> Susan J. Mielke Designs, Minneapolis

As an interior decorator you will have an exciting and rewarding career that lets you use your creativity to enhance people's lives.

Years ago, a famous psychologist named Abraham Maslow published a book titled *Motivation and Personality* which explains what humans need to have healthy and full lives. According to Maslow's "Hierarchy of Needs," once our basic needs for physical and emotional well-being are fulfilled (for example, once we have food, water, and security), we become concerned with "higher" needs. Among these higher needs are "aesthetic needs"—an appreciation and desire for beauty and order.

As an interior decorator, you will help people to achieve this important need. You will bring beauty, comfort and order into people's lives. You will discover how to get started and succeed in this fabulous career in the *FabJob Guide to Become an Interior Decorator.*

This chapter lays the foundation for the rest of the guide. In the pages that follow, you will learn some significant differences between interior decorating and interior design (and why interior decorating is the best career choice if you want to get started as quickly and easily as possible), read about the many benefits of the career, and discover the steps you will need to take to get started.

1.1   Interior Decorating vs. Interior Design

If you have been searching for information about interior decorating as a career, you have almost certainly come across the term *interior design*. While there are some similarities between the two careers, there are also some significant differences. It is important to know these differences because they have a direct impact on the types of jobs you can apply for. Here is a basic overview of the two careers:

Interior Decorator

Just as the job title says, an interior decorator decorates (or redecorates) interiors of buildings, with the aim of making rooms more attractive, comfortable and functional. Most interior decorators are hired to decorate homes, but they may also be hired to decorate the interiors of businesses such as boutiques, restaurants, and offices. They may work on the entire interior of a building or just a single room.

An interior decorator's work may involve a variety of design and room elements, including:

- space planning or "layout"

- color schemes
- furniture
- paint and wallpaper
- window coverings
- fabrics
- flooring and carpeting
- lighting
- art objects
- hardware fixtures
- accessories (e.g. vases, cushions, bookends)
- plants

A decorating job may be as simple as rearranging furniture yourself, or it may involve hiring and supervising contractors. As an interior decorator your tasks may include:

- meeting with clients to determine their wants and needs
- reviewing and taking measurements of the space you will be decorating
- preparing proposed room layouts
- obtaining cost estimates
- showing samples (e.g. colors, fabrics, tiles) to clients
- scheduling the work to be done
- arranging and overseeing painting, wallpapering, flooring, etc.
- shopping for and placing orders for furnishings and other items
- coordinating deliveries
- ensuring the decorating plan is put into action and runs smoothly until completion.

There are no formal educational requirements to enter this career. You can start calling yourself an interior decorator as soon as you start doing interior decorating.

This guide will tell you how to get started and succeed as an interior decorator. You will find resources to teach yourself any parts of the job you are not familiar with, information on how to get hired for a full-time job, and advice on how to start your own interior decorating business.

Interior Designer

While anyone can become an interior decorator, it is considerably more difficult to become a certified interior designer. Professional standards for the interior design profession are set by organizations such as the American Society of Interior Designers or the Interior Designers of Canada.

In both the U.S. and Canada, interior designers are certified through the National Council for Interior Design Qualification (NCIDQ) after passing an examination. To be eligible to write the examination, you must have an acceptable combination of full-time work experience and two to five years of post-secondary education in interior design. More information can be found at **www.ncidq.org**, or by calling NCIDQ at 202-721-0220 (Washington, D.C.).

While some people who call themselves interior designers are not certified, it is illegal in 18 states to call yourself an interior designer unless you are licensed.

You are probably wondering why it is so much more difficult to become an interior designer than an interior decorator. The reason is because interior design involves much more than decorating.

According to the official definition endorsed by the NCIDQ and the Council for Interior Design Accreditation (CIDA), "the interior design process follows a systematic and coordinated methodology, including research, analysis and integration of knowledge into the creative process." As a result of their education and experience, interior designers are qualified to "protect and enhance the life, health, safety and welfare of the public." Obviously this goes well beyond making an interior look more attractive!

Interior designers may work on a wide variety of interiors, such as office buildings, airport terminals, hospitals, manufacturing plants, government institutions, and many other types of buildings.

To do their job properly, interior designers must be educated in a number of areas. To quote from the official definition, the skills they need include:

- Research and analysis of the client's goals and requirements

- Development of documents, drawings and diagrams that outline clients' needs

- Ensuring that preliminary space plans and design concepts are safe, functional, aesthetically appropriate, and meet all public health, safety and welfare requirements, including construction code guidelines

- Coordination and collaboration with other allied design professionals who may be retained to provide consulting services, including but not limited to architects, structural, mechanical and electrical engineers, and various specialty consultants

In addition, their work can include interior decorating tasks such as the selection of furnishings, fixtures, and lighting. You can find the complete definition of an interior designer at the NCIDQ website at **www.ncidq. org/AboutUs/AboutInteriorDesign/DefinitionofInteriorDesign. aspx**.

Your Career

As you can see, the two careers are similar because they focus on improving interiors. A number of people who become interior designers also do interior decorating (the part of the job some find the most fun and interesting). In case you decide that you would like to become an interior designer, Chapter 2 contains information about interior design educational programs.

However, many people who want a career decorating homes or businesses do not want to become an interior designer. They may have thoughts similar to the following:

"Interior design doesn't sound like what I want to do. I don't want to have to spend years studying, worry about things like building codes, and write an examination to be certified. Can't I just start decorating people's houses without going through all that?"

The answer, of course, is "yes!" While some jobs clearly require the services of an interior designer (e.g. upgrading the interior of an airport terminal), there are many opportunities open to interior decorators. For example, if you want to start an interior decorating business, you can offer your services to the many people who want their home to be more attractive, but simply do not have the time or the skill to do it themselves.

As you will discover later in this guide, your services can benefit many people. In return, you can enjoy many benefits of this fabulous job.

1.2   Benefits of Being an Interior Decorator

As an interior decorator you will enjoy a career with tremendous benefits, including:

Exciting Work

As an interior decorator you will have an opportunity to do work that is fun and interesting. (Actually, "work" probably isn't the best term to use. Confucius is reported to have said: "If you enjoy what you do, you will never work another day in your life.") The career also offers plenty of variety. Chances are, no two jobs you work on will be exactly the same, and each one will give you an opportunity to learn and grow.

Personal Fulfillment

A job as an interior decorator allows you to use your creativity and other talents. This career also allows you to see the results of your efforts and have the satisfaction of making a design vision (yours and your client's) a reality.

Opportunities

The decorating business is a multi-billion dollar per year industry experiencing steady growth. According to Faith Popcorn, an expert in consumer trends, "Time is the new money: people would rather spend money than time." Rather than doing it themselves, more people are hiring interior decorators to beautify their homes.

People

You will likely meet and interact with a variety of interesting and successful people. Many of the people who hire interior decorators are wealthy, so you will spend time in many beautiful homes. Your work may also benefit other busy people who will appreciate your help in making their surroundings more attractive, functional, and comfortable.

Income

As an interior decorator, you can earn a comfortable living. If you start your own interior decorating business you could earn $100,000 or more per year. You will also get significant discounts on decorating materials you purchase.

Freedom

If you start your own interior decorating business, you will enjoy the freedom of being your own boss and choosing your own hours. You can also work on jobs that interest you and turn down work you don't want.

You Can Start Now

The interior decorating business is one that almost anyone can enter. No special education, experience, or connections are needed to get started and succeed. (As you will see, this guide will show you how to educate yourself, get experience, and make those important career connections.)

If any of these benefits interest you, read on to find out how this guide will help you break into interior decorating.

1.3   Inside This Guide

The *FabJob Guide to Become an Interior Decorator* is arranged to take you step-by-step through getting started and succeeding as an interior decorator. These steps, and the chapters they appear in, are as follows:

Chapter 2, *Getting Ready,* covers important preliminary steps to prepare you to become an interior decorator. Here you will discover the skills employers and clients are looking for, what you need to know about decorating, the best resources for learning interior decorating, and how to get decorating experience.

Chapter 3 offers tips on *How To Decorate.* You will learn some tools and tricks of the trade, including design and room elements. This chapter will also offer you step-by-step instructions on decorating and will give you some tips from the experts.

Chapter 4 focuses on *Getting Hired.* If you want the security of a full-time job, this chapter will give you information to help you land that job. You will discover who hires interior decorators, how to find out about job openings, how to prepare a portfolio and resume, and how to do well in an interview.

If you would like to *Start Your Own Business,* you will find some good advice in Chapter 5. You will find practical information on setting up your office. You will also learn how to set your rates, how to attract clients, and how to get discounts on furniture and materials. The information in this chapter alone could save you thousands of dollars.

Chapter 6, *Working With Clients,* will prepare you to do client consultations. You will learn to identify what your clients want, sell your services, and prepare decorating plans, design boards, budgets and contracts.

Included with this guide are many helpful samples, including forms and checklists you can use in your own decorating business. When you're finished with this guide you will know what steps to take next and where to go from there. By applying what you learn here, it's just a matter of time before you'll be where you want to be... in an exciting career as an Interior Decorator!

2. Getting Ready

Before you start applying for jobs or looking for clients, it's a good idea to take some preliminary steps to prepare yourself for an interior decorating career. By following the advice in this chapter, you could make yourself much more attractive to prospective employers and clients. In the pages that follow, you will discover how to develop essential skills and learn interior decorating.

Let's start by looking at how much you already have going for you...

2.1 Are You a "Born Decorator"?

Interior decorators need to use a variety of skills to do their job well. As you will read in this chapter, all the skills you need to succeed as an interior decorator can be learned. However, if you are a "born decorator" – in other words, if you already have a natural aptitude for decorating – entering this career will be even easier for you.

Here are a couple of ways to determine if you already have the basic skills you will need, or if you will need to brush up on them.

Signs of Decorating Talent

If you are a "born decorator" you likely have already demonstrated your ability in a number of ways. See how many of the following are true for you:

❑ You love to redecorate your own home. You may get the urge to rearrange the furniture even when other family members think it looks "just fine."

❑ You appreciate beauty — in art, in people, in nature, or in things.

❑ When you visit someone's house for the first time you notice ways they could make their home more attractive, functional, or comfortable. (Although you don't necessarily tell them unless they ask!)

❑ You are artistic or creative.

❑ If you belong to a social club, you are the one people turn to when they want decorations done for an event.

❑ You have a strong sense of the best placement for things within a particular space.

❑ Friends compliment you about how beautifully your home is decorated and may ask for your advice about how to decorate their own.

There is a common theme running through the above list. The most important trait for a decorator to have is a strong aesthetic sense--—also known as a "good eye." This comes naturally to some people, while others have to work to develop it. In this guide you will learn how to develop and improve this vital trait.

Personality Type

In addition to having a good eye, interior decorators typically have a number of other skills. The most important of these are interpersonal skills. A successful decorator must be an effective communicator in order to attract clients and develop relationships with suppliers (companies that supply decorating materials such as furniture, fabrics, etc.). Decorators who are skilled at reading people and negotiating can be tremendously successful.

These skills are typical of people with certain "personality types," as defined by the Myers-Briggs Type Indicator. A renowned system for measuring personality types, the MBTI looks at four dimensions of personality:

- Extraversion (E) vs. Introversion (I)

- Sensing (S) vs. Intuition (N)

- Thinking (T) vs. Feeling (F)

- Judging (J) vs. Perceiving (P)

You can come up with a four-letter "personality type" by determining your preferences for each of these four dimensions. Here are a few very basic examples, with the letters in brackets indicating what personality dimension each trait corresponds with.

- "Are you more extraverted (E) or more introverted (I)?"

- "Do you tend to trust your intuition (N) or trust what you see and hear (S)?"

- "Do you focus more on thoughts (T) or feelings (F)?"

- "Do you prefer life to be more structured (J) or more spontaneous (P)?"

You can take a quick quiz online to learn your personality type at **www.personalitytype.com/quiz.asp**. Out of the 16 possible personality types, one that is particularly well-suited to interior decorating is ENFP (Extraverted iNtuitive Feeling Perceiving), but it is important to remember that all kinds of people can and do succeed in this career. While someone with an ENFP or a similar personality type may be more naturally inclined to use skills such as persuasive communication, reading people, and negotiating, these skills can be developed by any personality type.

For example, someone who is an ISFJ type can do well in interior decorating because they have a natural aptitude for a very different type of skill needed by interior decorators—organizational ability. Again, this is a skill that can be learned using resources you will find in the next section of this guide.

2.2   Developing Your Skills

2.2.1   Training Your Eye

Since you are interested in a career as an interior decorator, chances are you already have a "good eye" for design. In other words, when you look at a room you can see what looks good and what could be improved.

No matter how naturally talented you are, you can continually "train your eye" and further develop your design skills. The best way to train your eye is to study what people consider to be good design. Seek out beautifully decorated interiors to look at. You can find numerous examples of beautiful interiors in the magazines, websites and other resources provided in section 2.3 of this guide (*"Teaching Yourself Interior Decorating"*).

To really train your eye, you will need to do more than simply look at designs. When you see a room, or a photo of a room, spend some time analyzing what you see.

First, notice the overall impression you have of the entire area you can see. Then start asking yourself questions. How does it make you feel? Does everything in the room work well together? What grabs your attention? Don't stop with the first answer that pops into your head. No matter what your response to each question, ask yourself "Why?"

Then notice the individual components—including the colors, textures, and how each element in the room is physically arranged. Once again, ask yourself questions. Why do you think the decorator made those particular choices? What changes would you make? Why?

You can find more exercises and questions to ask yourself at **www.sheffield. edu/htmlsrc/2eye.html**. It is a free excerpt from the "Eye of the Designer" lesson offered by the Sheffield School of Interior Design.

2.2.2 Interpersonal Skills

As an interior decorator, you will not just be working with things, you will also be working with people. In fact, good interpersonal skills can ensure you have many opportunities to do what you love—decorate. Here are some key skills and why they can be so helpful to your career:

Relationship Building

Think about the people you choose to do business with—whether it's your hair stylist, the person who runs the corner store you like to go to, or anyone else who you visit on a regular basis to purchase a product or service. If you are like most of us, one of the reasons you continue to do business with certain people is because you like them. If you don't like someone, chances are you would take your business elsewhere if you had another option.

When it comes to hiring a decorator, employers and clients usually have a number of decorators to choose from. Given a choice between two capable people, the job will usually go to the person who is well-liked. In fact, when people like you, their feelings toward you can extend to their perception of your work (this is called "the halo effect"). So they may actually see your work in a more positive light because they like you.

In addition to developing relationships with clients, self-employed decorators also need to develop relationships with suppliers and contractors. Suppliers are representatives of companies from which you purchase products such as fabric, furniture, and flooring. Contractors are individuals who do work such as renovations, painting, wallpapering, laying carpet, installing flooring, re-upholstery, etc.

Having a good relationship with suppliers and contractors can help you get what you want when you need something in a rush, that's difficult to get, or that a supplier won't make much commission on. A supplier or contractor who likes you will be more likely to go the extra mile for you, which in turn will help you look good to your client. (You will find more information about working with suppliers in section 5.5.)

Relationship building is also important for decorators employed by retail outlets, since this skill can help you get higher sales and repeat business. An excellent book about building relationships is *How to Win Friends and Influence People,* by Dale Carnegie.

Communication Skills

Verbal Skills

Verbal communication skills come into play when you are selling yourself to potential clients. Many people who hire interior decorators are wealthy. Chances are they are articulate and professional, and are likely to be comfortable hiring a decorator who "speaks their language."

To improve your verbal communication skills, ask friends or a vocal coach for feedback on any areas that could be improved, such as: use of slang, proper grammar, or altering your tone of voice to eliminate any harshness. (You can find vocal coaches in the Yellow Pages.)

Listening

Being a good listener can help you determine the best decorating solutions for people and ensure that you come up with something that the client wants. While listening seems like an easy skill to master, most of us experience challenges when it comes to paying attention, understanding, or remembering.

You can improve your listening skills by focusing fully on someone when they are speaking. Here are some ways to do that:

- Don't interrupt the other person. Keep listening to the other person, even if you think you know what they will say next. If you make assumptions, you might miss the point they're trying to make.

- Pay attention to the other person's nonverbal signals (tone of voice, facial expression, body language, etc.). These signals can give you valuable clues about what the other person is thinking.

- Ask questions in order to clarify what the other person has said. Try repeating what they have said in your own words to make sure you understand. Take notes if necessary.

- Don't be distracted by outside interference. Loud noises, the other person mispronouncing a word, or even an uncomfortable room temperature can break your concentration and distract you from the conversation.

- Give feedback to the other person. Nod occasionally, say things like "I see," and smile, if appropriate. Let them know you're listening.

Reading People

Being a skilled reader of people can not only help you get the job, it can help ensure you keep your clients satisfied. In addition to hearing what people say, a skilled decorator also notices non-verbal communication. For example, did a prospective client fold their arms when you made a particular suggestion? If so, they may be communicating that they disagree, even if they don't actually say so.

Although body language can't tell you precisely what someone is thinking, it can give you clues so you can ask follow-up questions, even as basic as "How do you feel about that?"

If you want to improve this skill, you can find some excellent advice in *Reading People,* a book by Jo-Ellan Dimitrius and Wendy Patrick Mazzarella.

Negotiation

As soon as a client or employer decides they would like to work with you, you will be faced with the issue of how much you will get paid. You will find information about standard fees for decorators later in this guide. However, no matter what fees are "standard," you may be able to get paid more through effective negotiation skills.

Likewise, being a good negotiator can help you save money on materials such as furniture, carpeting, wallpaper, etc. While suppliers offer discounts to decorators on many products, there may be occasions when you want to purchase something from a supplier that isn't used to giving discounts (for example, if you find a rare work of art that you want to buy for a client). In those cases, being a good negotiator may help you and your client save money.

If you want to improve your negotiating skills, read the book *Get Anyone to Do Anything,* by David J. Lieberman.

2.2.3   Organizational Ability

Being well organized will make your work much easier, especially if you have your own decorating business. As an interior decorator there will be times you'll have to juggle quite a few tasks at the same time, such as: meeting with clients, finding and ordering materials, arranging for shipping and delivery, scheduling tasks such as painting and installation, handling finances, and more. (Chapter 5 explains more about the specific tasks you'll be involved with if you start your own business.) You will have to keep track of paperwork and ensure that tasks are completed on time and on budget.

If you think your organizational skills could be better, you may be able to find some useful tips at websites such as **www.organizeyour world.com** and **www.getorganizednow.com**.

2.3   Teaching Yourself Interior Decorating

You can learn interior decorating by teaching yourself or by completing an educational program. In this section, you will learn about the first option. Section 2.4 will describe your many educational options.

To teach yourself interior decorating, start with Chapter 3 of this guide. The information in Chapter 3 comes from successful interior decorators and interior designers who have generously shared their expert tips and techniques to help you learn decorating as quickly as possible.

You can continue learning about interior decorating using any of the methods described below. We have also compiled a list of some of the best resources (websites, books, magazines, etc.) to save you hours of research time.

2.3.1   Places to Go

Open Houses

Open houses are an invitation to the public to view a home that's for sale. Show homes (also known as model homes) in new residential developments tend to be especially well-decorated. You may also be able to view beautiful decors in older homes for sale. While it is certainly possible to find attractive interiors in any community, you are most likely to find well-decorated homes in upscale communities.

The opportunity to view open houses in your own community (including homes of the wealthy) is probably available to you every weekend. Simply check the classifieds in the real estate section of your local newspaper, and you should be able to find a number of open houses you can attend. Remember to bring a notepad so you can take notes!

Other Beautiful Interiors

You can train your eye by visiting and observing a variety of well-decorated interiors in buildings such as historic homes, museums, art galleries, and offices of businesses that attract upscale clients. Types of businesses that usually have beautifully decorated offices include:

- interior designers and decorators (of course!)
- architectural firms
- law firms
- public relations agencies
- financial planners

Ask friends and family if they know anyone who works in any of these types of businesses. Using your persuasive communication skills, you may be able to arrange with the office manager for a tour of their boardroom and other areas. If not, the reception area alone may give you some good design ideas.

Showrooms

Furniture showrooms are another excellent place to train your eye. Showrooms are designed to sell furniture, so the furniture is displayed in the most beautiful settings possible. To find furniture showrooms, check the Yellow Pages under "furniture."

At a furniture showroom, especially one that sells very expensive pieces, you will usually find the decorators have chosen what they consider the best art, accessories, layout, colors, etc. to most effectively complement the furniture. Most furniture retail stores (with the exception of discount outlets) display their furniture in such settings.

Home Shows

A "home show" is a public event, usually held at a convention center, that features displays and demonstrations of products for home decorating and remodeling. Home shows are usually free to attend or have a small admission fee (about what you might pay to see a movie). They are a wonderful opportunity to learn about many aspects of home decorating.

Virtually every city has at least one major home show every year, and large cities may have several home shows. To find out about home shows in your community, check your local newspaper or contact your local convention center to ask for a schedule of upcoming events. (You can check the phone book to find local convention centers, or you can search for them online. You can also try searching online for "home show" and your city's name.)

Trade Shows

Trade shows are industry events that happen over a period of several days. They feature seminars and speakers talking about trends and developments in the interior design industry, along with exhibits of new products. The shows also provide an opportunity to network, and you may be able to attend for as little as $10. Major interior design shows include:

- NeoCon shows (Chicago, Los Angeles, Toronto, Baltimore)

- The International Home Furnishings Market (High Point, North Carolina)

- Chicago Design Show

These shows, as well as several others, are sponsored by a company called Merchandise Mart Properties. You can find dates and locations for these shows by visiting the Merchandise Mart Properties website at **www.mmart.com** or by calling 800-677-6278.

A number of trade shows are also held in Europe. You can find out about a variety of upcoming events, including international trade shows, at the American Society of Interior Designers website at **www.asid.org/events/national** or by calling their Washington, D.C. headquarters at 202-546-3480.

2.3.2   People to Speak With

Retailers

Furniture showrooms not only give you an opportunity to learn by viewing sample interiors, but they also give you an opportunity to learn from the people who work there. If the store employs decorators/salespeople, you can ask questions about decorating (you can also ask for advice for your job search!). You can do the same at any retail store that sells products used for home decorating (paint, carpet, lighting, building materials, hardware stores, etc.).

Even if the salesperson is not a decorator, they may be a good source of information about the products they are selling. They can answer questions and may be able to give you samples or written information. Be friendly and express appreciation for their help; remember, they are paid to make sales, and you will be asking for free advice.

> TIP: Retail staff are likely to have more time to spend with you if you go at a slower time of day (such as a weekday morning) instead of a Saturday afternoon when they are busy helping customers.

In section 6.5.3 (*"Prepare a Project Budget"*) you will find additional help-ful advice on how to contact retailers and other industry experts to learn about decorating costs.

Manufacturers

Companies that manufacture home decorating products – from flooring to fabrics – can provide a wealth of information about those particular products. Many manufacturers have local sales representatives (known as "manufacturers representatives") who may be willing to speak with you. However, these people are busy, and many prefer not to deal di-rectly with the public. (If you have ever tried to buy something directly from a large manufacturer, they probably referred you to a retail store.)

Put the word out to your network of contacts (friends, family, etc.) that you want to be introduced to people who work for manufacturers of home decorating products such as furniture, paint, or whatever prod-ucts you want to learn more about. If you don't have a personal connec-tion in a particular industry, another option is to try contacting a com-pany's public relations department. The public relations department may be able to answer your questions or refer you to someone who can. Or you can sign up to receive emails and newsletters from your favorite suppliers to get information on new products and trends before they even hit the stores.

You can find contact information for most manufacturers at their web-sites or through Hoover's Online (**www.hoovers.com**), a website which allows you to search for major U.S. companies by name or industry. For Canadian companies, go to the Globe and Mail site at **www.theglobe andmail.com/top1000**.

Interior Decorators and Interior Designers

Of course, you should also use your network of contacts to ask to be introduced to anyone working as an interior decorator or designer. If possible, go beyond getting a name and telephone number. Ask the in-dividual who personally knows the decorator to contact them, explain that you are learning about interior decorating, and see if you can call them to ask a few questions.

If absolutely no one in your network knows anyone who is a decorator or designer, you can try arranging a meeting with a cold call. Grab the Yellow Pages and start dialing. Explain that you are studying interior decorating and ask if you can arrange to meet with the decorator for 20 minutes to ask a few questions. People are much more likely to agree to a meeting if they know it won't take too much time.

Be prepared that the decorator may not be available for a personal meeting but may be willing to answer questions on the phone or by email. If they make such an offer, take them up on it! If you have your heart set on a personal meeting, try using your persuasive communication skills and say you would appreciate the opportunity to see how their office is decorated.

If a decorator agrees to a meeting, arrive on time and come prepared with a list of questions. At the 20-minute mark, acknowledge that your time is up, say you know the decorator is busy, and offer to leave. If the decorator doesn't have another appointment, they may be happy to extend the meeting. (If you want to make a good impression, it's usually not a good idea to stay longer than agreed without permission.) After the meeting, make sure you send a thank you note to the decorator and, if someone referred you, thank that person as well.

If you make a good impression on the decorator, it might lead to future opportunities such as an internship, mentoring, or even a job. Each of these are covered later in this guide.

2.3.3   What to Read and Watch

Most successful decorators read as much as possible. By reading about, and looking at, photographs of interiors created by top decorators, they can get ideas to use in their own designs. Here are some resources that can help you learn about decorating:

Magazines

There are scores of magazines that publish articles about homes and decorating. In addition to national magazines, there are regional and city magazines such as *Coastal Living, Colorado Homes & Lifestyle, Seattle Homes & Lifestyle, Southern Living*, and many others.

To make your research easier, we have reviewed the overwhelming number of choices, and compiled a list of top national magazines to give you a place to get started. Some contain photographs of beautiful interiors; others offer advice on how to decorate. You should be able to find most of these magazines at your local news stand or public library. You can even read portions of some magazines online.

- *Architectural Digest*
  www.architecturaldigest.com

- *Better Homes and Gardens*
  www.bhg.com

- *Country Home*
  www.countryhome.com

- *Country Living*
  www.countryliving.com

- *Elle Decor*
  www.elledecor.com

- *Florida Design*
  www.floridadesign.com

- *House Beautiful*
  www.housebeautiful.com

- *Metropolitan Home*
  www.methome.com

- *Romantic Homes*
  www.romantichomes.com

- *Southern Living*
  www.southernliving.com/southern

- *Town & Country*
  www.townandcountrymag.com

- *Traditional Home*
  www.traditionalhome.com

- *Veranda*
  www.veranda.com

- *Victorian Homes*
  www.victorianhomesmag.com

The following magazines are "trade magazines," which means they are read by people who work as professional interior designers or decorators. These are the magazines read by industry insiders to find design news, ideas, and information about suppliers. They include:

- *Home Furnishings News*
  www.hfnmag.com

- *Interior Design Magazine*
  www.interiordesign.net

- *Kitchen and Bath Design News*
  www.kbdn.net

- *Metropolis Magazine*
  www.metropolismag.com/cda/index.php

- *Window Fashion Vision Magazine*
  www.wf-vision.com

Websites

If you type "interior decorating" or "interior design" into a search engine, you will have literally thousands of websites to choose from. So here's a short list of the best websites for getting started learning about interior decorating. The following sites either provide detailed information, or links to detailed information, on numerous aspects of decorating.

- *About.com - Interior Decorating*
  Helpful decorating articles and links to hundreds of sites.
  http://interiordec.about.com

- *Debbie Travis' Painted House*
  Step-by step-instructions for decorating ideas featured on her PBS show.
  www.painted-house.com

- *Designers Portfolio at HGTV*
  www.hgtv.com/hgtv/designers_portfolio_main

- *HomePortfolio.com – Get Inspired*
  This site focuses on selling products, but you can find some good design ideas, and ask questions on the discussion boards.
  www.homeportfolio.com/GetInspired

- *House Beautiful Decorating*
  Excellent articles on many decorating topics.
  www.housebeautiful.com/decorating

- *Lowe's – Home Decor*
  This retail site has some of the Internet's best decorating advice.
  www.lowes.com

- *Move.com*
  Offers articles, advice and decorating tools.
  www.move.com/home-garden/decorate

- *MSN Lifestyle - Decorate*
  Decorating products and articles.
  http://lifestyle.msn.com/your-home/room-design

- *Rental Decorating Digest*
  Includes a helpful overview called "Interior Design 101."
  www.rentaldecorating.com

- *RONA – Decoration*
  Good advice from Canada's leading retailer of home improvement products. (Click on "Decoration")
  www.rona.ca

- *See My Design*
  This site is a great source of information about suppliers.
  www.seemydesign.com

Books

Amazon.com lists more than 4,600 books on the subject of interior decorating, but of course you do not have the time to read them all! So here is a selection of excellent books you may want to start with. Look for them at your local library, browse through them at a local bookstore, or order them online.

- *Christopher Lowell's Seven Layers of Design,*
  by Christopher Lowell

- *Debbie Travis' Painted House,*
  by Debbie Travis

- *Design Diary: Innovative Interiors,*
  by Noel Jeffrey

- *Designers' Houses,*
  by Dominic Bradbury and Mark Luscombe-Whyte

- *Easy and Elegant Home Decorating,*
  by Andrea Maflin

- *Elegant & Easy Rooms,*
  by Dylan Landis and David McGrievey

- *The Ultimate House Book: For Home Design
  in the Twenty-First Century,*
  by Terence Conran

- *A Handbook for Interior Designers,*
  by Jenny Gibbs

- *House & Garden Book of Style,*
  by Dominique Browning

- *101 Feng Shui Tips for the Home,*
  by Richard Webster

Watch TV

There are dozens of television shows that touch on some aspect of home decorating, from TLC's *Trading Spaces, Moving Up*, and *Stager Invasion* to PBS's *This Old House*. Check your local listings to find decorating shows, and if you don't already get the Home & Garden Television channel, consider contacting your cable company to order it.

In particular, check out the television program *Sensible Chic* on HGTV to get some great tips on achieving designer looks at reasonable prices. In each episode of *Sensible Chic,* the *Sensible Chic* crew recreates a big-budget inspiration room at a fraction of the cost.

One television program that can give you some great ideas for finding a compromise (without compromising style) in a situation where partners (normally a husband and wife) have extremely different tastes is the television program *Designing for the Sexes,* hosted by Rick Rifle and also airing on HGTV. You can learn new design and style techniques and how to handle compromising situations with each program you watch.

2.4   Educational Programs

While teaching yourself can be an inexpensive and fun way to learn interior decorating, you will probably be able to learn decorating more quickly from experts by taking an educational program. Educational programs take several different forms, including:

- four-year Bachelor's degree programs in interior design
- two-year Associate degree programs
- diploma programs
- certificate programs
- continuing education courses

In addition to offering on-site programs (where students attend classes in person), a number of organizations also offer decorating programs through distance learning.

2.4.1 What to Look For

To start with, what you will look for in a program will have a lot to do with you. Do you enjoy attending classes so you can interact with other people? Or do you prefer to work at your own pace? If you prefer to set your own pace, a distance learning program will obviously suit you better than a program offered in a traditional classroom setting.

How much time and money do you want to invest in your education? You could spend anywhere from a few hours to a few years, and anywhere from hundreds of dollars to thousands of dollars, on your education. Are you the type of person who prefers to learn by doing? If so, consider taking a program that offers an internship or work-study component.

All of these are factors to consider when you are evaluating different programs. In addition to your personal preferences, there are several questions you can ask to make you feel comfortable with the quality of a particular program. In this section we list a variety of educational programs. However, we cannot say which program, if any, will be best for you. You are the only one who can make that decision. You can ask some of the following questions and see if it is possible for you to speak with the instructor and former graduates of the program.

Is the Program Accredited?

Many educational programs are accredited by official organizations such as Accrediting Commission of the Distance Education and Training Council. Accreditation means that the program has met certain educational standards. (However, even if a program is not accredited, you may still find it to be valuable, depending on your personal goals.)

Is the Program Recognized in the Profession?

This question is best asked of people who are working in the profession. If you are conducting interviews with professional decorators, as discussed in section 2.3.2, you can ask them if they have heard of a program you are considering and, if so, what their opinion is.

What Does the Program Cover?

You may be able to save yourself some disappointment by finding out in advance what topics you will be expected to learn. If you want to focus on interior decorating you may not be happy with a program that includes interior design courses on such topics as building codes.

Many programs also include career advice and job placement services. While no program will guarantee a job upon graduation, this type of service may be helpful to your job hunt.

Who is Offering the Program?

Find out who is teaching the course. What are their credentials? How long have they been an interior decorator or designer? Do they have previous teaching experience?

If you are taking a program from a company find out how long they have been in business. You can also contact the Better Business Bureau. They can tell you whether there are any complaints lodged against the company. To locate a BBB anywhere in the U.S. or Canada, check the Yellow Pages or visit **www.bbb.org**.

2.4.2 Degree and Diploma Programs

As mentioned earlier in this guide, degree programs focus on interior design rather than interior decorating. If you decide at some point that you would like to earn a degree, you can find a list of programs from the Council for Interior Design Accreditation (CIDA) at the CIDA website. The site lists accredited programs in both the U.S. and Canada.

These are programs that provide academic preparation for professional interior designers. Visit **www.accredit-id.org/accredited-programs** for a that list includes more than 150 accredited college interior design programs, broken down by each U.S. state and Canada. As of 2010, all programs seeking accreditation from CIDA must culminate in a minimum of a bachelor's degree (e.g. Bachelor of Arts, Bachelor of Science, Bachelor of Fine Arts, or Bachelor of Interior Design). If you are considering a degree in interior design you should only choose a program that meets CIDA's current minimum standards.

Pre-Professional Assistant Level Programs

Although all programs seeking accreditation from CIDA must prove that they culminate in a bachelor's degree, there are a number of other programs available designed to prepare students for positions as design assistants or merchandisers rather than as professional interior designers. They may be useful for someone who doesn't want to go through a four-year program. For a list of diploma and two-year associate degree programs (e.g. Associate of Applied Science, Associate of Arts in Interior Design) in the U.S., visit **www.petersons.com/vpa/select/a1609se. asp**, or in Canada try **www.schoolfinder.com** (type "interior design" into the Quick Search box).

2.4.3   Certificate Programs

Dozens of universities, colleges and other organizations offer certificate programs in Interior Decorating. In many cases, earning a certificate can be an excellent way to get educational credentials as an interior decorator with a minimal investment of time and money.

To earn an Interior Decorating Certificate, you must complete a number of courses. The exact number and required subjects will vary from one educational institution to another, but you can expect the courses to be on the types of topics described in the next chapter, such as: color, lighting, furniture, fabrics, walls, window treatments, flooring, accessories, etc. Depending on the educational institution, other subjects offered may range from "Antiques Connoiseurship" to "Kitchen Renovations."

Most classes are held on evenings and weekends, although some educational institutions have daytime programs. An increasing number offer online courses as well.

The types of organizations that offer certificates in interior decorating range from small community colleges to well-known universities, including Auburn University, Philadelphia University, and the New York Institute of Technology. An Interior Decoration Certificate program is even offered by the continuing education department of one of the most famous and prestigious design schools in the world — Parsons The New School for Design in New York City. Phone 212-229-8900 to request a catalog or visit their website at **www.newschool.edu/parsons**.

Not surprisingly, the elite Parsons program is expensive (over $5,000 U.S.). If you are hoping to earn a certificate much less expensively, consider looking into programs at local community colleges or universities. You may be able to find local programs by doing an Internet search for any combination of the following terms: certificate, diploma, interior decorating, or interior decoration plus the name of your city.

However, new interior decorating programs are introduced frequently, and not all are advertised on the Internet, so if you want to get a certificate you should also contact local educational institutions directly. Phone local colleges and universities and ask for the continuing education department. That department should be able to tell you if they offer an interior decorating certificate or interior decorating courses.

There are several other organizations that offer certificates or diplomas in interior decorating.

2.4.4   Distance Learning

Distance learning may take the form of correspondence courses, where you receive materials by mail and can work at home, at any time of day, and at your own pace. Another option for distance education is online learning. With online learning you will typically enroll at the same time as other students and must meet course deadlines. Online learning allows you to interact with instructors and other classmates through chat sessions and email.

In this section you will find a list of interior decorating programs you can take from home. These programs teach standard decorating topics, such as color, lighting, floor plans, furniture, fabrics, walls, window treatments, flooring, accessories, etc. Most also teach various business aspects of interior decorating, such as consulting with clients and starting your own decorating business.

When considering costs, keep in mind that many programs will let you pay in installments (so you can spread out payments over a period of months or years). Also, some correspondence programs charge a nominal fee (e.g. $20-25) for shipping of materials.

As mentioned above, we cannot say whether any of the programs listed in this guide will be right for you. You are the only one who can make that decision. Program costs and other details can change, so make sure you confirm information about any program before registering.

Stratford Career Institute

Website:	**www.scitraining.com**
Program:	Interior Decorating Diploma
Format:	Online learning as described at **www.scitraining. com/Interior_Decorating/Outline**
Classes:	Four in-depth learning modules covering decorating topics, history of decorating, and business topics
Length:	You can finish in as little as six months. Students spend an estimated 6-12 hours per week on coursework.
Cost:	Regular tuition cost is $689 for the entire program of study. Stratford also offers an installment plan of 18 payments of around $37 per month.
Contact:	Email **admissions@scitraining.com** or call 800-254-4070.

Penn Foster Career School

Website:	**www.pennfoster.edu/decorator/index.html**
Program:	Diploma in Interior Decorating
Format:	Correspondence course
Classes:	Consists of 7 lessons (called "Instruction Sets") on decorating topics and running a business.
Length:	You can take from six months to two years to complete the program.

Cost:	At the time of printing, the U.S. program costs $498 U.S. while the Canadian program costs $950 CDN plus shipping. You can pay in install-ments.
Contact:	Contact through website or phone 800-275-4410.

Metropolitan Institute of Design

Website:	**www.met-design.com**
Program:	Courses in interior design, including decorating
Format:	Currently on site only; online courses will be of-fered in future according to the school
Classes:	Offers dozens of courses on various aspects of interior design. Two basic courses are *ID-1001 Part I Interior Design* and *ID-1002 Part II Interior Design*. ID-1001 teaches the history and practical aspects of design. ID-1002 covers decorating top-ics. A Feng Shui Program is also offered. You can see the complete list of courses by visiting their website and clicking on "Programs."
Length:	ID-1001 and ID-1002 are each 48-hour cours-es taken over 15 weeks. Other courses run 10 weeks.
Cost:	Practical Aspects of Interior Design sections are $1,250 each (there are three parts to this pro-gram). All Advanced Diploma 30-hour courses cost $750 each, and 20-hour classes and electives are $500 each. Books and study materials are ex-tra. Registration fee is $50.
Contact:	Email **mainoffice@met-design.com** or phone 516-845-4033.

Ashworth College

Website:	**www.ashworthcollege.edu/programs/ career-diploma/interior-decorating**

Program:	Diploma in Interior Decorating
Format:	Online or correspondence course
Classes:	Consists of 18 decorating lessons plus one unit on career information
Length:	Up to two years to complete.
Cost:	Tuition is $594 whether you choose online or correspondence. There is a $24 shipping and-handling fee for the print-based correspondence option. A monthly tuition installment option is available.
Contact:	Email **info@ashworthcollege.edu** or phone 1-888-231-6247.

Rhodec International

Website:	**www.rhodec.org**
Program:	Associate Diploma Course, Professional Diploma Course, or Bachelor of Arts in Interior Design
Format:	Correspondence course
Classes:	The Associate Professional Diploma consists of 12 lessons on design and decorating topics. The Diploma course consists of 64 lessons and a final test. See the website for full details of the Bachelor's program.
Length:	One year for the Associate Professional Diploma. Two to three years for the Diploma. Three to four years for the Bachelor.
Cost:	The cost for the Associate Diploma program starts at $955 U.S. Sixty credits consisting of 10 subject modules are required for completion of the diploma. If paid in full on enrollment, 6-credit modules are $894 and 3-credit modules are $447. The final, 12-credit module, including the final test, costs

	$1,118. See Rhodec's website for further payment details and options.
Contact:	Email **uscontact@rhodec.edu** or phone 1-877-274-6332

Sheffield School of Interior Design

Website:	**www.sheffield.edu/htmlsrc/2outline.html**
Program:	Certificate
Format:	Correspondence course
Classes:	30 lessons on decorating topics and running a business. For a list of lessons, including two excellent sample lessons, visit the website above.
Length:	According to the school, you can complete the program in 6-8 months if you study about two hours per week. You have up to three years to complete the program.
Cost:	The cost is $848 if paid up front, but by registering online you can save an additional $50. Or you can make payments of about $35 per month over 28 months (a total of $998).
Contact:	Email **info@sheffield.edu** or phone 212-661-7270

2.4.5   Continuing Education Courses

Your local college or university may offer interior decorating courses, even if it doesn't offer a certificate in interior decorating. Through the continuing education department you may be able to take a single course on a Saturday or over several evenings, and learn about color, wall coverings, or other decorating topics. Not only can this be a valuable learning experience, you can also list any decorating courses you have taken on your resume.

If you can't find a listing for the continuing education department in your local phone book, call the college's main switchboard and ask for the continuing education department. They will be able to tell you about upcoming courses. In addition to colleges and universities, you may find courses in basic decorating techniques offered by local high schools, business colleges (check the Yellow Pages under "schools"), or retailers such as fabric stores.

2.5 How to Get Experience

Here is some good news for aspiring interior decorators: It is easy to get interior decorating experience. Unlike some careers – where it is very difficult to get hired without experience, but very difficult to get experience without a job – you can get all the experience you need now to help you break into a fab job in interior decorating. In this section of the guide you will discover a variety of ways to get experience. Of course, you are not expected to do everything we suggest below. Choose the ones that fit best with your personal interests.

To get the most benefit from these activities, make sure you arrange to have photographs taken of everything you decorate. The photos will be proof of your interior decorating experience to show to prospective clients and employers. (See section 4.1 for details about how to get photographs and prepare a portfolio.)

2.5.1 Decorate for Family and Friends

Decorate Your Own Home

Most interior decorators get their first decorating experience working on their own homes. Even if you feel every room in your home looks perfect the way it is now, redecorating your home can be useful to you in a couple of ways. (You can always change it back later!)

First, it gives you an opportunity to practice decorating while you are learning more about it. Even if you have just one small room to experiment with, you can get "hands-on" experience with a variety of decorating techiques. For example, you may have heard you can make a dramatic change to any room, quickly and inexpensively, simply by rearranging the furniture or painting the walls a new color. Give it a try! Experiment with techniques you wouldn't ordinarily use. Consider this room your "lab" where you can try things out before recommending them to a client.

Redecorating your home is valuable for another reason — you can get more photographs of "your work" to show to employers or clients. Imagine being able to show photos of one room with several different looks. This can be a great way to impress employers with your versatility and your ability to decorate for a variety of clients with different tastes.

Homes of Friends and Family

Your friends and family members may already have asked for your advice about decorating matters, but if they haven't yet asked you to actually decorate their homes, why not offer?

Of course you wouldn't say something like "Gee, I've noticed your home doesn't look very good. Why don't I come over and make it look better?" To avoid offending anyone who feels their home is already well-decorated, simply ask for their help spreading the word that you are looking for opportunities to volunteer your services as a decorator.

Explain that you need to get practical experience to help you become a professional interior decorator. The people who care about you want you to achieve your dreams, and eventually they – or someone they know – will want to redecorate. Some of the times your family or friends may need to redecorate are when they are experiencing transitions in life, such as:

- marriage or co-habitation (help them merge two households into one)

- moving into a new home

- childbirth (offer to decorate the baby's room)

- hosting a special event (such as a wedding or dinner party)

- starting a home business (you could decorate their new office)

- selling a home (explain how a well-decorated home can attract buyers)

Also remember that the definition of "home" can go beyond what we usually think of. For example, see if anyone you know can use your services to decorate any of the following (you can probably think of other possibilities):

- basement suites for renters

- guest houses

- cottages

- mobile homes

- yachts

When someone wants to use your services, try to treat them the way you would treat a "real" client. Meet to discuss their needs, and make sure you discuss any budget. If they want you to buy materials for them, arrange to receive payment for materials in advance. To avoid misunderstandings, it's a good idea to prepare a simple contract even if you're working with family members. (Let them know you need the practice.) See Chapter 6 for detailed advice about working with clients.

Another thing to let your friends and family know in advance is that you will want to take "before" and "after" photos for your portfolio. You can also ask for a letter of recommendation once you have finished decorating for anyone who has a different last name than yours. (Unfortunately, a recommendation letter from your mom probably won't impress future employers.) See Chapter 4 for more information about photos and letters of recommendation.

Businesses of Family and Friends

When you put the word out that you are looking for interiors to decorate, you can let your friends and family members know you are available to decorate their businesses as well as their homes. Here are some possibilities:

- offices

- restaurants

- retail stores

- hotels and motels

- model homes (also known as "show homes")

- model suites of properties for sale

- booths at trade shows or conferences

As mentioned in the last section, when you find someone who wants to use your decorating services, work with them the same way you would with a paying client. Also let them know that you will want to use them as a reference if they are happy with your services.

2.5.2   Volunteer for Charity

Imagine being able to do what you love, get valuable experience, and make a difference in your community at the same time. You can do all of these things by volunteering to decorate interiors for charity. While opportunities will vary from one community to another, here are some possibilities:

Habitat for Humanity

Habitat for Humanity is an international non-profit organization dedicated to helping people have "decent, affordable houses." In each Habitat for Humanity community, groups of volunteers build houses from the ground up. (More than 350,000 homes have been built so far.) The houses are then sold to needy families at no profit, through no-interest loans.

Habitat for Humanity needs volunteers to work in all areas of home construction, including the interior. This could be an opportunity to meet people and learn more about how new homes are constructed, as well as get decorating experience. Even Martha Stewart and Rosie O'Donnell have decorated a Habitat home. (They teamed up to decorate the home's interior in a "who's the craftiest of them all" contest against *This Old House* host Norm Abram and talk show host Sally Jesse Raphael who helped build the exterior.)

There are Habitat for Humanity chapters in every U.S. state and nearly 90 other countries. To find one near you, visit **www.habitat.org/local** or call 800-422-4828.

Home Raffles

Some communities have fund-raisers in which a house is raffled off (usually for $100 per ticket) to raise money for a local charity. Home raffles may be promoted through flyers delivered door-to-door, news-paper or television advertising, booths in shopping malls, etc. If you hear about a home raffle, you could call the organizer and volunteer to help decorate the interior.

Other Volunteer Opportunities

In every community there are scores of charitable organizations that need volunteers. When you find a cause you believe in, see if there is any opportunity to volunteer your decorating services. If your timing is right, you might end up with the chance to decorate the organization's offices. Even if they don't need an office decorator, you could volunteer to be the decorator for special events. You won't have much of a bud-get to work with (if any) but the experience can be valuable in many ways.

2.5.3   Internships

What They Are

An internship is a short-term, entry-level position that gives you hands-on work experience. As an intern you would go to work for a company at regularly scheduled times (although you might work as few as eight hours per week) and carry out tasks assigned by your supervisor. The main difference between an internship and a regular job is that most interns are not paid.

Although you will likely be volunteering your services to a company, you get practical work experience that can be very helpful once you start applying for jobs or start looking for clients for your own decorat-ing business. As an intern you can make valuable industry contacts, learn new decorating skills, and build your resume and portfolio.

You can offer your services for as little as a week; however, you will have the opportunity to learn more if you can arrange a longer intern-ship. (For example, the Metropolitan Institute of Design arranges ten-week internships for its students.)

Finding an Internship

If you take an interior decorating program through a college, they may arrange internships for students. Ask if they have an internship program when you register.

Assuming you are not attending a college that arranges internships, there are a couple of ways to set one up yourself. First, decide which companies you would like to work with. (See Chapter 4 for information about different types of companies that hire interior decorators.) Then start calling. If it's a large company (such as a manufacturer of home decorating products), you can ask their human resources department if they have an internship program. If they do have such a program they will tell you how to apply.

If you want to work with a small company such as an interior decorating or interior design firm, ask to speak with one of the owners. (To find out the owner's name, ask the receptionist or look the company up on the Internet first.) Whether you get through to the owner, or speak with someone else in the company, explain that you would like to volunteer your services as an intern.

While you might think any company would jump at the chance for free labor, some companies are so busy the owner may feel they don't have time to train an intern. (In a few cases an interior designer may not want to help train a potential competitor, either.) So be prepared to sell yourself, using your persuasive communication skills. Explain why you will bring value to the company.

One thing that most companies need is help doing the tasks that no one else wants to do. If you are willing to answer telephones, make copies, run errands, do the filing – in other words, if you are willing to do "whatever it takes" to help them out – say so.

If someone is interested in having you intern for them, they will ask you to come in for an interview and may ask to see your resume and portfolio. In many ways, applying for an internship is similar to applying for a job. You will learn more about that in Chapter 4.

Making the Most of an Internship

Once you have an internship, do a first-class job with every task you are given, even the menial tasks. Everyone "pays their dues" when they are starting a new career, and those who do it with a positive attitude can make a great impression.

Look for any opportunities to get actual decorating experience—even if it means working a few more hours than you originally agreed to. Volunteer to help out whenever you can. Be someone who does such a great job that you will be missed when the internship is over.

Here are some tips for making the most of your internship:

- Don't forget to ask questions. If you are unsure about a task you have to complete, or even if you're just curious about some aspect of the decorating business, ask your supervisor. It's their job to supervise you, but they can also be a valuable source of information, as well.

- Work on what interests you. If a project comes up that you would like to work on, ask your supervisor if you can get involved.

- Get organized. Keep records of your work. Consider starting a journal of your internship activities, and try to document every project you work on for your portfolio. Keeping track of everything you've learned can help you when you apply for a job in the future.

- Set up evaluation sessions with your supervisor. This gives you a chance to ask about projects or assignments and get feedback on your performance.

- Learn what the other employees in the company are responsible for. This will give you an idea of what other types of jobs there are in the decorating industry.

- Attend professional association meetings. Your company likely belongs to at least one; ask your supervisor about attending a meeting.

- Keep a list of networking contacts.

At the end of the internship, ask your supervisor for a written letter of reference. If you have done exceptional work, you may even get a job offer from the company you interned for.

Job Shadowing

For some companies, it may be easier to have you spend a short period of time with an employee than to find someone to supervise you for an internship.

Job shadowing involves spending a day, a week, or some other limited period of time observing someone work. It allows you to learn more about a career, ask questions, and actually see what a job entails on a daily basis. Most job shadowing is arranged through personal connections, although you might be able to arrange a job shadow by calling companies that interest you.

2.5.4   Get a Part-Time Job

Another good way to get related experience is by taking a part-time job for a company involved in the interior decorating industry. Even if the job doesn't focus on decorating, it can give you an opportunity to learn valuable skills that could help with your future job hunt.

One of the easiest ways to get this kind of experience is by applying for a part-time retail sales job. Many retailers have high rates of staff turnover, so they are always hiring. While the starting pay won't be high, you will get the kind of experience that employers and clients look for.

The types of retailers that can best prepare you for an interior decorating career are those that sell related products, such as: home furnishings, lighting, fabrics, house paint, housewares, art, antiques, etc. If you have the opportunity, look for a position where you will have an opportunity to work with and learn about a broad range of decorating styles. See chapter 4 of this guide for detailed step-by-step advice to help you find a job.

3. How to Decorate

This chapter of the guide explains what you need to know about decorating, and gives step-by-step instructions on how to decorate.

3.1 Tools of the Trade

Essential Decorating Tools

Following is a list of some of the supplies and/or tools you will need to decorate and may wish to include in a "decorating kit":

- Paint chip fan deck (a master paint sampler with hundreds of shades)

- Color wheel

- Manufacturers catalogs

- Paper (including both plain white paper and graph paper)

- Notepad

- Pencils (with erasers) and pens

- Measuring tapes — both a good firm metal one (at least 25' long) with a lock on it and a soft flexible cloth one

- Rulers (including a scale ruler and a straight edge)

- Calculator

- Furniture templates

- Fabric swatches

- Sample floor coverings

Ideally, you should keep these "decorating tools" in a briefcase (your "decorating kit") that you take with you each time you are working— whether you are going to a furniture store, a client's home or a show-room. (You will borrow fabric swatches and floor coverings samples from wholesalers on an as-needed basis to show clients for consultations or once you've been hired, so these items will change from client to client.)

You may be amazed at how many times you end up pulling out your measuring tape, notepad and pen in various settings to measure and record the dimensions of either a wall or window or a piece of furniture or even an accessory. The cloth measuring tape is great for measuring soft items such as cushions. The graph paper (and white paper), ruler, pencil, calculator and furniture template are great for drawing out decorating floor plans.

You can pick up a furniture template and a scale ruler at a home improvement store such as The Home Depot, Lowe's, Rona (in Canada) or Homebase or B&Q (in England). The scale ruler is extremely helpful when you are drawing odd-sized furnishings to scale such as occasional tables and chairs, etc.

You can find out where to get a color wheel in the section on color. You should be able to pick up the sampler paint chips from a large paint store. Let them know you are in the interior decorating business and this may help with you obtaining a full paint sampler.

One company that supplies paint samplers to tradesworkers is Pittsburgh Paints. You can contact them directly at 1-800-441-9695 or visit their website at **www.pittsburghpaints.com**. Pittsburgh Paints has

1,800 color samples in their "The Voice of Color Design Collection". There are seven different complimenting colors on each 9" x 2" sampler and each sampler is hole punched and placed together on a large ring for a total of 1,800 color paint samples to choose from.

You may also want to include some or all of the following items in your "decorating kit":

- Felt furniture protectors (these stick on to the bottom of chair legs and table legs and protect the floor from scratches)

- Clear flat stick-on plastic protectors (these protect furniture and walls from scratches and raise and level items such as glass table tops to prevent slippage)

- Picture hanging kit, including a hammer, variety of nails and hooks, wire, etc.

- Small sewing kit with scissors, thread, needles, straight pins and safety pins (for quick repairs or to pin fabrics, etc. to get an idea of a particular look)

- Level (for hanging pictures)

In addition to the above, some decorators also find it useful to have a drawing table (a table that you can put on an angle for easier drawing) together with a good desk lamp that will illuminate the area where you are drawing your plans. This would be kept at your office (or home if you work from home). You can purchase a drawing table at an art supply store. Otherwise, a nice size desk or kitchen table will work just fine for drawing plans.

3.2   Design Elements

To be a successful decorator, there are a number of design elements you need to know about. When decorating a room, there are important design elements that must be taken into consideration. Design elements affect the entire room and include space, balance, color, and texture.

In this part of the guide, you will learn these basic principles of design. In section 3.5 (*"Step-by-Step Decorating Instructions"*) you will find out how to apply them to an actual decorating project.

A Few Words About Feng Shui

As an interior decorator you can expect that, sooner or later, one of your clients will ask you about Feng Shui (Chinese for "wind and water").

Pronounced "fung schway," Feng Shui is a Chinese art that has been practiced for thousands of years. The Chinese believe that a life energy flows through all people and things. This energy is known as Qi or Chi (pronounced "chee"). When Chi flows freely through the spaces we inhabit, it helps our personal Chi stay balanced, and we experience happiness, health, wealth, and good luck.

Chi enters a home through the doors and windows. Where it flows from there depends on the placement of objects within the home. It is believed a properly decorated home can attract more positive Chi and improve the lives of the people who live in the home. Decorators who practice the art of Feng Shui, sometimes called the "Chinese art of placement," ensure that furniture and other room elements are placed so that the energy can flow freely.

The flow of energy is also affected by the location and construction of the home. You can compensate for design problems by adding, or changing the placement of, certain elements within the home. For example, you might rearrange furniture, remove clutter, or add items such as mirrors, plants, lights, or fountains.

To ensure proper balance of Chi, each home must contain the five elements of fire, wood, water, earth, and metal, which can be added through such things as colors, fabrics, and accessories. In deciding where to place items in a home, Feng Shui practitioners use a tool called a "Bagua," a type of map that shows which parts of a home represent the different life areas (such as wealth, relationship, health, and career).

For more information visit **www.fengshuipalace.com** or go to **www.lowes.com** and search for "feng shui."

3.2.1   Space

At its most basic level, interior decorating involves changing something within a space. However, beyond making a space attractive, effective decorating ensures that a space is functional—that it can be used for its intended purpose. Following are two different scenarios relating to making a room functional:

> **SCENARIO 1:**
> You are decorating a living room which your clients have told you they intend to entertain in. You arrange the furniture so people can sit close enough to carry on conversations. Near the seats, you place tables which can hold drinks and small plates. Is this room functional?

> **SCENARIO 2:**
> You are decorating a family room. Your clients have told you they want to be able to watch television in the room, have an area for playing games and a reading area. You decorate a fabulous looking family room with a games table area and a reading area. The TV does not look very good in this room, so you put it up high, far from the seating area. Is this room functional?

In the first scenario, by setting up the room so it is conducive to conversation, you have made the room functional according to your clients' wishes. In the second scenario, if you neglect to set up a comfortable seating area in range of television viewing, you will fail to accomplish your client's decorating wishes because the set up of the room will not be totally functional.

Later in this guide you will learn ways to ask clients what functions they want a room to serve, how to measure space, and how to arrange the best layout.

3.2.2   Balance

When decorating it is vitally important to take into consideration visually balancing a room to create a feeling of equilibrium and harmony. Whatever you decide to use in your decorating equation, your goal is to balance the look and create a sense of harmony with what is placed within the room.

Each object in a room carries a different weight (large objects carry more weight than small objects; bright and warm colors carry more weight than pale or cool colors; shiny objects carry more weight than dull or flat objects; rough textures carry more weight than smooth textures; a busy pattern carries more weight than a simple pattern, etc.). Your goal is to balance the visual weight in a room and colors, textures, patterns and objects are all part of the balance equation.

When deciding where to place an item, some questions you may want to ask are: What is the visual weight of the item? Where will the item look best? What will need to be placed around the item to give it balance?

There are two types of visual balance that are important when decorating: symmetrical balance and asymmetrical balance. It is ideal to have a variety of both symmetrical and asymmetrical balance within a room to give it more depth and interest.

Symmetrical Balance

Symmetrical balance is achieved when two identical items are placed on two opposite sides of an imaginary line. For example, placing identical matching candleholders on each side of a fireplace mantel creates a symmetrical balance (which is also considered a formal balance). In the photo on the next page, the pictures placed on each side of the mirror are symmetrical.

Asymmetrical Balance

Decorating only with symmetrical balance leads to a more formal and somewhat stuffy (possibly even boring) look, which is why it is ideal to also have arrangements that are asymmetrical.

Asymmetrical balance occurs when you have varied pieces of different sizes and shapes placed to create an equilibrium. For example, on a consul table, you may decide to place a decorative box in the middle and then place a lamp on one side and a vase of flowers on the other side. The vase of flowers will most likely be a different size and shape than the lamp, however, the differing sizes and shapes on each side of the decorative box balance each other and create the asymmetrical balance. In the photo shown here, the bust and lamp create asymmetrical balance:

This photo shows both symmetrical balance (the pictures beside the mirror) and asymmetrical balance (the items on the table).

All elements and objects within a room are taken into consideration when balancing a room, and even a small accessory or plant can be used to bring balance. A large neutral colored painting can be balanced by a small, bright and colorful accessory. If you place a large sofa on one side of the room, you may want to balance it with another large sofa (or a loveseat with an occasional table) on the other side of the room.

Over a fireplace, you may decide to hang a fabulous piece of art and place a vase with flowers on one side of the mantel and a large candle-holder with a bright candle on the other side. However, if you decided to place a large vase with flowers on one side of a fireplace mantel and nothing on the other side, this would look off balance and not create a sense of harmony.

As mentioned, besides shape and size, you will also need to balance colors, textures and patterns throughout the space to create harmony.

For example, if one side of your room is totally decorated in red cotton upholstered furnishings while the other side is in gold striped silk, the room will look out of harmony (and out of balance), however, if you mix these colors and fabrics and bring in some complimenting patterns and/or colors (possibly by scattering decorative cushions on each side), you can balance the look.

3.2.3   Color

Color is one of the most complex design elements and there is a lot that new decorators need to know to understand how colors work when decorating.

Colors can not only make a room more attractive, they can actually affect the way people feel. For example, reds and oranges are stimulating, while shades of blue can make people feel more relaxed. So a bedroom decorated entirely in bright orange is not going to be very relaxing!

To choose colors that work well together, start with a tool known as the color wheel. A color wheel can take several different forms, and contain dozens of shades. You can get a color wheel at an art supply or craft store, or try the Color Wheel Company which offers basic color wheels as well as an Interior Design Wheel just for interior decorators for $9.00. Visit **www.colorwheelco.com** or phone 541-929-7526.

The color wheel includes the three *primary*, or pure, colors: red, yellow, and blue. It also includes the secondary colors which are equal combinations of two primary colors:

- red + blue = purple

- red + yellow = orange

- blue + yellow = green

Intermediate (also known as *tertiary*) colors are an equal combination of a primary color and a secondary color next to it on the ring. For example, blue (a primary color) and purple (a secondary color) combine to make blue-purple. The six intermediate colors are: blue-purple, blue-green, yellow-green, yellow-orange, red-orange, and red-purple.

Primary, secondary and intermediate colors can be mixed together, or mixed with neutral colors such as black or white, to form all the other colors. (Other colors sometimes referred to as neutrals include gray, beige, brown, and taupe.) Reds and oranges are typically considered warm colors; while blues and greens are typically considered cool colors.

In the excerpt that follows, Homestore, Inc. provides excellent resource information about "the characteristics of color and the qualities that give colors personality and character" and they have defined some technical terms relating to color:

Hue

Hue is just another word for color. Turquoise and crimson are hues; so are softer colors like lilac and butter cream. The terms hue and color are used interchangeably in art and interior design.

Value

Value refers to the lightness or darkness of a color. Of course, there are infinite variations in value, from the lightest lights to the darkest darks. Mint, for example, is a light value of green. Navy is a dark value of blue. If you look at the Color Ring (see the color section of this book), you'll notice that each pure color has a natural value; that is, yellow is naturally light, while violet is naturally dark.

Temperature

This aspect of color is easy to grasp, even for novices. Refer to the Color Ring (in the color section in the middle of this book) as you read about visual temperature.

If you draw an imaginary line on the color ring from red-violet to yellow-green, the colors on one side of that line – yellows, reds and oranges – seem warm. Warm colors are considered to be "advancing" because they seem as though they are coming closer to the viewer. On walls, warm colors can make a room feel cozy and enveloping.

The colors on the other side of that imaginary line on the color ring – greens, blues and violets – are the cool hues. They appear to be farther away, which is why they are called "receding" colors. On walls, cool colors can make a room feel spacious and calm.

Visual temperature is relative. Red-violet and yellow-green may seem warm or cool, depending on the presence of other colors. Next to orange, red-violet looks cool; next to blue, it looks warm.

Visual temperature comes into play when you combine colors in a decorating scheme. In general, the juxtaposition of warm and cool color intensifies each. If you paint one room a warm red and an adjoining room a cool green, each will seem more intensely warm or cool. This effect also works within a room: Cool walls make a warm wood floor seem even warmer.

Intensity

So far, you've learned that value is the lightness or darkness of color, and temperature is the warmth or coolness of color. Intensity is the third color characteristic, and it can be confusing for the novice. Examples make it easier to understand.

Intensity is about the purity or brightness of color. It's relatively easy to spot intense colors: These are the "cartoon colors" of childhood and the brilliant hues of tropical fish. Lacquer red, lemon yellow and cobalt blue are examples of intense red, yellow and blue. Low-intensity colors are by comparison quiet and subdued. Brick, gold and cadet blue are low-intensity versions of red, yellow and blue.

Intensity is an important color concept because, more than value or temperature, it sets the mood in a color scheme. Intense colors are fresh and vivid, while low-intensity colors are quiet and understated. Varying intensity – introducing a slightly brighter green among duller greens, for example – can bring life to a scheme and keep it from looking like a color formula.

As you search for materials, analyze the colors you see in terms of value, temperature and intensity. Once you can say to yourself, "That's a light value," "This is a warm color," "Here's an intense red," you'll be able to manipulate color for successful effects, rather than relying on luck.

It's easy to confuse the terms value and intensity. Value is about the lightness or darkness of a color. Intensity is about its brightness or dullness. Try thinking of the characteristics separately. First ask yourself, is it light, medium or dark? That's the value of a color. Then ask, is it bright or dull? That's the intensity.

Neutrals

The true neutrals – black, white and gray – don't have a place on the color rings, but they play an essential role in decorating. Sometimes called "the non-colors," true neutrals provide visual relief in a scheme with color, without altering the color relationships. Imagine a black leather chair in the company of a red sofa, or soft gray walls as a backdrop for blue furnishings.

True neutrals are stark and sophisticated. In the absence of color, a true-neutral scheme depends on pattern, texture and finish for visual interest, so be sure to collect a generous mix of materials for your clients to consider.

Just as true neutrals can calm a colorful scheme, color can enliven a true neutral scheme. One spot of intense color – from a favorite painting, for example, or other eye-catching artwork – in a neutral scheme can be stunning. Or try repeating small bits of the color in the room so that it becomes an integral part of the scheme.

Undertones

Interior Designers sometimes say, "This green has blue undertones; that gray is yellowish." What difference does it make? It makes a big difference. The term undertones refers to the subtle, underlying color of a color. How can a color have another color? Few colors, especially those in interiors, are pure. Instead, they are mixtures of several colors, and the undertones reflect that mix. Put another way, the undertone of a mixed color is the minor color that influences the main color. Pure red has no undertones because it is a primary color. But terra-cotta, a version of red-orange, has yellow undertones. Where does the yellow come from? Red-orange is half orange, and orange is half yellow.

Discerning undertones is a challenge for the novice, but practice will sharpen your eye and build your confidence. The key is to really look at colors and analyze their content. Think of it as a game: Can you see the red undertones in a blue-violet fabric? (Remember, violet is made up of red and blue.) That hint of red might cue you to consider adding other colors with red undertones, such as peach (made up of red and yellow) or melon (a lighter value of red-orange). Both colors are harmonious with blue-violet.

Undertones are especially important when considering wall color. If you love yellow but are reluctant to use it on your walls, look for a near-white with yellow undertones, a color you might call French vanilla. If you're using a patterned fabric with a neutral background, study its undertones and choose a wall color with a similar color bias.

Neutrals can have undertones, too, and it is often easier to spot the undertones in a neutral than in a more vivid color. Comparing neutrals side by side helps; the green undertones in a greenish gray are obvious next to a true gray, which has no color.

If you're still having trouble identifying the undertones of colors, simplify the exercise and ask, "Are the undertones warm or cool?" That information alone can help you choose compatible hues. Apple green, for instance, has warm undertones; aqua blue has cool undertones.

In reality, identifying undertones is more about avoiding disaster than anything else. Undertones that clash – a bluish white next to a yellowish white, for example – may look unpleasant. Even slight differences in the undertones of wall and trim colors can be noticeable.

3.2.4   Texture

Texture is another important element to take into consideration when decorating a space because texture adds both visual and tactile interest. Texture can stimulate emotions, create a feeling of warmth and harmony and can provide sensual pleasure.

Textures can be found in the flooring, area rugs, walls, fabrics, draperies, furnishings, etc. Visual texture may be seen in paint, wood furnishings, certain fabrics (such as smooth or satiny looking fabrics or rough or coarse looking fabrics). Tactile textures stimulate your sense of touch depending on materials used (for example leathers, silks, burlaps, velvets, chenille, etc., all have a different sense of touch). Textures can be rough or smooth, hard or soft, coarse or fine, shiny or flat, etc.

Using the same texture throughout an entire room can be boring. A mix of textures can help to bring a room to life. Textures can be combined in many different ways and it is ideal to use a variety and combination of textures when decorating to add excitement and interest and to bring together the desired look and feel for the room, however, don't overdo it. An example of how textures can be combined is by taking a sofa that is upholstered in richly patterned damask fabric and adding a few cushions of varying materials (possibly a couple damask cushions combined with a couple of velvet cushions and one chenille cushion).

A mixture of hard fabrics (such as leather) with soft fabrics (such as chenille, linen or cotton) can also work well even if the soft fabrics only appear in cushions and pillows.

When putting together a decorating plan, it is ideal to create a design board in advance with the various textures you wish to use to see how the combinations will work together. For more information about design boards, see section 6.5.2.

3.2.5   Pattern

One design element that you can have fun experimenting with is using different patterns and combining them with varying colors. The fabric patterns that are selected for a room will have an impact on the feel of the room. For example:

- patterns with geometric shapes will give the room a contemporary look

- patterns with checks will give the room a casual look

- patterns with tapestries or paisleys will give the room a more formal look

- fabrics with a light airy pattern such as florals will give a room a more airy, open and casual look

- some patterns (such as stripes) can give either a formal or casual look depending on the type of fabric used.

Don't be afraid to combine stripes and plaids or checks and florals or reverse patterns (such as a yellow floral on a blue background with a blue floral on a yellow background) to add interest and variety. However, you do need to anchor the varying patterns together so that the combination doesn't look like a bunch of clashing patterns. For example, you can anchor a dark color in some of the fabric patterns and it can help to anchor some of the dark pieces of furniture in a room. You can also pick one color that unifies all the varying patterns (even if only the smallest amount of that unifying color is found within the patterns).

Some enduring and more popular traditional patterns for fabrics are plaids, stripes, gingham checks, florals and color printing in fabrics. Some newer and popular trends for patterns right now are leopard print (or any type of African print), palm trees and other tropical type patterns and patterns with bumblebees or butterflies. One thing to keep in mind when mixing patterns is to ensure the mixture is anchored with a solid color.

The mix of different patterns will also have an affect on how the room flows. Again, when putting together a decorating plan, it is ideal to create a design board in advance with the various fabrics/patterns, textures, paint colors, flooring, window coverings, etc. to see how the combinations will work together.

3.2.6   Scale

Scale in decorating refers to the relative sizes of different items in a room in relation to each other, in relation to the room and in relation to the individuals who will be using the items. Homestore, Inc. defines scale more specifically at their Homestore.com website as: "The proportion or size of a piece of furniture as it relates to a room."

The size of a room (and the size of the individuals using the room) will factor into whether large scale furnishings or smaller scale furnishings are used. Large objects look smaller when placed in a big space while small items look bigger when placed in a small space. For example, if you place a small accent chair in a huge room with very high ceilings, the chair will look dwarfed and out of place, yet if you place that same chair in a small space, it will likely look fabulous.

In a large family room, a large oversized sofa and loveseat and chaise lounge with solid wooden tables can be used, but this type of furniture would not work in a small room. In a small room it would be better to use a smaller scale sofa with a low back and low arms or a love seat or a couple of open legged chairs together with tables with glass tops (to give the appearance of openness). Also, a petite woman might choose to have smaller scale furnishings while a large man may choose larger scale furnishings.

It is best to keep pieces of similar scale together. For example, a small occasional chair will look better next to a floor lamp or an occasional or accent table than next to a large piece of furniture like an entertainment center or an oversized sofa.

Scale is also important when decorating with accessories. Placing a large piece of artwork or a grouping of artwork on a large wall can look fabulous. However, placing a small piece of artwork on that same large wall (without any of the other pieces of art) can look out of place and off scale.

3.2.7   Line and Form

Line

Lines can be vertical, horizontal or even diagonal and can be curvy or straight. All of the elements within a room can contain lines including the flooring, wall coverings, window coverings, furniture, accessories and fabrics. Additionally, the architecture within a room (doors, archways, windows, columns and even moldings) have lines in them. Curvy lines in a room (such as the lines in archways or rounded off furniture) are softer and more feminine while straight lines (such as doors, chair molding, square tables) are more masculine and have a feeling of strength.

Lines create movement within a room. The eye follows the lines and is directed towards the focal point in a room. Too many lines within one space can look busy while not enough lines in a room can make a room look boring and bare. Therefore, as a decorator, your job is to create a space that has enough lines within it to add interest and give the eye directions about where to look, without overdoing it.

Form

Form relates to the shape of an item or room element (whether it be a piece of furniture or accessory or lamp or window covering or wall, etc.) within a room.

When decorating, you should select items (e.g. furnishings and accessories, etc.) that go with the architectural form within the room regardless of the decorating style. For example, if the room has rounded corners and archways, furnishings with curves and rounded shapes will work well while furnishings that are boxy with hard edges won't. If the walls of the room are high yet narrow, then the furnishings should also be tall and narrow. By following the form of the room with items of similar shape and form, you will create a space that is in harmony.

You and your client will know that you have successfully decorated a room when you have a good feeling about how the room looks and the look is pleasing to your eyes. However, if something seems off kilter when you look into the room, you know that you have further rearranging to do.

3.3   Decorating Styles

As an interior decorator, you will be expected to know about different decorating styles. Styles can relate to:

- a particular regional style (i.e. styles influenced by a certain region such as American, French or English Country)

- a particular historical style, also called a period style (i.e styles from or influenced by a certain time period such as Neo-classical, Victorian, Colonial and Modern, to name a few), or

- the general appearance of the furniture.

Of the numerous decorating styles, most of them are categorized as being either casual, contemporary or traditional. Some of the popular style trends today are Modern (a contemporary style), Country (a casual style) and traditional styles such as Neo-classical, Victorian and Colonial. Eclectic is another popular decorating style that is created by mixing elements from two or more of the main styles (contemporary, traditional and casual). Descriptions of the most popular styles begin on the next page.

Among other things, the style can determine whether you'll be shopping for antiques or looking for modern furniture. It is important to note that when your client is deciding which period or regional style to go with, they should take into consideration the current architecture of their home. For instance, if your client lives in an open-beamed log home, it makes more sense to go with a Country style. If they live in a home with high ceilings, arches, pillars and columns, a Neo-classical look might work best.

However, it is totally suitable to decorate using more than one period or regional style. Keep in mind that your client may wish to mix and match various styles to create a very unique décor and Eclectic look.

3.3.1 Colonial

The Colonial style has been around since the 1600's yet evolved somewhat in the middle of the 18th century. This style is traditional and formal and reflects simple elegance. It is a popular style that is often used today.

Rooms that are decorated in Colonial style are simple but classic. High quality fabrics and materials (such as silk damask and brocades), fine furniture and exquisite draperies are used to decorate a room to give it a simple, yet rich, look.

Colonial style furnishings are often made of cherry wood or mahogany and have classic designs such as the Queen Anne style or Chippendale style. Queen Anne style furniture has curvy and dainty shaped legs (this style of leg is called cabriole) or "S shaped" legs on chairs, tables, sofas and chests and sometimes the cabriole legs have claw and ball feet. The Chippendale style has linear shaped furnishings including chairs with bow backs and straight front legs.

Other furnishings you might see in Colonial style decorating are high Queen Anne style chests, a double chest of drawers, loveseat, wing chair, dressing table, drop-leaf table with cabriole legs, and tables that stand on pedestals (or on cabriole legs).

The floors may be hardwood, or even tiled (with a marble look) and beautiful oriental rugs are often part of the flooring.

Walls may be covered in Georgian styled panels (from floor to ceiling) or they may be plastered in earthy tones or bright yellows, blues or greens. Alternatively, walls may be wallpapered or painted with a marbelized look. Moldings are sometimes used, particularly cornice and crown moldings.

Accessories that can be found in Colonial style homes are grandfather clocks, wall mirrors, sconces, chandeliers and silver service ware.

3.3.2   Country

Country style is normally casual, rustic and slightly cluttered yet can provide a real sense of warmth and comfort. This style is becoming increasingly popular. It is reflected by natural fabrics and materials and is emphasized by a sense of place (e.g. American, English, or French).

Furnishings are often made with stripped or antique pine or are sometimes made from maple, oak or wicker. Some pieces of wood furniture might be painted (blue is a popular color for this). Some other types of furnishing materials that are returning for a more back-to-nature feel are rattan, rod iron, distressed wood, teak and even log. If metals are used with these types of materials, they often have an antiqued or rusty looking finish to them.

Although the Country style was inspired by traditional styles, with time it is becoming more contemporary and floral fabrics (such as those created by designer Laura Ashley) are popular, as are vintage fabrics and laces. Preferred colors are off-whites, apple green, blues, pinks and pastel colors and earthy colors such as autumn reds, oranges and yellows.

Often beams on the ceiling are exposed, or the ceiling may even be made of cedar. Flooring is often pine or hardwood or stone or tile while window coverings are often wooden blinds or shutters.

Accessories are typically items from nature such as wreaths made from twigs or berries, dried flowers (which are quickly being replaced by fresh flowers), birds nests, sea shells, bowls of fresh fruit, displays of fresh vegetables, etc. Antiques and vintage accessories are also popular such as vintage signs or toys. Additionally, crafts play a part in country decorating (particularly quilts).

American Country

American Country style celebrates the spirit of America and started becoming popular just over 25 years ago (around bicentennial time). This style is charming, warm, relaxed, comfortable and eclectic and honors handcrafted items, memorabilia, past and simple pleasures and traditions.

Wicker chairs, twig furniture, stripped or antique pine, painted furnishings, Shaker cabinets, and floral upholstered furnishings can all be found in American Country homes.

Common fabric choices are linen, vintage cottons, lace or aged leather. Floor coverings may be wood or tile floors with hooked or homespun area rugs. Wall coverings can range from a pastel painted wall to a wall that has been stenciled in places (such as on the borders) to wallpapered.

Quilts, throws, cushions made with weathered fabrics, duck decoys, vintage signs, game boards, wooden trunks, vintage clothing and any objects made by American ancestors are popular accessories used within this style. Even the Southwestern influence of Native American items including motifs, or cowhides and bright colors are considered part of the American Country style.

English Country

English Country is a relaxed, comfortable and unpretentious style, yet is somewhat more cluttered. In English Country style, you will find mainly pine furniture, and overstuffed upholstered furnishings in casual pastel colors in chintz fabrics. Floral patterns are extremely popular (including the Laura Ashley type look as mentioned earlier) as are paisleys.

Furnishings in the kitchen may include a large pine kitchen table and open china cabinet displaying dishes with a mismatch of chairs (there could be a couple of antique chairs, and a couple of British colonial style chairs, mixed with some pine chairs, etc.). The furniture is normally solid and sturdy and, as mentioned, made from pine (or it can be made from oak).

Colors in English country style are normally soft and/or natural (such as off whites, pale yellows, mossy greens, earthy reds and taupes). Open beamed ceilings and whitewashed walls are trademarks of the English Country look.

The English decorate and accessorize with more of an eclectic style— mixing antique pieces, collectibles, Chinese porcelain, fancy tea pots, blue and white china, stacked books and mementos, with newer items.

French Country

French Country style is growing in popularity. It is warm, inviting and casual but unlike English Country, the colors are much more vibrant with blues and yellows dominating, and reds and greens also commonly used (influenced by colors of the Provencal countryside).

Furniture is often made out of chestnut, walnut or pine and although most of the furniture is fairly simple, chair legs are often curved. Some popular French Country furniture pieces are: an armoire (sometimes painted), sleigh bed or a white painted iron bed (with bed canopies or curtains), long walnut dining table with mismatched chairs, skirted round tables, buffets, bench with a floral upholstered seat and in a living room you may find classic Louis IV pieces.

Some other pieces commonly seen in a French Country style home are a wrought iron chandelier, French doors and copper pots hanging from pot racks.

Common fabrics used are lace and linens. Bedding is often traditional white with pillowcases trimmed in lace and embroidered. Popular patterns in fabrics are checks, florals and *toile de Jouy* (which has scenic designs in contrasting and vibrant colors).

Wall to wall carpet is not commonly used with this style and normally rough textures are used for walls and floors including stone, slate or brick tiles or ceramic tiles (sometimes with area rugs covering the flooring). Walls may also be stenciled or finished with a plastering look or whitewashed or colorwashed.

Popular accessories are blue and white Chinese pottery, copper pots, baskets, wine racks, candelabras, dried flowers and collections of glass bottles (such as perfume bottles).

3.3.3   Eclectic

Eclectic style is one of the most popular styles. In essence, this style is created when items from two or more different styles are combined together. It is often the most natural way to decorate because you can use items that your client already has and add different style items to them.

Although this style can offer you the most unique and interesting way to decorate that can characterize the personality of your client and include the items they love, it needs to be brought together with the important design elements of decorating kept in mind such as balance, scale, color, line, form, and texture. If these are not taken into consideration, the final effect can be a mismatched mess. However, if basic decorating principles are used when decorating Eclectic style, the outcome can be both fabulous and interesting.

For example, a casual Southwestern style Armoire can be mixed with a contemporary sofa (similar to a contemporary style you might find at Ikea) and combined with a coffee table that has a contemporary looking rounded glass table top sitting on a base made of two casual Southwestern style pots.

The lighting could include a contemporary looking floor lamp and table lamp and accessories could include plants in pots, contemporary candleholders with colored candles, Southwestern style pieces of art, a contemporary glass vase filled with calla lilies, decorative boxes, stacked books, etc. The combination is a mix of two different styles (one being the casual Southwestern style and the other being a contemporary more modern style).

Although it might seem that decorating with an Eclectic style will be the easiest, it is in fact one of the hardest styles to pull off successfully and that is why it is key to remember to take into consideration the design elements to ensure that the look is finished and pulls together to create a fabulous looking space.

3.3.4 Modern

The Modern style first originated in the 1920's to 1950's. In Modern style, the space is kept simplistic (pared down) and basic with little or no decoration and limited color is used. Clutter is definitely not part of the Modern look.

Furnishings have clean, no fuss lines, with rounded corners. Fabrics are often monochromatic. Chrome and glass are used for tables, as are lacquer and plastic laminate. Furnishings are "geometrically useful" and leather is a popular choice for upholstery with black, gray, white or brown being the most common colors. However, leathers and other upholstery can also be found in striking primary colors. Teakwood is often used with this style, or other neutral toned woods can be used for tables and cabinets.

Built-in shelving, built-in beds and other built-in units such as cabinets and cupboards are commonly seen in Modern decorating as are modular units. Other items seen in Modern style homes are mirrors and glass block (glass brick) to reflect and let in light.

Floors are kept simple (either hardwood or polished parquet) and if carpet is used it can be found in neutral colors. Sometimes bright colored area rugs are used that have abstract patterns or geometric shapes on them.

Often walls are painted white and windows are covered in blinds or simple drapes or they are left bare all together to let in the light. Accessories are used sparingly and often have geometric shapes or curves and can be found in vibrant colors. Glass is a popular accessory choice.

3.3.5 Neo-Classical

The Neo-Classical style is traditional and formal and it originated from the influence of ancient Greece and Rome (and Egypt, to a degree). The Neo-Classical look is fresh and clean, not fussy, while at the same time it is formal, dignified and classic. Symmetrical balance is an important element of Neo-Classical decorating.

Furnishings are normally in light woods and can have simple lines, however, furnishings can also be quite ornate with curvy lines and ornate detailing. Cream and natural color fabrics are very common within this style and other colors that are used within this style are reds, yellows, golds and greens. Additionally, Egyptian or Greek motifs can be used either in fabrics or on wall coverings. Window coverings are normally sheer, light and airy fabrics that hang symmetrically.

Common architectural elements within a Neo-classical designed home are columns, archways, crown moldings, rosettes and ceiling medallions. Rich and elegant fabrics in silks, velvets and brocades are used and predominant colors are gold, black and red.

Marble (or faux finished marble) is a popular flooring choice as are tile and wood or parquet. Marble, stone tile or faux finished marble paint are popular on walls. Popular accessories are urns, mythological figures, Greek style vases, Greek and Roman artwork and Greek style busts and sculptures.

3.3.6   Victorian

The Victorian style is traditional and formal, even somewhat fussy, and originated in the 19th Century (when Queen Victoria reigned in England). The Victorian style is reflected by ornate furnishings in dark woods, patterned area rugs, and lots of accessories.

Furniture is solid and large (somewhat bulging in shape) and often made from mahogany or walnut (dark woods). Upholstered furnishings have curvy shapes and deep buttons on them and they stand on cabriole or fluted legs. Popular furnishings are settees, marble topped chests and tables, armoires, corner cupboards, small writing desks and bathtubs with ball and claw feet.

The fabrics are deep colored, heavy and rich, such as velvet, silk, satin, damask and chintz, and are often trimmed with cording, tassels or fringe although lacey fabrics are also used quite a bit. Popular patterns found on fabrics are florals, birds, landscapes, scenes of animals or scenes of children. Needlepoint, whether it is on cushions, furnishings, or even wall hangings, is also a reflection of the Victorian style.

Floors are often covered in wood or parquet (in main areas) or tile or linoleum in kitchens and bathrooms. Oriental rugs or other patterned area rugs are often found on floors.

Walls are often covered in boldly colored wallpaper or are painted in cheery colors (such as crimson, vibrant greens, yellows and blues) in main rooms while bedrooms often have cooler and lighter shades of blues, greens, pinks and grays. Paneled wood may be used on the walls in some rooms (such as studies) while tiles may be used on the walls in kitchens and bathrooms.

Windows are covered with luxurious drapes or curtains (again with fringe and tassel and rope trimmings) and stained glass windows are commonly found in Victorian style homes.

Popular accessories of the Victorian style are a pitcher sitting inside a wash bowl, bottle collections, silver framed photographs, wooden toys, china door knobs, landscape paintings, brass clocks, bronze statues, candelabras and silver dinnerware.

3.3.7   Other Decorating Styles

There are many other styles in addition to the ones listed above. The following information from Homestore, Inc. describes the Art Deco, Arts & Crafts, Baroque, Contemporary, Georgian, Mexican and Southwestern, Oriental and Tudor styles.

Art Deco

The quintessential 1920s and 1930s style for skyscrapers, homes, cinemas, even cruise ships, Art Deco is glamorous, modern and dramatic. French designers mixed classical and contemporary elements, including the passionate colors of Fauvist paintings, sensuous fabrics, exotic artifacts of Egypt, Mexico, and the Middle and Far East, and Cubist painters' geometric shapes in round mirrors, floor treatments and barrel-shaped chairs.

American designers streamlined the style with modular and built-in chrome and aluminum furniture, while British designers contributed sleek materials like Bakelite and commercialized motifs like zigzags and chevrons.

Arts and Crafts

The Arts and Crafts style in England and America from 1860 through 1925 embraced quality materials, craftsmanship, and simple lines and forms to fashion one lovely harmonious interior. Fabrics and wallpapers with Gothic, floral and Japanese designs complement rather than overwhelm rooms, especially those created by movement founder William Morris. Furniture was block-shaped, usually oak, like Gustav Stickley's Mission pieces. Lighting was beautiful and useful, especially Louis Comfort Tiffany's stained-glass lamps and Dick Van Erp's hammered copper lamps.

Baroque

The Baroque style is theatrical and extravagant. Decorative elements are intended to startle, electrify—and flaunt wealth. This was also true for the European courts and aristocracy that embraced the 18th-century style. Furniture is massive and opulent, textiles are luxurious and expensive, colors are royally rich and glittery, accessories are exotic and sparkling, floors are dramatic. The style was most magnificently showcased at France's Louis XIVs palace at Versailles.

Contemporary

The Contemporary style honors current living and values. In the 1990s and today, interiors are functional, physically comfortable, environmentally conscious, and versatile to suit the hurried individual's idiosyncratic tastes and needs of the moment. Bright, airy and uncluttered, the style embraces white walls, blonde woods, fresh colors, sensual textiles and hi-tech fabrics, deep cushions, open or lightly draped windows, clean-lined mobile furniture, and materials that are natural, recyclable, or industrial such as glass and steel. The result: eclectic yet cozy retreats from fast-paced pressures.

Georgian Style

The Georgian style of 18th-century England revived classical Grecian and Roman principles of proportion and symmetry. Traces of other flamboyant styles surface in the details, including French Rococo ornamentation, medieval Gothic motifs and Chinese lacquerwork. Still, the Georgian look is mostly simple, uncluttered, sophisticated, and elegant. It features urn designs in wall moldings, timeless Wedgwood china and delicate furniture by then world-renowned master designers Thomas Chippendale, George Hepplewhite and Thomas Sheraton.

Mexican and Southwestern

Influenced by indigenous Indian and Spanish cultures, the Mexican and Southwestern styles are earthy, sophisticated and soulful. Furniture is rough-and-ready wood with decorative carvings; wool textiles are hand-woven with geometric motifs of nature; light fixtures are ornamental tin and wrought iron. But there are differences. The passionate Mexican style's loud colors, painted furniture and exuberant use of handcrafted decorative objects celebrate a folk heritage.

The Southwestern adobe style exudes a peaceful panache with subdued tones of surrounding mesas. Select accessories, especially chic pottery, paintings and sculptures from New Mexico's art and Indian colonies, epitomize the style.

Oriental Style

The Oriental style is mystical, meditative and calming, from ornately decorated palaces and temples to minimalist interiors of the common man. Though the Orient spans countries from China to Indonesia, certain elements are common to the diverse styles of each. Materials are natural, bamboo being a staple. Craftsmanship of furniture, ornaments and textiles is splendid. Lacquerwork and batik are distinctive. Colors are subdued or vibrant. And there is a respect for spirituality inherent in the symbolism for patterns, colors, artifacts and placement of objects.

Tudor Style

Stylistic freedom colored Englands Tudor period from 1485 to 1603. Fueled by political stability, international trade and prosperity, a building boom of multistory individual manors and townhouses introduced signature design features for long-term living and comfort: the wall fireplace, wall and ceiling ornamentation like strapwork, and ornate permanent furniture. Other decorative elements are a hodgepodge of influences from Gothic Europe, Italian and German Renaissance, the Orient and the Middle East.

Further Information

In addition to the styles listed above, there are a number of other styles (although many not as common) which you can read more about at **www.move.com/home-garden/decorate/style-guide**.

3.4   Room Elements

No matter what decorating style you use, there are a variety of room elements to consider. These are the specific items within a room, including:

- furniture
- flooring
- lighting
- walls
- window coverings
- accessories
- fabrics

3.4.1   Furniture

In the furniture industry, furniture is often categorized as either *soft goods* (which includes upholstered items such as sofas, ottomans and chairs and also beds) or *hard goods* (which includes desks, tables, chairs, chests, etc.). Hard goods are also often referred to as "case" goods.

Furniture selections are normally made based on style and how a piece looks (whether it is aesthetically pleasing); however, comfort, durability and function are other important factors to take into consideration. Accordingly, in addition to style, you'll need to know about furniture materials, features and construction, as these affect function, comfort and durability.

When purchasing furniture, one thing to keep in mind is that the quality of an item should match up with the price (or, even better, the price should be good for the quality of the product). Just because a piece of furniture is priced highly doesn't mean that it is of great quality. In fact, the quality of the furniture item could range from very poor to excellent. Following is some information about furniture qualities; however, you should also be familiar with the manufacturer's reputation. You can learn more about various aspects of wood furniture from the information provided below by Homestore, Inc.:

Wood Furniture

Types of Wood

The quality of the wood used for furniture is measured by its beauty, its stability (how well it wears over time), how easy it is to work with, how well it resists shrinking and cracking and how well it takes stain and finish.

HARDWOODS

Hardwoods are not necessarily hard, nor are softwoods always soft. A hardwood comes from a broadleafed, or nonneedled tree, like maple, cherry or mahogany. These woods are frequently used in furniture construction and usually don't have a hard surface. This can indicate a greater strength or stability; but those very qualities can also make hardwoods difficult to work with for certain purposes, such as intricate carving and detail work.

SOFTWOODS

Softwoods, or wood from needle-bearing trees such as pine or cedar, are also used in furniture making, frequently when easily carved or worked wood is needed. Since their surfaces are often soft, they are more susceptible to marks and dings, but these marks can result in a weathered or worn quality that is appropriate or appealing in certain pieces.

SOLID WOOD

The term *solid wood* does not mean that one single piece of wood was used throughout the piece, nor does it necessarily mean that all the wood throughout the piece is solid. Generally the term means that all the exposed pieces of wood are solid; those areas of the piece that are hidden from view, like the back of an armoire, for example, may be something else, like plywood.

PLYWOOD

Plywood is made from thin sheets of wood material that have been bonded together, usually with heat and glue. Frequently a plywood will be surfaced with a high-grade veneer. Construction of five-ply or seven-ply boards can offer great strength, stability and durability, so the use of plywood (as opposed to solid wood) in furniture construction is not necessarily a bad thing. Some plywoods are stronger and lighter than wood, and they are usually less expensive. For these reasons, manufacturers sometimes use plywood in non-visible areas of furniture construction where strength is paramount.

Finishes

Finishes can be decorative or protective or both. Oil and wax protect while giving a soft, matte finish. Oil and shellac or varnish give a soft, slightly higher sheen and also help protect wood. Lacquer gives the highest gloss and a hard coating. Any finish should be evenly applied, without apparent brush strokes or drips.

STAINS

A stain penetrates the wood, and provides an even color without hiding the grain or decorative figuring of the wood. When purchasing stained wood furniture, be careful that the stain has not been applied to make an inferior wood resemble a good one. Stain colors can mimic almost any wood, but it should always be clear at the time of purchase whether "mahogany," for example, refers to the finish or the wood. A stain should be an enhancement, not a disguise.

For an even, long-wearing finish, the process entails many steps: To pre-pare the wood, it needs to be sponged, sanded and dusted to open the wood pores; clean the wood and bring out the natural figuring. Next, the stain is hand-applied and allowed to dry thoroughly. Then it is sanded and rubbed down. This process is repeated, often as many as fif-teen or more times on fine furniture. Lesser pieces will use fewer coats, or machine-applied stains. Finishes should be smooth, bubble-free and crack-free (unless the piece is distressed). But it is also important to un-derstand that furniture stains are not permanent and unchangeable— they fade and alter from contact with sunlight and air.

PAINTS

Paints are intended to cover the surface of the wood, usually with opaque color. Paints can be water-based or oil-based (oil-based paint is generally used on furniture, and is usually easier to clean). Paint fin-ishes can be smooth and solid, which generally requires several coats, or distressed (weathered, pocked or otherwise made to look old), either intentionally or through actual age.

LACQUERS

This is varnish applied to wood in numerous thin coats; after each ap-plication, the coat is allowed to dry before being polished. The resulting finish is very hard and, frequently, highly glossy. Lacquer is often tinted (red and black are the most common colors), decorated, painted, gilded and inlaid. The use of lacquer originated in Asia and is most closely as-sociated with Asian furniture.

Construction

Many museums have furniture on display that is thousands of years old. And while we don't buy furniture with the expectation that it will last through the millennia, there is no reason that a piece of fine wood furniture can't get handed down to your great-great-grandchildren. The way a piece of furniture is built will affect whether your descendants get a treasured antique or a garage-sale reject.

The joins, or places where two pieces of wood connect, determine whether a piece will stand firm and strong, or wobble with use and age. Note that in a piece of quality furniture, wherever two or more pieces of wood join, the grains should match up. Common joins include:

MORTISE AND TENON

One side of a solid piece of wood is cut to fit a notch in an adjoining piece. The fit should be tight, and then the joint should be glued for further support.

DOUBLE DOWEL

Two wooden pins are cut and fit snugly into holes in both pieces of wood being joined. These joints are usually glued for extra security. Wooden dowels should be at least two inches long and 7/8" in diameter.

TONGUE-IN-GROOVE

A join used in places where two boards fit together side-by-side, as in the top of a table. This kind of joint is not used where the join must support weight or form an angle.

DOVETAIL

Used primarily in drawers, a dovetail joint has notches cut into the two pieces of wood that are to be joined. These notches must be accurately cut to interweave securely.

MITER JOINT

Two boards are angled to fit at a perfect 90 degrees. This joint may be reinforced with dowels, screws or nails.

CORNER BLOCKS

These are triangular wood blocks that are cut to fit corners, and are then glued or screwed into place. They should be used to further secure weight-bearing joints, especially those found in chairs.

Upholstered Furniture

Following is some excellent information and advice provided by Homestore, Inc. about upholstered furniture, or "soft goods." The upholstered furniture in your house, from sofas and chairs to the mattresses on your beds, are usually big-ticket household investments. For this reason, it pays to understand the basics of furniture fabrics and construction before you buy and to take good care of your furniture once you take it home.

Choosing Upholstered Furniture

Upholstered furniture is composed of three elements: frame, support system and fabric cover. Furniture prices generally vary depending on the quality of these elements. Here are the options.

FRAME

Furniture frames (also called the "carcass" or "bones") for top-of-the-line pieces are made of hardwoods, slowly dried in a kiln to prevent warping. Cheaper frames are made of softer wood and may be assembled in a less-than-durable construction.

SUPPORT SYSTEM

Springs, webbing and padding are the invisible but critical elements of upholstered furniture. Traditionally, expensive furniture has been constructed with hourglass-shaped, individually-tied coil springs. Many manufacturers now use "zigzag" or sinuous-wire springs or rubberized webbing strips—less expensive but strong alternatives.

The soft innards of upholstered furniture come from stuffing placed over the springs and padding under the outside fabric. Separate cushions on high end pieces use either down feathers or a feathers "plus" combination, though foam, covered with a layer of fiberfill, is the most common cushion stuffing.

FABRIC

Upholstery fabrics are tough as well as good-looking. Blends of natural and manufactured fibers, treated to block stains, make upholstery long-wearing and easy to clean. Here are some fibers and their common characteristics.

- Silk is a strong, resilient, luxury fiber with a natural luster. Fiber size varies from fine to heavy, as in raw silk.

- Cotton is a versatile fiber, used for prints and wovens, and is comfortable to use in all climates. It, as well as any untreated natural fiber, is less stain-resistant than synthetic fibers.

- Linen, a high-end fiber, is prized for its crispness, strength and durability.

- Wool is strong, durable, soft to the touch and naturally resists water.

- Rayon is a smooth, soft, lustrous and comfortable manufactured fiber. It wrinkles easily when used alone. Blended with other fibers, it adds silk-like luster to the finished fabric.

- Nylon is strong and resistant to abrasion, rot, and mildew. It has a low absorption for water and other liquids.

- Acrylic, a manufactured fiber, can offer many of the qualities of wool, a natural fiber. It is often used in plush or fleecy fabrics. Acrylic resists fading but is prone to pilling, the creation of small balls of fiber on the fabric's surface.

- Olefin is a strong, soil-resistant manufactured fiber that is used alone or blended with other fibers.

- Polyester is a strong, resilient and abrasion-resistant fiber that adds luster when blended with other fibers.

Protecting Fabrics

Most fabrics designed for upholstery come from the manufacturer with a stain- and soil-repellent finish. When it is missing, the store should be able to add the treatment with a warranty when you buy a piece of upholstered furniture, or you can buy a spray-on form at a hardware store and apply it yourself. Fabric protection gives you time to pick up or blot away spills before they soak in. It cannot totally prevent damage to the fabric.

If you are considering buying a warrantied fabric-protection treatment, read your fiber and fabric information carefully. If a fabric was treated at the mill, a second treatment is unnecessary.

Furniture Terms

Following is a list of various furniture terms (as defined by Homestore, Inc.) to assist you with recognizing different items or characteristics of furniture.

Armoire	A large cabinet or wardrobe, with two doors and shelves on the interior for storing clothes or electronic equipment.
Banding	Inlay or marquetry that produces a color or grain contrasting with the surface it decorates.
Bombé	(French) An outward swelling. Applies to commodes, bureaus, and armoires.
Bowfront	A cabinet front that curves outward to appear convex.
Break front	A bookcase or china cabinet made of three vertical sections, the center one projecting forward beyond the two end sections.
Buffet	A small cupboard. The French definition of the word is "a small sideboard, a place for keeping dishes."
Bun foot	A flattened ball, or bun-shaped, foot.
Bureau	In America, the name refers to a bedroom storage piece commonly known as a "dresser." The French word, however, originally designated the red cloth covering for a writing desk, and, later, was used to refer to the desk itself.
Cabriole	A graceful, curving type of leg that swells outward at the knee and inward at the ankle.
Camelback	A curved sofa back characterized by a large central hump.
Case goods	Specifically, storage pieces made primarily of wood. More generally, refers to entire collections of wood bedroom and dining room furniture, including some pieces that are not storage, such as headboards and dining tables.
Couch	A 17th- and 18th-Century term for a daybed. Not used as a term for a sofa until recent times.

Credenza	A sideboard or buffet.
Dowel	Headless pin, usually made of wood, used in furniture construction.
Eight-way, hand-tied springs	Each coil spring is hand-tied into place with twine, interlocking it with other coils. Using a set of knots, the coils are tied front to back, side to side, and diagonally across.
Etagere	A set of open shelves for displaying small objects and sometimes having an enclosed cabinet as a base.
Gateleg table	A table with a folding leaf upheld by a leg that swings out like a gate. Popular in Colonial America.
Highboy	A high chest of drawers, deriving its name from haut bois, which in French means "high wood."
KD	"Knocked down." Term applied to furniture sold unassembled or only partially assembled.
Motion upholstery	An upholstered piece with reclining or inclining seating features.
Occasional	A term applied loosely to any small tables, such as coffee tables, lamp tables and consoles.
Patina	A surface texture produced by age, wear or rubbing.
RTA	"Ready-to-assemble." Term applied to furniture sold unassembled or only partially assembled.
Secretary	A drop front desk, often with book shelves above and drawers below.
Settee	A long seat or bench with a high back and often with arms.
Sideboard	A dining room piece with a long flat top for serving and usually equipped with drawers or cabinets for storing china.

Trundle bed	A low bed, which, during the daytime, is rolled under a larger bed.
Veneer	Thin sheets of wood applied to the surface of furniture for decorative effect.
Windsor chair	A chair with a wooden or rush seat, pegged legs, and a back of turned spindles.
Wing chair	An upholstered chair with a high back, stuffed arms and wing-shaped projectors at head level.

As you will see from all of the information provided above, there is a lot to know about furniture and there are many aspects to furniture including style, construction, durability, comfort, function and materials used. Refer to the information on selecting furnishings in section 3.5 (*"Step-by-Step Decorating Instructions"*) for information on how to select furniture and find furniture suppliers and stores.

3.4.2   Flooring

When it comes to floor coverings you have a tremendous number of options. In addition to different colors, textures and patterns, there are many different types of flooring. Common choices include carpet, wood, vinyl, laminate, tiles and area rugs. Less common choices include bamboo and cork.

What you recommend to your client will depend on their needs and wants. Flooring choices are made for both decorative and practical reasons. Not only does flooring need to look good but it also needs to fit the purposes of your client.

For example, if your client wants to decorate a bathroom or kitchen, you need to take into consideration not only how the flooring will look but also how the flooring will perform in these rooms. In a kitchen and/or bathroom, the flooring must also resist moisture so, although it might feel warm and soft underfoot, carpet is not a good choice for either of these rooms. Following is some information about the most common flooring choices:

Carpet

Many people like the color options, warmth, comfort, texture and feel of carpet. Additionally, carpet is quiet underfoot, acts as a form of insulation from both cold and heat and absorbs sound (which is great if your client has a two-story home or lives in an apartment or condominium). Another advantage is that carpeting can be relatively inexpensive.

If the above advantages of carpeting appeal to your client, they may wish to have wall-to-wall carpeting installed. There are two commonly used types of wall-to-wall carpet in North America: berber and broadloom. Berber carpet is often made from a synthetic fiber and has looped pile that runs in parallel lines and it has a tweedy look to it. Berber is becoming increasingly popular and, although it is more casual, it is very durable and often has a stain-resistant finish which makes cleaning spills much easier. Broadloom carpet is any carpet that is made on a broad (wide) loom and the carpet can either be tufted or woven. Normally, broadloom carpet is anywhere between 12 to 15 feet wide, which minimizes seaming on wall-to-wall carpeting.

Another type of carpet is Axminster carpet (this originated in Axminster, England in the 1700's) and this is a patterned, woven carpet that can be used as wall-to-wall carpet or can be custom cut for area rugs. This type of carpeting isn't as popular as berber or broadloom for homes; however, because of its durability and ease of cleaning and the wide range of patterns and colors, it is often used in commercial areas (such as hotel lobbies, etc.).

The expense of carpeting depends on the carpet's fiber, finish and construction including the pile (height of the fiber), density (the amount of fiber tufts per square inch) and texture (how the fibers are twisted or looped).

Some of the synthetic fiber types are nylon, acrylic, polyester and olefin (also known as polypropylene) and a natural fiber type is wool (which is often more expensive). Carpet manufacturers are making carpets more durable and stain-resistant nowadays which, besides the advantages listed above, is why carpet remains a popular flooring choice.

TIP: Carpeting experts recommend that good quality underlay (also known as padding) be used especially in areas with high traffic (to increase the durability of the carpet), in areas where your client wants a soft and cushy feel under their feet and in areas where they want extra sound absorption. It is important to note that good quality underlay will increase the life of a carpet.

Wood

Wood flooring in either hardwood or softwood is a great way to add a naturally beautiful product while adding warmth and charm to a home. Hardwood floors are normally made of oak, maple or birch while softwood floors are made of pine, cedar, spruce or fir. After wood flooring is installed, it is often treated with a sealant and finished off with clear urethane. It is also possible to buy pre-finished wood flooring.

If your clients are interested in wood floors, they should be made aware of the fact that wood floors need to be maintained by coating them with a polyurethane every year or so and the floors should be waxed and buffed on occasion.

Wood floors are growing in popularity and this has helped with manufacturers being able to produce better finishes and more options for where wood flooring can be installed. Wood flooring can now be bought in long-strip planks, engineered planks and 3/4" solid wood and the end results of each look very similar.

Besides looking wonderful, elegant and charming, wood floors are also quite easy to clean as long as they are properly maintained.

Vinyl

Vinyl flooring is made from synthetic materials. There are a number of advantages to using vinyl flooring. It is inexpensive, durable, easy to clean and maintain and it is good for high traffic areas and areas where moisture might build up, such as bathrooms, kitchens, laundry rooms, etc.

The look of vinyl is more casual than tile or wood yet there are many options for patterns and colors including looks of marble, wood, tile, brick, stone and many others. The disadvantages of vinyl flooring are that it can get scratched (and torn) and it can also stain.

Laminate

Laminate flooring is a great option for flooring because not only does it look like real hardwood but it is much more durable, easier to maintain and easier to clean than real hardwood. Additionally, laminate flooring is highly stain and fade resistant and it is more affordable than real hardwood. Although laminate flooring has numerous benefits and closely resembles the look of hardwood, keep in mind that it is not a true wood product and is therefore not the "real" thing. If this doesn't bother your client, laminate flooring may be a great choice for them.

A couple of the more well known manufacturers of laminate flooring are Pergo (**www.pergo.com**) and Formica (**www.formicaflooring.com**). You can view samples of laminate flooring at each of their websites.

Tile

There are many different types of tiles to choose from, including ceramic, marble, stone, mosaic, clay, slate, granite, etc. One of the biggest benefits of tile is being able to select from a number of various pattern options. Additionally, tile looks beautiful, is durable (in most cases), is easy to clean and requires minimal upkeep.

There are disadvantages to tile and the most notable ones are the expense, the coldness of tiles under an individual's feet (unless they have under-floor heating) and the fact that things can break if they are dropped on tiles or the tiles might possibly chip if they are not the most durable type.

When selecting tiles for the floor, always make sure that you select flooring tiles (as opposed to decorative tiles for showers, walls, backsplashes, etc.). Besides selecting tiles, you will also want to help your client with selecting a grout color that will go well with the desired look.

TIP: Tiling experts recommend that you order approximately 10 percent more tiles than you require so that there are extras in case of breakage. After all of the tile is installed, your client should keep any leftover tiles because these can always be used as replacement tiles if any of the installed tiles chip over time. A good tile layer can cut out the chipped tile and replace it with one of the extras.

Area Rugs

A quick and easy way to add color, texture, warmth and character to a room is to place an area rug within the room. Additionally, area rugs can cover problem areas (stained carpets, for example) or scratched hardwood or vinyl. Some other reasons to use an area rug are to create intimacy or a feeling of coziness, to create a seating area, to define a space, to provide warmth for your client's feet, to reduce the noise in the room, to create a focal point, to establish a color direction or to bring colors in a room together and to protect flooring.

Area rugs can be purchased in varying sizes and shapes and in varying materials and the costs can range from inexpensive to very costly. As with carpeting, area rugs are also available in many different fibers including both synthetic fibers – such as acrylic, nylon and olefin – and natural fibers – such as wool, cotton or sisal (plant fibers) or jute.

TIP: It is important to always use a similar sized nonskid pad underneath an area rug. This pad will prevent the rug (and people) from slipping, make it easier to vacuum, and most importantly protect the area rug from wear. Additionally, a pad will protect hardwood floors, laminate or vinyl flooring underneath from scratches from the coarse bottom of an area rug.

As mentioned, there are many different flooring options, and choices are made for both practical and aesthetic reasons depending on what is required and desired. Refer to section 3.5 (*"Step-by-Step Decorating Instructions"*) for information on selecting flooring.

3.4.3   Lighting

Lighting serves more than one purpose in a room. In addition to ensuring people can see, it also contributes to the mood of a room. Imagine, for example, the difference between a room softly illuminated with candlelight compared to a room lit up with bright spotlights.

Sunlight can be used to illuminate a room, but it is difficult to control. While natural daylight can be included in your decorating project, you may also be concerned with three types of artificial lighting.

General Lighting

Also known as ambient lighting, general lighting is indirect lighting that brightens an entire room. It can be provided by lights mounted on the wall or ceiling or by large lamps. Your choices for general lighting range from chandeliers to track lights to floor lamps or large table lamps.

Task Lighting

Task lighting is direct lighting that provides enough illumination for people to carry out specific tasks such as reading, studying, or working. It is focused in the direction of where the task will be carried out. It is often provided by small lamps, but can also be provided by other types of lighting such as track lighting.

Accent Lighting

If there is something interesting in the room that you want people to notice – such as a work of art – you can draw attention to it with accent lighting. Accent lighting involves focusing three times as much light on the object as the area around it. The lighting can be provided by spot lights or other lights that will illuminate it sufficiently.

Color and Light

It is important to know how lighting in a room can affect the colors. Homestore, Inc. provides the following excellent insight into how light works with color in a room:

Thanks to light, we see color. The science of color and light is not that simple, of course, but a basic understanding of how light influences color can help you make wise color and lighting choices.

Most light in your home is artificial, and the color of that light varies. Warm light from incandescent bulbs intensifies yellows and reds but dulls the cooler colors. Halogen bulbs, a special category of incandescents, produce a whiter, brighter light. The cool blue light of standard fluorescent bulbs amplifies blues and greens but muddies warm yellows and reds. Newer "soft white" fluorescents come closer to the warmth of incandescents.

Light fixtures themselves contribute color to a room. Pendant lights can have brightly colored glass. A warm-hued lamp shade will cast its own glow, influencing other colors and helping to set a mood. Be aware, however, that strongly colored lamp shades tend to soak up the light. White or cream shades have become classic because they yield maximum light.

A room's exposure determines the quality of its natural light, which can influence your color choices. North-facing rooms receive less direct sunlight, and that light tends to be cool, while south-facing rooms get inherently warmer light. The conventional wisdom is to balance the temperature in a room, using warm colors in north-facing rooms and cool colors in south-facing ones. You are free to ignore that advice, of course, and enhance the natural temperature of a room with colors of a similar temperature.

The way materials and surfaces reflect light also affects color. A shiny red lacquer table will reflect light and appear brighter, while the same red rendered in a heavily textured fabric will be comparatively dull.

3.4.4   Walls

As with other room elements, you have many choices when it comes to decorating walls. Your options for decorating walls go well beyond deciding what color to paint them. (Although painting the walls a different color is a relatively quick and inexpensive way to make a dramatic change to a room.)

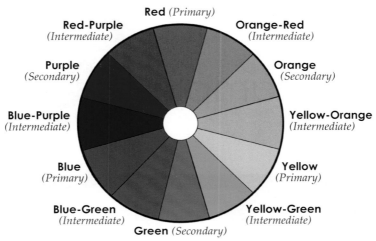

Red *(Primary)*

Red-Purple *(Intermediate)*

Orange-Red *(Intermediate)*

Purple *(Secondary)*

Orange *(Secondary)*

Blue-Purple *(Intermediate)*

Yellow-Orange *(Intermediate)*

Blue *(Primary)*

Yellow *(Primary)*

Blue-Green *(Intermediate)*

Yellow-Green *(Intermediate)*

Green *(Secondary)*

Above is a basic color wheel that includes the three primary colors (red, yellow and blue), the three secondary colors (purple, orange and green) and six intermediate (also known as "tertiary") colors that are an equal combination of a primary color and a secondary color next to the intermediate color on the color wheel.

Design Samples

The stunning living room above shows a floating sofa (a sofa pulled away from the wall) covered in decorative cushions to add color and texture. A soft shawl drapes an exquisite bench for added interest. Notice the greenery, flowers and accessories spread throughout the space to personalize the look.

Leading by Example

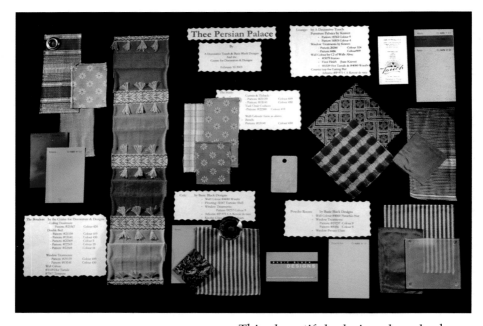

This beautiful design board shows samples of paint chips and flooring and countertop materials together with the numerous luxurious fabrics to be used in the decorating plan. By putting together a design board like this, you can show your clients how the different colors, patterns and textures will all work together.

Design board courtesy of Sallie M. Ritchey, D.I.D., of A Decorative Touch at the Centre for Decorators & Designs, 304 - 1235 - 26 Avenue SE, Calgary, Alberta.

If you want examples of your work to show clients, but don't have design boards from an actual decorating project, you can produce sample design boards with pictures and materials you might use to decorate a room.

This design board shows a photograph of the desired look (a Neoclassical style with a Victorian bust for an accessory) together with the different materials and fabrics recommended for use.

This design board shows the type of look (Shaker style) that a decorator might recommend to a client together with the sample materials to be used.

Design boards created by Wade Steel, student of Sallie M. Ritchey, D.I.D., of A Decorative Touch at the Centre for Decorators & Designs.

A sensual Asian theme infuses the room with rich colors and understated drama. The botanical design of the area rug echoes the curvy lines of the armchair.

Asian
Inspiration

BEFORE: This nondescript living room in a vintage Manhattan building showed no personality.

Interior Decorating by Keith Lichtman, KL INTERIORS, New York, NY, www.KL-Interiors.com.

A citrus inspired color palette along with contemporary furniture breathes life into the space. The geometric rug and clean-lined window dressings keep the room grounded.

Citrus
Flavor

BEFORE: The black leather furniture and bare walls shouted "bachelor pad" in this high-rise condominium home.

Interior Decorating by Keith Lichtman, KL INTERIORS, New York, NY, www.KL-Interiors.com.

The chocolate and tan living space is now more transitional. A clean-lined coffee table balances the traditional elements in the room such as the fireplace mantle and paisley armchair fabric.

Sweet
Temptation

BEFORE: This traditional living room was pleasant, but the client wanted a richer color palette.

Interior Decorating by Bobbie Lyons, Owner of Affordable Elegance Room Design, LLC, Stamford, CT, www.affordableeleganceroomdesign.com.

An elegant transitional statement has been created with chocolate velvet sofas, modern lamps, and varied accent tables. The room is capped off by a custom valance and drapes at the patio door for a sophisticated look that echoes the new color scheme.

BEFORE: This bland living room was lacking a dynamic color palette and a distinct style.

Interior Decorating by Keith Lichtman, KL INTERIORS, New York, NY, www.KL-Interiors.com.

A warm traditional style is showcased with the wood and leather dining set along with ornate buffet and mirror. Soft jade walls are complementary to the red tones in the furniture and flooring. A new patio door updates the room while moldings around the doorways create drama.

BEFORE: This formal dining room was overdue for a remodel.

Interior Decorating by Marlaina Teich, Owner of Marlaina Teich Designs, Merrick, NY, www.MTDNY.com. Photography of 'Before', Marlaina Teich Designs. Photography of 'After', Oleg March Photography.

Rich mocha walls soften the room along with a wooden and upholstered dining table set with extra seating. New custom window valances unite the updated color scheme.

Dining
with
Style

BEFORE: Red walls were clashing with this client's new cabinets and granite countertops.

Interior Decorating by Barbara Green, Sensibly Chic Interior Design, Cornelius, NC, www.sensiblychic.biz.

Kitchen
Magic

BEFORE: This purely utilitarian kitchen was a blank slate in this New York City high-rise condo.

Mosaic glass tile walls and a new layout have transformed this kitchen into a chef-worthy space. New cabinetry, crown molding, granite countertops, flooring, and appliances come together for a declaration of modern style.

Interior Decorating by Keith Lichtman, KL INTERIORS, New York, NY, www.KL-Interiors.com.

This beautifully decorated children's bedroom looks fabulous with the teddy bear collections, area rug, plenty of decorative cushions, artwork and plants. Don't forget to add art to the walls and decorative cushions when decorating a child's bedroom and ensure there is plenty of storage space.

Sweet
Dreams

Interior Decorating of child's room by Jan L. Riddell, Jazz It Up Interiors, and Catherine Goulet. Photography by David Watt of David Watt Photography.

A glamorous master bedroom retreat has been created using soft colors and sweeping lines. The diamond quilting on the headboard repeats the subtle wallpaper pattern. Citron silk curtains tie it all together.

BEFORE: The master bedroom of this 1790's Berkshire, Massachusetts, house had spartan country decor.

Interior Decorating by Keith Lichtman, KL INTERIORS, New York, NY, www.KL-Interiors.com.

A hotel chic, gender-neutral guest suite now cordially receives visitors. Textured wallpaper, neutral colors, and luxurious fabrics are the highlights of this room.

Spartan to Spectacular

BEFORE: This no-frills guest bedroom feels uninspired and unwelcoming.

Interior Decorating by Keith Lichtman, KL INTERIORS, New York, NY, www.KL-Interiors.com.

BEFORE: The owners of this whimsical bird-themed guest bathroom were ready for a new look.

AFTER: A warm tan color sets the tone for this sophisticated bathroom. Botanical-themed wall art retains a nod to nature while showcasing a contemporary style.

Beautiful
Bathrooms

Interior Decorating of bathroom on this page by Gail Mayhugh, GMJ Interiors, LLC, Las Vegas, Nevada, www.GMJinteriors.com.

The mature trees and landscaping surrounding these clients' home provided the inspiration for this design concept. The graceful whorls within the marble appear to be branches amongst the surrounding trees, giving the feeling of being nestled in the branches of one of those trees itself.

This beach-themed powder room was created under stairs. It captures the elements of the ocean with sea forms, starfish, and nautical plants. The countertops and backsplash are made of pool tile to stand up to daily usage by the family's children and friends.

TOP: Interior Decorating by Judson Rothschild, Rothschild Interiors, Beverly Hills, CA, www.RothschildInteriors.com. Photography by Everett Fenton Gidley, LLC.

BOTTOM: Interior Decorating by Jeanine Naviaux, President, On The Inside Design, La Jolla, CA, www.ontheinsidedesign.com.

This graceful room abounds in opulent materials including marble clad walls, glimmering surfaces, fine woods, and supple furnishings. All this echoes the precious quality of the Goldberg collection while providing a warm environment for this private retail setting.

Business Class

BEFORE: For this commercial project, William Goldberg Diamond Company wanted to transform their very traditional conference area into a luxurious boutique for their private clientele.

Interior Decorating by William Green & Associates, New York, NY, www.wga architects.net.

Walls can also be covered with wall coverings, fabric, tiles or wood. They can also be decorated with stencil designs, or covered with a "faux finish" that can create looks ranging from a stone wall to a villa in Tuscany.

Paint

As Debbie Travis (from the popular TV show *Debbie Travis' Painted House)* says, painting a room is one of the easiest ways to transform a space. It is also one of the easiest ways to bring in color and add life to a room. Some of the advantages of painting a room are that it is relatively inexpensive and it doesn't take much time (compared to some of the other wall treatment options).

Many people prefer to have their room(s) painted the traditional way with brushes and rollers. Depending on your client's wishes, they may choose to use an oil-based paint (which takes longer to paint with but is durable) or water-based paint (latex) which is a lot quicker to paint with and easier to work with. You may need to help your client with choosing what type of finish to have (from flat, to semi-gloss, to gloss to high gloss).

It is preferable to use flat or semi-gloss paints in main living areas such as a living room, dining room or family room and a higher gloss paint (which are easier to clean) in an area like the kitchen, however, everyone has their personal tastes and preferences.

There are many different colors and types of paints to choose from. Some of the more popular paints used today are Benjamin Moore, Behr, Martha Stewart, Pittsburgh Paints, Pratt & Lambert and Ralph Lauren (this line has some incredible suede style paints!).

These paint manufactures also offer a wealth of information on their websites about paints and decorating with paints.

- *Benjamin Moore*
  www.benjaminmoore.com

- *Behr*
  www.behr.com

- *Martha Stewart*
  www.marthastewart.com

- *Pittsburgh Paints*
  www.pittsburghpaints.com

- *Pratt & Lambert*
  www.prattandlambert.com

- *Ralph Lauren*
  www.ralphlaurenhome.com/products/paint

If your client wants to have their room painted but would prefer something more unique, there are a variety of decorative faux techniques that can be used to add depth, interest and beauty to a room. To create a faux finish, a water-based paint color is mixed together with a "faux" glaze (the ratio is normally one part paint to four parts glaze) and then the mixed glaze is applied in various ways. Some of the more popular techniques are:

Ragging On

This involves painting the wall with a base coat color and letting it dry (or using the base coat that is already on the wall) and then using a damp rag dipped in the mixed glaze and applying the glaze mix to the wall by blotting the rag either evenly or randomly over the wall to get the desired effect.

Ragging Off

This involves painting the wall with a base coat and letting it dry (or using the base coat that is already on the wall) and then rolling on the glaze mix and then using a rag (or crumpled up plastic bag) to blot off the glaze mix.

Sponging On

This involves painting the wall with a base coat color and letting it dry (or using the base coat that is already on the wall) and then using a dampened sponge dipped in the mixed glaze and applying the glaze mix to the wall by blotting the sponge either evenly or randomly over the wall to get the desired effect. Although this sounds the same as ragging on, the effect looks quite different.

Sponging Off

This involves painting the wall with a base coat and letting it dry (or using the base coat that is already on the wall) and then rolling on the glaze mix and then using a dampened sponge to blot off the glaze mix in either a random or even pattern. This sounds the same as ragging off; however, the end result is different.

Dragging

This technique is used to give a distressed or antique-like look and involves painting the space with a base coat and letting it dry (or using the base coat that is already on the wall) and using a nylon or polyester brush (approximately six inches wide) dipped in the glaze mix and then dragging the wet brush around, followed by using a dry brush to drag the glaze mix around until it dries and until the desired look is achieved.

Combing

This technique is virtually identical to dragging, however, instead of using a wet brush, an item with teeth is used to drag until the desired effect is achieved.

Color Washing

This technique is used to give a rustic, worn, faded and "washed" look and involves painting the wall with a base coat color, letting it dry (or using the base coat that is already on the wall) and then using either a nylon or polyester paint brush to apply the glaze mix with random brush strokes and altered stroke patterns to get the desired look. Alternatively, instead of a paint brush, a wet rag dipped in the glaze mix can be used and by simulating washing motions (or outlining figure 8's) over the wall, can give the desired "washed" look.

Spattering

This involves painting the wall with a base coat color and letting it dry (or using the base coat that is already on the wall) and then using a damp paint brush dipped in the mixed glaze and spraying on the glaze mix by flicking the brush with your fingers or simply flicking the brush to apply the spattered paint.

Wall Coverings

Wall coverings (or wallpapers) are not as popular as they were a number of years ago; however, they are still a good option to consider when decorating a wall because there are many different patterns, textures and colors to choose from to fit any budget. Additionally, wall coverings can add interest to a room and they can also cover any defects on a wall.

Wall coverings come in vinyl, papers (with vinyl backed coating) and handprinted papers, grass cloth, and other natural fibres such as linen, etc. Wall coverings that are inexpensive are usually hard to work with, not as durable and more difficult to apply.

Fabrics

Another option for covering a wall is to apply fabric, which adds interest, texture, ambience and a unique look. Besides adding flare and warmth to a room, fabric can also cover an imperfect wall. Fabric can be stapled directly to a wall, hung like drapes, glued to a wall, gathered or shirred (a form of gathering) to create the desired look.

Different fabrics can be chosen from to cover a wall. Some of the more popular choices are linens, cottons (particularly muslin), silks and sheer fabrics. Depending on the fabric chosen, you can either create a soft and airy looking wall or an exquisite luxurious looking wall. However, one of the disadvantages is that placing fabric on a wall can be quite costly and time consuming (particularly if there is a lot of sewing of the fabric involved).

Tile

Different types of tile (such as stone, clay, ceramic, granite or even mosaic) can be applied to a wall to give a more natural type look or a more decorative type look (with ceramic tiles there are many different colors and patterns to choose from).

Often tiles are used on only a portion of a wall as opposed to all the way up a wall and are mainly used on walls in the kitchen or bathroom (where surfaces need to be kept clean and can be easily wiped down). Additionally, tiles are often used on fireplaces to give a more dramatic look.

One of the biggest advantages of using tiles is that they look fabulous and, depending on the finish, can either add warmth, color, texture or pattern to a wall. However, one of the disadvantages is that tile can be one of the more costly choices for walls.

Wood

Adding wood to a wall can add a beautiful natural warmth to a room. Wood paneling can be used to cover the whole wall or it can be used to cover the lower part of the wall (this technique is called wainscoting and can look fabulous and elegant in a room). Wainscot panels can be ordered pre-cut or they can be custom ordered to match the other woods within the room (for example, doors and/or moldings).

If wood is going to be added to walls, it is most likely going to be added to walls in the living room, dining room, study, family room or even in basements.

Some of the other benefits of using wood are that it acts as a great insulator and it can cover flaws and imperfections on a wall. One of the disadvantages of wood paneling is the cost, as it can be expensive to cover a wall in wood.

Moldings

In addition to the above, you can also give a wall a more finished look by adding trim and moldings (such as chair molding, crown molding, baseboards and case molding). Chair molding is a molding strip that runs the width of the walls and is normally about 30" to 36" off the floor. Chair molding looks fabulous when it is similar to the other moldings used in a room and is painted the same color. Chair molding creates a line for the eye to follow.

Additionally, crown moldings and cornice moldings can beautifully finish off the top of a wall and give an elegant look. Baseboard moldings (especially nice wide ones) can add a finished appearance to the bottom of a wall and case moldings can nicely trim doors and windows.

One thing to keep in mind when putting various types of molding within a room is to ensure they are of the same color and similar styles.

Refer to the information on determining wall treatments in section 3.5 (*"Step-by-Step Decorating Instructions"*) for advice on selecting wall treatments.

3.4.5 Window Coverings

Window coverings are part of any good decorating plan and they can add texture, color, drama and interest to any room while also serving a functional purpose.

There are a number of factors you will need to take into consideration when selecting window coverings and the most important of these are privacy, function, style and how much light you want to allow in. When it comes to decorating windows, your options for window treatments are extensive and include:

Curtains

Curtains are a window dressing attached to a rod that are opened and closed by hand. Curtains normally cover all of a window or can be two tiered and can either be casual or formal and may be lined or unlined and can either be bought already made to size or can be custom made with a fabric of your client's choice.

Drapes

Drapes are a window dressing set up on a pulley cord system where a rod is pulled to open and close the drapes. Drapes are normally more formal than curtains and are usually lined and are often at least the length of the window and sometimes even go all the way to the floor and sometimes even spread on to the floor (this is called puddling and can have a really dramatic look!). There are a number of different drapery style options from pleated to tabbed to smocked styled draperies and often drapes are custom made with select fabrics which can really bring in texture and color if desired.

Blinds

Blinds come in a number of different colors and options, including venetian blinds (which are made from wood, metal or plastic and have two-inch slats and hang horizontally over windows), mini blinds (which are made from wood, metal or plastic and normally have one-inch slats and hang horizontally over windows), vertical blinds (which are normally made in three-inch wide slats made from fabric or PVC that hang vertically), and matchstick blinds (which are made from split bamboo and hang horizontally). Most blinds often have an informal look about them.

Shades

Shades cover the window and close from top to bottom. They can be made from select fabric or can be purchased pre-made in solid colors in fabrics like linen. Additionally, shades may work on a basic roller system or on a more elaborate cord and drawstring system such as with Roman shades (these have horizontal folds), Festoon shades (these have billowy folds) and Pleated shades (these normally have permanent pleats).

Sheers

Sheers are translucent and airy looking window coverings made from any sheer fabric.

Shutters

Window treatments normally made from solid panels of wood or wooden slats on two separate shutters that are mounted on opposite sides of the inside of a window. These can look quite casual.

Decorative Accents

A number of different decorative accents are available for dressing up windows, including:

Tie backs   Fabric pieces of material that "tie back" the curtains from the window

Decorative rods   Can be made from varying metals or wood and curtains or drapes hang from them

Sconces	Stone, plastic, wooden or ceramic sconces with openings can be hung on the outside edges of a rod or they can be hung outside the top of the window trim and have long scarves run through them to "frame" the window
Valances	Fabric headers that cover the top of drapes or curtains and/or the hanging hardware
Cornices	Fabric-covered wooden boxes that sit out over the top part of a window and overtop of drapes and hardware

You will see from the information provided above that there are many different options to choose from (including color, fabrics, and textures) when selecting window coverings and the choice of style will really depend on the look and functionality required. Refer to the information in section 3.5 (*"Step-by-Step Decorating Instructions"*) for advice on selecting window coverings.

3.4.6   Accessories

Accessories are one of the most important items in making a house a home. After all, accessories express the personality and individuality of a home-owner. They can include unique decorative items, cushions, throws, lamps, mirrors, plants, flowers, candles, artwork, screens, sculptures, heirlooms, collectibles, etc.

One of the keys to bringing the decorative look together is to have a balance of complementing items with contrasting items. For example, if your client wants to decorate a family room with a "tropical and worldly feel about it," you may decide to place complementing cushions decorated with palm trees on each side of the sofa and love seat and add a contrasting cushion with pineapples (contrasting in pattern, texture and color) in the middle of the sofa to add interest and finish off the look. Some important tips to keep in mind when accessorizing are:

- Group items together. If your client has a variety of objects of similar color, shape and/or design, group them together to show them off. It is ideal to group items in combinations of three or five (or some odd number).

- Place items of varying heights together to add interest, placing the taller pieces behind the shorter pieces to add depth.

- It looks better to keep collections (such as a collection of glass bottles) grouped together than to spread the items throughout the house. When collections are scattered, the feel and look is more of clutter as opposed to a lovely collection.

- Use plenty of artwork and, again, group artwork together (unless a piece is large enough to stand on its own).

- Use mirrors to open up a space and make it look larger, however, always make sure that whatever the mirror is reflecting is something that is appealing to look at (not the ceiling or a back door, etc.).

- Use plenty of greenery and plants of varying sizes and shapes to add warmth and texture.

- Use silk and/or fresh flowers to add color, vibrance and life to a room (and place the flowers in a beautiful and/or decorative vase or jug).

- Try hanging decorative wall sconces (with or without lights) on either side of a piece of artwork or mirror.

- Use decorative cushions (don't be afraid to use a lot) and throws to bring in texture, color and interest.

- Use lighting, floor lamps, table lamps, candles to add warmth and to create a mood.

- When decorating a bathroom, don't forget to add accessories such as candleholders, candles, plants, vases, flowers, artwork, baskets with rolled towels, etc. to liven the room.

- Books can be used as decorative accessories; a colorful coffee table book can be placed at an angle on a table to add interest or hard cover books (with their glossy covers removed so that the gold embossed print on the book can be seen) can be stacked and/or angled or used to elevate smaller items in a family room or office.

- Avoid over-accessorizing with small items that will appear as clutter.

Adding accessories to a room can be one of the most fun and rewarding parts of decorating because accessories can breathe life into a room, and add color, warmth, texture, drama, personality and pizzazz.

3.4.7   Fabrics

A number of room elements involve fabrics (also known as *textiles*). There are fabrics made of natural fibers such as silk, wool, cotton and linen and there are synthetic fabrics made from manufactured fibers such as polyester, nylon and acrylic. You may need to choose fabrics for furniture upholstery, wall treatments, bed linens, window coverings, decorative cushions, etc. In addition to ensuring the fabrics work well together in terms of design elements (such as color, texture, and pattern), you'll need to ensure they will stand up well. Susan J. Mielke, an interior decorator in Minneapolis, says "Know your fibres! Know how they react to light, water, humidity, and different climate changes."

Fabrics can add warmth and color and ambiance to a room while bringing in different patterns and textures. Expensive, exquisite and luxurious fabrics can add a look of elegance and formality to a room while casual fabrics such as cotton or linens can add a look of comfort to a room.

Depending on the weave, the weight and the type of fabric, this can affect the cost, use and durability of the fabric. Tightly woven fabrics (such as brocades and damask) are more durable and can be used to upholster furniture, while loosely woven fabrics (such as burlap or chenille) would not hold up that well on furniture but would work well for curtains and drapes (burlap) and decorative cushions and throws (chenille).

Following is a list of popular fabric terms defined by Homestore, Inc.:

Batik   Hand-printed material colored by dipping the fabric into dye.

Brocade	Originally heavy silk with an elaborate pattern in silver or gold threads. Brocade fabric has an embossed appearance.
Chenille	From the French word for "caterpillar," so named because chenille yarn is plush and fuzzy. Also used to denote fabrics made with chenille yarn.
Chintz	Originally any printed, cotton fabric. Now refers to fabric with a glazed or "polished" surface.
Damask	Named for the ancient city of Damascus where elaborate floral designs were woven in silk. Damask is flatter than brocade and is reversible. The pattern changes color on the wrong side.
Jacquard	Damasks, tapestries, brocades, matelass and all cloths with elaborate figures woven on a jacquard loom.
Matelass	French, meaning "to cushion or pad." Refers to fabric with a quilted surface produced on the loom. A figured or brocaded cloth with a raised pattern.
Moire	A fabric, particularly silk, with a watered or wavy pattern.
Ticking	A strong cotton fabric used to cover mattresses.
Toile	A sheer cotton or linen fabric.

When decorating, use a variety of fabrics (just as you would use a variety of patterns and textures) to add interest, warmth and color. Again, when putting together the decorating plan, it is ideal to create a design board in advance with the various fabrics/patterns, textures, paint colors, flooring, window coverings, etc. to see how the combinations will work together.

3.5   Step-by-Step Decorating Instructions

While each decorating project will be unique, there are a number of basic steps which you will likely need to take on many projects. They are:

1. Do Space Planning

2. Determine the Best Layout

3. Choose a Color Scheme

4. Determine Flooring Requirements

5. Select Wall Treatments

6. Determine Lighting Requirements

7. Complete any Repairs or Renovations

8. Select Furnishings

9. Choose Window Coverings

10. Arrange the Furniture (using the Layering Process)

11. Accessorize

12. Evaluate the Decorating

This section of the guide explains each of these steps in detail, and in Chapter 6 you will get advice on customizing these steps to each particular client's needs.

3.5.1   Do Space Planning

Before you begin decorating and laying out furniture in a room, you will need to do space planning to know how much space you have to work with so you can plan what to do with it. Space planning will allow you to try out different alternatives for room layout. It will also help you in budgeting as you will know how much will be needed of different types of materials (e.g. carpet, flooring, wallpaper or paint).

The three basic steps in space planning are:

• measure the area

• draw plans

• determine the best layout (covered in the next section)

Measure the Area

You will need to measure the space to be decorated so that you can draw the room to scale (i.e. make floor plans). To do this you will need to accurately measure the room and ideally you should do this with a 25' (or longer) metal tape measure with a lock on it. You will need to ensure that you measure and record the dimensions of all parts of the room, including walls, doors, windows, closets, any openings such as arch ways, electrical outlets, locations of switches, and any other items and/or permanent fixtures (such as fireplaces) in the room.

It is helpful and makes the job a lot easier to have a second person (possibly your client) assist with the measuring. The helper can hold one end of the measuring tape, when needed, while you read and record each measurement. Ensure that you not only measure the width and length of each room but also find out and record the height of the walls. Get into the habit of measuring everything twice to verify that each measurement is accurate.

Draw Plans

After you have completed measuring and recording all measurements, the next step is to prepare two plans. In addition to a floor plan (also called a base plan or base map), you will need to prepare an elevation plan showing locations of windows, doors, cupboards and other vertical items.

Floor Plan

Having a floor plan of the room drawn to scale will help you visualize the whole room. It is best to draw a rough floor plan while at your client's (at the same meeting that you take measurements) to ensure that you draw in all of the fixtures, openings, outlets, heat registers, doors, windows, etc. However, you will likely want to draw a more refined and thorough floor plan at your office (on your drawing table, if you have one), after meeting with your client using the rough drawing as a starting point.

Most interior decorators use 1/4-inch grid graph paper (available at any office products store); however, many choose to draw to 1/2-inch scale with each 1/2-inch representing one foot within the room and, in such a case, each box on the 1/4-inch grid graph paper would represent six inches (half a foot) within the room. This means that two squares (on 1/4-inch grid graph paper) will equal 1/2-inch, which will equate to one foot within the room.

For example, if the width of the room is 12 feet, you would draw a line 24 boxes wide (to represent 12 feet wide). It is easiest to draw a straight line with your ruler (or better yet, with a straight edge). After drawing the width of the room, then draw the length of the room. After you have drawn the dimensions, draw in any windows, doors (including which way the door swings), fireplaces and other openings, cupboards, built-in bookshelves, or other permanent fixtures, fireplaces, electrical, cable and telephone outlets, switches, heating ducts and returns, etc.

Elevation Plan

Elevations are particularly important when planning cabinets or wall systems. Here are a couple of tips from Homestore, Inc.:

- Try an elevation sketch of your proposed wall arrangement. How do the vertical lines created by cabinets, windows, doors, and appliances fit together? It is not necessary for them to align perfectly, but you should consider adjusting the width of a wall cabinet to line it up with the edge of a sink, range, or base cabinet.

- Follow a similar process to smooth out horizontal lines. Does the top of the window match the top of the wall cabinets? You might want to adjust the cabinet height, or add trim or a soffit.

Another option, instead of drawing the floor plan, is to use computer software for home design. With this type of software you can even draw 3D plans. Chapter 5 has advice on finding design software. While making an accurate drawing (floor plan) is an important first step in space planning, most decorators will also take pictures with a digital camera to use as a memory aid (these images can then be used as "before" pictures for your portfolio).

3.5.2 Determine the Best Layout

After you have drawn the room to scale, you can then experiment with layout. To determine the best layout for the space you will be decorating, you will need to do the following (each of these is discussed in detail below):

1. Determine the balance lines of the room

2. Determine the traffic patterns

3. Determine the desired focal point

4. Determine what the room will be used for

5. Experiment with different furniture arrangements

Determine the Balance Lines of the Room

To determine the balance lines of a room, take your floor plan (i.e. the scale drawing) of the room and divide the room into four equal quadrants. In other words, on your floor plan, draw a line (in pencil) down the center of the width of the room and draw a line across the center of the length of the room to divide the room into four equal sized areas. Where the two lines cross is your midpoint and you can use the midpoint as a starting point for planning where to place your furniture around.

Drawing the balance lines (and determining the mid-point) will keep you in check so that you don't weigh down any one side of the room, but work towards keeping a balance of the furnishings within the whole room. The weight of the furniture should be more or less equal on opposite sides of the room to keep the room in "balance." For example, if one side of the room has a large sofa in it, the opposite side of the room may have two chairs with an occasional table between them that face the sofa. The two chairs and occasional table balance out the large sofa.

Determine the Traffic Patterns

The next thing to determine is where the traffic patterns will be within the room. You need to take into consideration the location of doors (and which ways they swing), windows (your client will need to have access to open their windows), fireplaces, etc. This will tell you where you can't put any furniture because it would block the traffic flow of individuals moving around the room.

If a door opens into a room, you will need to give at least 36" of space before placing a piece of furniture or else a person entering the room will have difficulties maneuvering around.

Other things to take into consideration when determining traffic patterns are the placement of heating and cooling vents and units, where a television might be placed if there will be one in the room you are decorating and where conversation areas will be (avoid having traffic walk through conversation areas or in front of a television). You can re-direct traffic away from these areas depending on where the furniture is placed. Ideally, individuals should be able to "go with the flow" and the pathway from one place within the room to another should be unimpeded.

> **TIP:** 30" is about the minimum path width to walk around within a room, however, 48" is desired for major traffic paths in a room.

Determine the Desired Focal Point

A focal point is any interesting fixture or item that individuals will focus on within a room. In other words, it is the area that your client will want to be looking at when they are sitting in the room. Some examples of focal points are:

- A beautiful fireplace

- An amazing view

- An interesting or large piece of artwork or furniture

- A television

Most of the time there is one main focal point within a room; however, if a room is large, sometimes there can be a secondary focal point. For example, in a large living room that has a spectacular ocean view or mountain view and a dramatic fireplace within the same room, the view might be the primary focal point with the fireplace being the secondary focal point. In such a case, the focal points have been predetermined.

Other times, a focal point can be created within a room. For example, using a large and interesting piece of artwork or a television can create a focal point. After you have determined the focal point, it will be much easier to plan furniture arrangements around it because you will then know where to start placing seating arrangements (to face the focal point), etc.

Determine What the Room Will Be Used for

When making plans for the layout of a room, it is important to find out what the room will be used for. For example, if the room that you are decorating is a living room that will mainly be used for watching television, then you may decide to place an entertainment center with a television in it on one of the largest walls and have a sofa facing the television, etc.

On the other hand, if a living room will be used mainly for entertaining and reading, then the layout will be very different and seating areas will need to be set up for both. Further information on furniture placement is included later in this guide.

Experiment with Different Furniture Arrangements

After you have drawn a floor plan, determined the balance lines of the room, traffic patterns, focal point and what the room will be used for, you can then start experimenting with the different options for furniture placement. You can do this by drawing different pieces of furniture in pencil onto your floor plan, using a furniture template. When using a furniture template, ensure that you use one in the same scale as your floor plan. If you have drawn your floor plan to 1/2-inch scale, ensure you use a 1/2-inch scale furniture template.

Start by placing the largest pieces of wooden furniture, then the largest upholstered items, smaller upholstered items, then tables and so on. If an arrangement looks too cramped or doesn't look good, you can erase or move the furnishings and start again until you end up with an arrangement that works great within the room.

As mentioned earlier, computer planning can make your job a lot easier by allowing you to quickly move objects around on your screen.

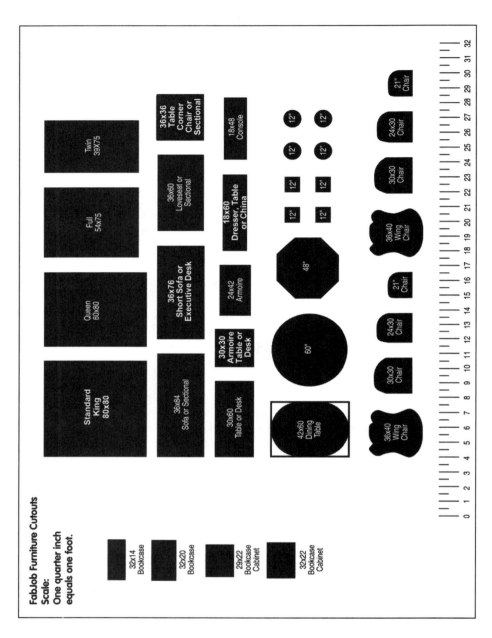

TIP: Instead of drawing furniture with a template, you can print and use these furniture cut-outs. (If you are reading the print version of this book, the cutouts are included on the CD-ROM.)

3.5.3   Choose a Color Scheme

A color scheme is the color palette used in a home (or a single room). Color preferences can be very different from person to person and the main colors in a color scheme may have already been pre-determined by your client before you even begin the decorating process based on the current wall colors, furnishings, and/or area rugs already chosen or staying in the area to be decorated.

If your client's color scheme is dated or doesn't work or they are looking for a change, you will then be in a position to help influence the color scheme. Walls can always be painted, area rugs can be replaced and furniture colors can be changed somewhat by adding decorative cushions or even reupholstering or replacing pieces.

There are many options for color schemes. Many people choose to go with the 60-30-10 rule with a dominant color making up 60 percent of the room, a secondary color making up 30 percent of the room, and an accent color used in about 10 percent of the room. Other alternatives for color schemes are to use complementary colors (colors opposite each other on the color wheel such as purple and yellow), contrasting colors (such as red and pink), colors with a monochromatic look (i.e. colors in the same family such as light and dark green), or related colors (i.e. colors next to each other on the color wheel, such as orange and red).

One thing to keep in mind is that you can and should combine various colors however, it works well to choose one dominating color scattered throughout the room to tie the look together and then add accent colors that can be repeated from place to place.

To assist you (and your client) with selecting colors, following are some things you may want to keep in mind:

1.   Determine what the room will be used for. It is best to keep cool colors (such as greens, blues and violets) in rooms that will be used for relaxing (such as bedrooms and retreat areas), and warm colors (such as yellows, reds and oranges) in rooms where there will be lots of activity (such as play rooms, family rooms, etc.).

2. When deciding on a color scheme for a room, determine what type of sunlight exposure the room gets. If there is little sunlight exposure it is best to include warm color schemes, and if there is a lot of sunlight exposure (for example, in a south exposure room), then cool colors will work well.

3. If the room you will be decorating is large, you may want to use warm colors, which will appear to bring the walls closer in and add a feeling of coziness within a large room. However, if the room is quite small and your client would like it to look larger, you should use cool colors (which are receding colors) that give the appearance of the walls being farther away so that the room appears more spacious.

4. Is there a particular color that your client loves or feels good around that they would like to use in the space? Or does your client have a particular piece of art or a beautiful area rug or an upholstered piece of furniture (or even a fabric swatch) that they want you to use as a starting point for the color scheme?

TIP: Once you have selected the colors, make sure you check them out in the room in daylight to make sure they still work well for the space. On another note, make sure the colors flow from one room to the next to give the home a feeling of harmony.

Once you determine the main color to be used, you can come up with various pleasing and complementary (or contrasting) color combination possibilities and you can then present the options to your client and have them decide on the color combination that will work best for them. Here are some excellent color combination tips from Homestore, Inc.

All colors go together if you know how to combine them. Sound simple? It is, once you know the Language of Color. Finding the right colors is as much about choosing harmonious values and intensities as it is specific hues. Just as important are the proportions of colors in a combination. Following are simple guidelines for creating successful schemes. Keep in mind that, although color theory tends to focus on pure colors, in the real world – in your home – colors are almost always softened and diluted.

Use similar values to link different colors. Light colors from all around the color ring naturally go together because they share a common value. That's why willow, maize and lilac, all light-value colors, are pleasing together. Deep colors, such as claret, spruce and navy, likewise have an affinity, their dark value.

When you use sharply contrasting values in a scheme – dark green furnishings in a white room, for instance – your eye may jump from one element or area to another, an effect you may or may not like.

Use similar intensities to link different colors. In other words, use clear colors with clear colors and grayed colors with grayed colors. Like value, intensity is a unifying factor. Burgundy and hunter, low-intensity versions of red and green, are congenial colors. This approach – combining different colors of similar intensities – is just as effective when the colors are opposite on the color ring as when they are side by side.

Of course, identical values and intensities aren't always desirable—too much sameness can lead to boredom. To a group of light values, throw in a few darker colors. Or punch up a low-intensity scheme with a bit of more intense color. Fortunately, with so many materials and textures available, you'll automatically achieve variation in value and intensity when you gather samples.

Use your colors in unequal quantities. Equal amounts of color fight for attention; unequal amounts are more pleasing. A large expanse of green, for example, with smaller amounts of violet and coral, is harmonious, whereas equal quantities of green, violet and coral are likely to be unpleasantly competitive. The secret is to let one color dominate while the others play supporting roles.

Where you place colors in a room is just as important as their proportions. Imagine pink and green in two hypothetical schemes. One room has pale green walls and soft pink furnishings; the other has pale pink walls and soft green furnishings. Although the same two hues are involved, the effects are dramatically different.

For now, as you consider different color combinations, keep in mind that color placement has everything to do with the visual impact of a scheme.

Once you have determined the color scheme, you can then select fabrics, textures and patterns to work within your decorating plan.

3.5.4   Determine Flooring Requirements

Flooring is one of the most important room elements because it is the foundation of the room and will help to establish color direction and add texture to the room (and possibly even add warmth and comfort depending on the type of flooring chosen).

Your client may be happy with their current flooring and there may be no need to change it, although they may want to add a decorative touch such as an area rug. If your client does want or need a flooring change, the information below will help you with assisting your client.

As mentioned earlier, there are many different options when selecting flooring, such as carpet, tile, vinyl, laminate, area rugs, wood and cork. Flooring needs to be chosen not only for the decorative aspect but also needs to be chosen with practicality of use in mind.

Some questions you may want to ask your client about their desired flooring before making recommendations are:

- Does the flooring need to be durable? If so, laminate or tile might be good options as these are both durable products.

- Does the flooring need to be easy to clean? If so, vinyl, tile, laminate or wood might be good options.

- Does anyone in the household have allergies? If so, you might recommend hardwood or tile instead of carpet.

- Is it important for the flooring to be warm under your feet? If so carpet or area rugs might be best.

- Is it important for flooring to be soft under your feet? If so, once again, carpet or area rugs might be best.

- Are color and design important factors in your flooring? If so, carpet, area rugs, vinyl or tile can all offer a variety of color and design options.

- Does the flooring need to absorb sound? If so, carpet and area rugs are great at absorbing sound.

- Does the flooring need to be easy to maintain? If so, vinyl, laminate and tile might be good options and wood is not a very good option.

- Is it important that the flooring be quiet to walk on? If so, carpet or area rugs (and even vinyl) might be the best options.

When selecting flooring, you will also want to take into consideration how color and pattern can affect the look of a room. Light colored carpet, laminate, vinyl or tile with no pattern can make a room look larger, while darker colored patterned carpet or dark wood floors or dark busy patterned tiles or vinyl can make a room look smaller. Flooring with a horizontal linear pattern (running the width of the room) can make a room look wider while flooring with a vertical linear pattern (running the length of the room) can make a room look longer.

> TIP: Sometimes flooring (such as carpet) is sold with the square yard charge including installation while other times the installation charges are in addition to the materials ordered. You should ask about installation charges when ordering carpet (or other flooring) and also about removal of any old carpeting, plus delivery and installation timing.

Select the Area Rug

Adding an area rug to a room is a quick and easy way to add color, texture, warmth and character to the room. However, this being said, not all rooms will require an area rug and, if this is the case in a room you will be decorating for your client, you can skip over this section.

One of the most important decorating concepts is to select the right area rug for a room and it is important to do this in the early stages of decorating. In fact, it is suggested that you have your client purchase the area rug before they purchase the remaining pieces of furniture required. Often a large area rug will be your starting point for establishing the color direction, fabrics, textures and patterns to include within a room. However, if some of these elements have already been pre-chosen, you will need to work around them.

Following are some tips for selecting area rugs for your client:

- When selecting an area rug for your client, you will need to take into account their budget. Area rugs are available in many different fibers including both synthetic fibers (such as acrylic, nylon and olefin) and natural fibers (such as wool, cotton or jute) and the costs can range from inexpensive to very costly.

- A large area rug normally establishes the color direction for the room. Given this, it is ideal if the area rug contains most or all of the colors that are to be included in the room. For example, if you plan to decorate a room using taupe, gold and black, most or all of these colors should be included in the area rug. However, if you have an accent color (such as red) that will only be used in about 10 percent of the room, it is not essential to have this color within the area rug.

- All elements within the room will need to be taken into consideration, such as any current flooring, wall treatments, upholstery, etc. that are staying. If the flooring or wall treatments are busy or have an ornate pattern, it is best to choose an area rug with a subtle pattern. However, if the flooring and walls are quite simple, a more patterned area rug can be chosen.

- When shopping for area rugs, it is helpful to bring swatches of fabrics, wall coverings and/or paint and flooring that are already being used in the space or that you propose to use in the space to ensure that the colors in the area rug will coordinate with the other room elements.

- When looking for an area rug, remember to look for rugs that have a lot of texture (this can be found when the rug is carved in various areas and when many different fibers are used within the rug).

- Another factor to take into consideration is how much traffic the area will get. It is ideal to include a more detailed patterned area rug in high traffic areas because this type of pattern will require less maintenance (e.g. dirt does not show up as easily, etc.).

- It is also important to determine the purpose for the rug. If you are trying to define a cozy conversation area with the rug, then a dark colored rug would work best. If you want a more open spacious look, than a lighter-colored area rug would be better. If you are looking to add drama or pizzazz to a room, then a colorful and/or uniquely patterned area rug may be the best choice.

- Area rugs can be purchased in varying sizes and shapes and you are not limited to rectangular shaped rugs. Circular or octagonal rugs can look very dramatic and add a unique look to the room.

NOTE: One of this guide's contributing decorators had a client with an exquisite octagonal shaped kitchen nook with a layered octagonal ceiling. When their client was looking for an area rug to go over the marble floor and underneath the round kitchen table, the decorator sought out and found the most perfect octagonal area rug that worked fabulously in that area.

- When purchasing an area rug for under a coffee table, you should purchase a 6' x 9' rug or larger (depending on the size of the room and other surrounding furnishings). All four legs of the coffee table should sit on the rug and it is ideal to have the rug run just short of the width and length of the other furniture within the space where the area rug will be laid so that there is a small amount of flooring exposed between the furniture and the area rug so that the area rug stands out more.

- When purchasing an area rug for under a dining room table, you will typically require an 8' x 10' rug or larger (depending on the size of the dining room table). Prior to going shopping to select an area rug for under a dining room table, you will need to measure the width and length of the dining room table (with all leafs that will be used). You will need to allow at least an extra two feet on each side of the table so that individuals can pull out their chairs while dining and have their chair legs stay on the rug.

What this means is that if your client has a table that is five feet wide by seven feet long, the area rug will need to be at least nine feet wide by eleven feet long. This calculates out by adding two feet to each side of the width of the table (5 feet wide + 2 feet + 2 feet = 9 feet wide required) and adding two feet to each side of the length of the table (7 feet long + 2 feet + 2 feet = 11 feet length required).

TIP: When purchasing an area rug, don't forget to also buy a similar sized nonskid pad to go underneath the area rug to prevent the rug (and people) from slipping, make it easier to vacuum, and most importantly protect the area rug from wear.

3.5.5   Select Wall Treatments

After you and your client have determined the color scheme for the room and selected an area rug, then you are in a better position to determine wall treatments. However, if your client is happy with their current walls (possibly they had them freshly painted before hiring you), there may be no need to make any changes if the wall treatments will work within the decorating plan.

If your client does want or need a change to the walls, there are many different options when it comes to decorating walls including paint, wall coverings, fabric, tiles or wood.

Some things you might want to take into consideration with determining the wall treatments for the room are as follows:

- What color walls will look best within the color scheme? After you have selected the color scheme for the room and determined flooring requirements and selected an area rug, you will then have a better idea of what color to choose for the walls. The color will need to complement the other elements within the room.

- Are there any defects in the walls that should be covered? If there are any defects in the walls, then wallpaper, wood or fabric might be the best choice.

- Is it preferable to have a cozy feel or a spacious, airy feel in the room? If a room is to have a cozy feel, then darker and warmer colors will draw the room in while cool and pale colors will draw the room out if a more spacious look is desired.

- Does the room need more texture? If so, fabric, wallpaper or tile can provide both tactile and visual texture while a faux finish can provide visual texture.

- Is there any requirement or desire to have tiles on the walls? If you are decorating a kitchen or bathroom, there may be a desire to include tiles on the wall.

- Would the style of the room warrant wood walls? The style you and your client have chosen to decorate with will determine whether wood walls will work within the space. For example, in a Colonial style room, wood wainscoting would look fabulous, while in a Country style room, cedar wood paneling would also look great. However, in a Modern style or Neo-classical style room, wood walls would not be a good choice.

- Is a faux finish look desired? If a faux finish look is desired and will look good within the space and with the style of decorating, then you will need to determine with your client what type of faux finishing technique to use. If you are decorating a Neo-classical style living room, then a marble faux finish would look fabulous. If you are decorating a Southwestern style room, then a colorwashed faux finish would look great.

- Are any moldings required to give the room a more elegant and finished look? Once again, the style chosen to decorate the room and any finishing touches that are needed will factor into whether any additional moldings should be added to the walls. Traditional style rooms would look great with additional crown, chair and case moldings.

Have your client take the time to answer the above questions with you. After you have explored the various options, you will then be in a better position to recommend wall treatments.

3.5.6 Determine Lighting Requirements

Lighting in a room is another very important element both for functionality (for example, being able to read) and for setting a mood and creating an atmosphere.

To determine lighting requirements, you first need to know what the room will be used for. This will likely have been determined earlier through meetings with your client.

If the space will be used for entertaining, reading, and watching television, the needs will be very different than if it will only be used for watching television or for working. For entertaining purposes, your client will likely want to create an ambience through the lighting. For working purposes, your client will need sufficient task lighting (i.e. lighting that is bright enough to be able to work).

Next, assess what lighting is already available. Some things to consider are:

- How much natural daylight is there within the room?
- Where are the current light fixtures?
- Will more light fixtures need to be installed?
- What floor and/or table lamps will be used for the space and will more need to be purchased?
- Will candles be used to add mood lighting?
- Where will all the activities take place (for example, working, reading, eating, etc.)?
- Is any accent lighting desired (to highlight a prized possession or piece of art)?

After the above items have been considered, you will then be in a better position to determine what lighting is still required for the room. You will do this based on the lighting that is already available and the activities to take place in the room.

For any additional lighting required, you will then need to determine whether lighting fixtures and/or lamps will work best for each given situation. Following is some information about lamps and light fixtures to help you determine what type of lighting to select.

Using Lamps for Lighting

One easy way to add lighting to a room is to use lamps. Lamps can be considered decorative accessories as well. When selecting a lamp for your client, you will want to take into consideration the style and color of the lamp (and shade) together with what type of light the lamp generates. Following are some tips about the various types of lamps that you can choose from to add a variety of lighting to a client's home.

Floor and table lamps are usually used for general lighting purposes in living rooms, dining rooms and family rooms. Often a floor lamp will illuminate an area that doesn't get much light. Table lamps can also be used in bedrooms. The advantage of using floor and table lamps is that they can easily be brought into a room (with no need for an electrician) and can be moved from place to place, if needed, to add lighting.

Additionally, table and floor lamps can add color, texture, interest and a whole new decorative element to a room. The average height of a table lamp ranges from 24" to 32" while the average height of a floor lamp ranges from 62" to 72".

Desk lamps are often used in an office space or a space where hobbies are performed or studying or reading is done. These lamps are normally between 12" to 20" high and are used as task lighting to illuminate a specific area.

Table accent lamps (i.e. occasional table lamps) are normally under 22" high and are often used in bedrooms, entranceways, hallways and other areas that need extra lighting.

Accent lamps (i.e. lamps used for direct accent lighting) are used to "accent" a particular piece of artwork or sculpture, etc.

One thing to keep in mind is that most people do not use enough lighting while decorating. Using lamps in a space serves two functions: (1) adding more lighting and (2) adding another decorative element.

For a small to mid-size room, consider using two to three floor and/or table lamps in addition to the light fixtures already present in the room. In a large room, consider using three to five floor and/or table lamps in addition to the light fixtures present.

You will have previously determined the lighting required for the room and whether it is best to bring in additional lighting through light fixtures or through lamps. If you have determined that you will need some additional floor and/or table lamps, you can now purchase the lamps selecting styles and colors that will work with the other pieces in the room.

However, besides appearance, you will need to take into consideration how much and what type of lighting is required for an area (whether it be general, task or accent lighting) and how much light and what type of light the particular lamp you are selecting gives off to determine if a selected lamp is a good fit for the area.

When purchasing lamps, most lamps will come with a shade; however, if the lamp base is sold separately, ensure that you purchase a properly scaled shade to the lamp base. In other words, don't buy a shade that is too small (or too large) for the base.

Shades come in many different sizes and colors and can be found with fabrics made from many different patterns and textures. When selecting lamps and shades, make sure that you bring fabric swatches of your furniture, flooring, and other room elements to ensure that the lamp and shade will work with the other items.

Another thing to take into consideration is the types of light bulbs you choose to place in the lamps for your client. This will depend on whether you plan to set a mood or accent a particular space with the lamp or whether the lamp is being used for a specific activity, such as reading. Light bulbs can give off different color (from white to yellow and beyond) and can give a warm effect (yellow tinted light bulbs) or cool effect (white light bulbs or light bulbs with a slight blue tint).

Lower wattage/lower voltage lighting is becoming increasingly popular with today's energy conscious consumer. You should keep this is mind when looking for lighting options. Ask the lighting salesperson if these bulbs will be an option for a particular lamp or type of lighting.

To find lamps, check out lighting stores, lighting showrooms, furniture stores, home décor stores and even home improvement stores.

Light Fixtures

Besides using lamps, there are a variety of ceiling and wall-mounted light fixtures that may be suitable for decorating and lighting up your client's home.

Ceiling Light Fixtures

Some options for ceiling light fixtures are:

Chandeliers	These hang from the ceiling and are often found in dining rooms, living rooms or foyers and are normally quite decorative and are used for general lighting.
Pendant lights	Pendant lights are popular and a great alternative to pot lights in a kitchen (especially on an island). They will help bring task lighting right where you need it most – close to the surface you are working on.
Track lighting	This is a fixture that has a number of adjustable lights attached to a track and this type of lighting can provide accent, task or general lighting.
Spotlights	These can be placed on tracks or recessed into the ceiling and are often used for accent lighting.
Globe ceiling fixtures	This type of lighting provides general lighting and you normally find these in hallways, bathrooms, bedrooms and laundry rooms. Often these fixtures can look like a half rounded fixture or fully rounded fixture that sits close to the ceiling.

Wall-Mounted Light Fixtures

Other forms of light fixtures that can be quite decorative to use are wall sconces (these are great for accent lighting and/or to add ambience) or wall lamps (for more general lighting). These types of light fixtures can be added when there is limited table space for a lamp or when a decorative look is wanted in a space, especially with wall sconces. Living rooms and dining rooms are popular places for wall sconces while bedrooms are often where you will use wall lamps. These types of fixtures are called wall-mounted fixtures.

When considering wall options keep in mind that unless you are working on a renovation project and included in the early planning stages, wall mounted lighting (particularly wall sconces) will be difficult to install. They will need to be hard-wired in by a qualified electrician, unless you use the type of wall sconces where the electrical cord is encased in metal or plastic tubing that will then scale down the wall to the nearest plug.

Another form of light fixture is an undershelf or undercabinet fixture that can provide both task and accent lighting. You will often find undercabinet lighting in kitchens and undershelf lighting in display cabinets to accent treasures.

> **TIP:** A great way to add versatility to your light fixtures is to install dimmer switches so that the amount of light can be varied depending on the activity and mood/ambience desired.

When determining lighting required for a space, first determine all types of lighting required (general, task and/or accent) and then determine how you would like the various types of lighting brought into the room (whether through ceiling fixtures, wall-mounted fixtures, table or floor lamps, desk lamps, accent lamps, etc.).

Lamps and light fixtures can be found at lighting stores, lighting showrooms and home improvement stores. Additionally, you can often find a number of decorative lamps at furniture stores and stores like The Bombay Co. and Bowring (in Canada). To find lighting stores in your area check the yellow pages under "Lighting Fixtures" and "Lamps."

3.5.7   Complete any Repairs or Renovations

Determine if anything needs to be repaired (such as a crack in the wall or ceiling) or if any renovations and/or installations are to be done and have these co-ordinated and completed before decorating begins. For example, if an archway is being added, this will need to be handled at this stage and prior to any further decorating or placement of furniture. You will need to coordinate any repairs or renovations with your preferred contractor and suppliers and develop a schedule that will work with your client as well.

In addition to the above, you will have previously determined if there is enough lighting in the space to be decorated or whether any new light fixtures need be added. If new light fixtures are required, this is the time to have the electrician come in and wire them in and also have the fixtures installed.

On the next few pages is a checklist of possible repairs or renovations that may (or may not) be required for a particular decorating project. If required, these repairs and renovations should be scheduled in within your decorating plan and completed before the furniture is brought in and arranged.

Repairs and Renovation Checklist

Walls and Ceiling

❑ Have any repairs completed (e.g. fixing cracks in the wall or ceiling)

❑ Arrange for any painting required on walls or ceiling

❑ Arrange for installation of any wall coverings (wallpaper)

❑ Arrange for installation of any tile or wood on walls

❑ Have any fabric sewn and applied to the walls

❑ Arrange for installation of any moldings (crown, chair, baseboard, case)

❑ Have any archways constructed

Flooring

❑ Have any repairs completed (e.g. replacing a cracked tile)

❑ Have any carpet installed

❑ Have any hardwood or softwood installed

❑ Have wood treated with a sealant and finished off

❑ Have any tiles laid and grouted

❑ Have any vinyl or laminate or other type of flooring installed

Windows

❑ Have any new windows installed

Lighting

- ❑ Have any ceiling light fixtures installed

- ❑ Have any wall-mounted light fixtures installed

- ❑ Have any under-cabinet or under-shelf lighting fixtures installed

Kitchen and/or Bathroom Specific

- ❑ Have any cabinets or countertops installed

- ❑ Have any sinks, tubs, toilets installed

Miscellaneous

- ❑ Have any additional electrical work completed

- ❑ Have any required plumbing work completed

- ❑ Have any heating work completed

- ❑ Have any built-in units constructed

- ❑ Have any new doors installed

3.5.8   Select Furnishings

Another part of decorating that can be quite enjoyable is selecting furnishings for the area being decorated. As mentioned earlier, a number of factors are involved in furniture, including the construction and durability, materials used (wood, upholstery, etc.), functionality, comfort, cost, and the one that's most personal to your client—style!

Before you even set off with your client to select furnishings, there are a few things that should be determined:

1. You will need to find out which furniture items, if any, will be staying or have already been purchased for the area being decorated. It is important to know this because any new furnishings will have to work with the current furnishings. It is ideal to

bring a photo of any current furnishings that can be pulled out and compared with desired furniture items to ensure that the colors, fabrics, patterns, style, etc. will work together.

2. You will need to determine what items of furniture are still required and what each item will be used for. This is important to know because if your client wants a chair for their living room to be used for reading or relaxing, then comfort will be an important factor. However, if the chair is being purchased to make a statement and to look aesthetically pleasing but will rarely be used, comfort will not be a priority.

3. You will need to determine your client's decorating style preference for any new furniture items. Ideally you will have already determined this from earlier meetings with your client. If this isn't yet clear, you can always have your client flip through a few interior decorating books or magazines and have them point out what type of furniture they want to purchase. By knowing this information up-front, this will help narrow down the types of furniture stores you will want to look at.

When shopping for furniture, it will be helpful to come prepared with items that will help with your selection. For example, if a sofa will be staying in the room to be decorated and you are out looking for two occasional chairs to go in the room, it will be helpful to bring a cushion (or fabric swatch) from the sofa to help with matching up colors, etc. Additionally, it will also help to bring swatches or samples of other elements being used in the room (such as flooring samples, wall coverings, other fabrics, etc.) so that you can determine whether any desired furnishings will work with the other elements in the room.

When shopping for furniture, you will need to be familiar with the types of materials that can be used (both woods and upholstery fabrics) and it is also beneficial to know about quality, construction and comfort. Refer to section 3.4.1 for more information.

Selecting Case Goods

As mentioned in section 3.4.1, case goods (also known as hard goods) are furniture items mainly made from wood such as tables, chests, chairs, desks, dressers, armoires, etc. However, case goods can also incorporate other "hard" items such as hard plastic, wrought iron and brass and other metals, and glass and marble for table tops, etc.

When you are shopping for case goods, there are a number of different types of woods to select from. They are classified into hard woods (such as cherry, mahogany, maple, birch and oak), soft woods (such as pine, cedar and fir) and wood products (such as plywood, particle board, etc.). When selecting wood furnishings, it is helpful to be familiar with the construction method used and to be aware of the long-term durability of the product.

Some things to look for when selecting well-constructed and durable furniture are:

1. How sturdy is the item? (Put your hand on the edge of the item and press up and down—does the item wobble or does it stand firm?)

2. How are the pieces joined together and is a strong joint used? (A strong joint would be a dowel joint, a mortise and tenon joint, or a tongue and groove joint, but not a butt joint.)

3. Does the wood grain match up where it should?

4. Do drawers and doors open easily and properly?

5. Is the piece finished off nicely? (For example, is any stain evenly applied?)

Selecting Upholstered Furniture

When selecting upholstered furniture, you will often be able to select the upholstery (i.e. fabric) from a number of options that are available with the particular furniture line. You will want to select a fabric that has a texture, design, color and pattern that will harmonize with other items in the room being decorated and fits with the style of your client.

When you are selecting fabrics there are certain things to keep in mind. Just because a certain fabric costs more (particularly higher grade fabrics) doesn't mean that the fabric is more durable or of a higher quality than a lower priced (lower grade) fabric. The pricing of higher grade fabrics is often based on how difficult it is to make the fabric and on the availability.

For example, fabrics made with silk are expensive because of the difficulty in making the fabric; however, silk itself is not a very durable fabric. Fabrics that are tightly woven (such as cotton and linens) are much more durable and can cost much less. Cotton is a readily available fabric and is very durable and much less expensive than silk, but cotton certainly doesn't have the same feel and look as silk.

> **TIP:** Fabrics used for upholstery are given durability ratings. Ask salespeople what those ratings are for the available fabric choices.

To determine if an item will be comfortable for your client, make sure that they try it out. For example, if they are purchasing a mattress, have them lie down on the in-store sample. If they are purchasing a sofa, have them sit on it and make sure that they are able to sit back far enough to be able to relax and feel comfortable while still feeling supported on the piece. Have them run their hand over the fabric selected and make sure that it feels comfortable to them (not too rough and not too soft to touch).

As you can see, there are many factors to take into consideration when assisting your client with selecting furnishings. Once you have determined the color scheme and style for the area being decorated, you are in a great position to start looking for furniture. You can then select a piece of furniture that is suitable as far as the look and style, comfort, construction and durability go.

For upholstered items, you can then select desired upholstery with the texture, pattern and color preferred. You can then ask about ordering in the piece, and find out about the return policy and any warranties given. See section 5.5 for detailed advice about how to shop for furniture.

3.5.9   Choose Window Coverings

Window coverings can add texture, color, drama and interest to any room while also serving a functional purpose.

There are a number of factors you will need to take into consideration when selecting window coverings and the most important of these are privacy, function, style and how much light you want to allow in.

Privacy

One of the main reasons for using window coverings is for privacy, unless your client lives in a remote area and this is not an issue. To get complete privacy, it is ideal to select a window covering that will provide complete opaque covering, such as shades, or lined drapes or curtains. A level of privacy can also be obtained by using blinds and shutters.

Function

For the window covering to work, it needs to be functional. For example, your client will need to be able to open and close the window coverings as they require. The window coverings will need to serve the purpose your client intends for them to serve (such as blocking out light in a nursery when a young child is sleeping, etc.).

Light Control

Another reason to include window coverings is to control the amount of sunlight that is allowed into a room. During the bright of day, your client may want the option to tilt blinds or close curtains and drapes to keep the glare down, especially in rooms with TVs and computers.

Additionally, your client may wish to protect furnishings, carpets and fabrics from fading due to excessive UV rays from sunlight. Also, in the summer months, when the sun rises early (often before most individuals plan to awake), having window coverings that completely block out the sunlight – such as shades or heavily lined drapes – may be important to some people.

Style

Besides having window coverings that block sunlight, provide privacy and are functional, it is ideal to select window coverings that are aesthetically pleasing and offer a decorative element.

Some options for window coverings are set out below with comments to take into consideration when determining which type of window covering to select:

Curtains

Curtains can be used for either a formal or casual style depending on the type of fabric (and pattern) selected. Many styles of curtains can be bought pre-made or fabric can be chosen to have curtains custom made. Curtains can be lined to block out the sunlight, if required, and they can be wide enough so that they close fully and provide complete privacy.

Drapes

Drapes are normally used in formal decorating styles such as Colonial or Victorian and they are typically custom made with exquisite and luxurious fabrics filled with texture. Drapes are often lined and can provide excellent blockage of sunlight and privacy.

Blinds

Blinds are often used for casual decorating styles such as Country or Modern. Numerous color options are available and although blinds do provide a level of privacy and some blockage of sunlight, they do not provide complete coverage. Accordingly, if these are critical factors for your client, then this type of window covering should not be selected. Blinds can be custom ordered; however, venetian blinds can often be purchased directly from a home improvement store where they will cut the blinds to size while you wait.

Shades

Shades can be used for both casual and formal styles. If they are used for casual styles, they would likely be used on their own while if they are used for formal styles, they would likely be used to add an extra element of privacy and sunlight blockage behind formal curtains, sheers or drapes. Some shades can be bought pre-made but often they need to be ordered to size and fabrics can be selected for custom made shades.

Sheers

Sheers can look fabulous and offer a great decorative element. Sheers do filter and soften the sunlight, but they are not very effective in providing privacy and blocking out total sunlight. This type of window treatment would normally only be purchased for aesthetic reasons. Sheers can often be purchased pre-made or they may need to be custom made if they do not fit the window they are required for.

Shutters

Shutters are often used for casual decorating styles (such as Country) and like blinds they do provide a level of privacy and some blockage of sunlight. However, shutters with slats do not provide complete coverage. Accordingly, if these are critical factors for your client, then this type of window covering should not be selected.

Shutters can be custom ordered and sometimes you can even find pre-made shutters that fit the windows you require them for.

Decorative Accents

As you can probably tell by the name of this category, decorative accents are normally selected to provide a decorative element and not for privacy or sunlight blockage.

Some decorative window accents – such as tie backs, decorative rods, sconces and often scarves – can be bought pre-made, while other decorative window accents such as valances and cornices often need to be custom made.

You will see from the information provided above that there are several different options to choose from when selecting window coverings and the choice of style will really depend on the look and functionality (i.e. privacy and sunlight blockage) required.

Depending on the type of window treatment selected, there may be several options in colors, fabrics and textures to choose from. As indicated, some of the window coverings listed above can be bought pre-made, but some need to be ordered or custom made.

In such cases, you will normally need to allow up to two weeks (and sometimes even much longer) to get the desired window covering in. This should be taken into consideration when selecting window coverings.

3.5.10 Arrange the Furniture

As mentioned under "Space Planning," before placing any furniture, you should take the time to draw some plans. You can do this by taking your "base" floor plan (referred to above) and, using a furniture template in the same scale, you can draw in the various furniture items (in pencil) right on to a copy of your floor plan. If something doesn't work, you can erase it and make a different arrangement. By doing this in advance of placing any furniture, you will ultimately be saving time in the long run.

When planning the placement of furniture, ensure that there is a mix of symmetrical and asymmetrical balance to create a visual balance and harmony.

When arranging furniture, always remember to use the "layering" process by placing items in the following order: (1) place the area rug first, then (2) place the large wooden furniture items, (3) place the upholstered furniture items, (4) place the tables, and (5) place the lamps.

Place the Area Rug First

Make sure that the area rug is placed exactly where you want it before any furnishings are placed in the room. The area rug will ground the room and establish the color direction.

Place the Large Wooden Furniture Items

The next step is to place the large wooden furniture items such as an armoire or an entertainment center (in a living room or family room) or a bed (in a bedroom) or a desk (in an office). A common mistake that some people make is putting the largest piece of furniture on one of the smallest walls or trying to place large furniture items in a room that is too small to handle it. Ensure that the largest wooden furniture items are placed against the larger walls.

> **TIP:** Large pieces of furniture should be evenly distributed within in a room to keep the room balanced. Leave room around large furniture pieces for the best effect.

After you have placed the large furniture items, you can then place other pieces in relation to them.

Place the Upholstered Furniture Items

The next step is to bring the upholstered furniture item(s) into the room, whether it be a couch/sofa, loveseat, chair, ottoman, bench, chaise lounge or settee. Start with the largest upholstery items first. For example, if there is a sofa, loveseat, large chair and two occasional chairs to go into the room, first you would bring in the sofa, then the loveseat, then the large chair and finally the occasional chairs. Don't line up the furniture around the perimeter of the room — use the center of the room also.

> **TIP:** A lot of open floor space isn't a good thing. One thing you should do in a mid- to large-size room and should probably do even in a smaller room is move the sofa away from the wall (that is, "float" the sofa in the room) and move it towards the center of the room to make a conversation area.

If you place the sofa and a loveseat in an "L" shape, you can often create, depending on the size of a room, a second seating area. It is ideal to have a second and even a third seating area in a very large room.

It is likely, in most cases, that the largest upholstered item (such as the sofa or loveseat) will be facing the focal point of the room. For example, in a family room, the large sofa will likely face the television while in a living room, the sofa may face the fireplace, etc.

One practice that is becoming more common and adds interest to a room is using an oversized upholstered ottoman as either a seating area or even as a coffee table.

In a bedroom, it is best to place an item at the end of the bed (such as an upholstered bench or a small chest) to anchor the bed and to add some dimension to the room. Another option is to place a small area rug, either on its own or under the bench, at the end of the bed.

Place the Tables

Next, bring in your cocktail table, end tables, occasional tables, sofa tables, consuls, etc. In a living room, a cocktail table can be centered in front of a sofa while an end table can be placed at the end of a sofa and an occasional table can be placed between two chairs. If you are "floating" a sofa (placing the sofa away from the wall), make sure that you also pull the end table(s) out and "float" them beside the sofa.

One thing to keep in mind is that your end tables do not need to match each other or even the other tables in the room. Unique tables can add variety to the room and can make for a much more interesting look when they complement other furniture in the room. It is ideal, when you do have a second seating area, if you can make it functional by placing a games table in between a couple of chairs.

Another thing to keep in mind when placing tables is if your client plans to eat or drink or entertain in that particular room. If so, is there a place to set down a glass or plate near each seat? If not, another table should be placed.

Place the Lamps

Bring in and place any floor lamps and/or table lamps. When placing lamps, you need to determine where the activities will be taking place. For example, if there is an area for reading or an area for doing hobbies or an area for doing work, a task lamp will need to be placed in the specific area. If there is one area of the room that doesn't get enough general lighting, it would be ideal to add a floor lamp to that area.

As you will see from the information provided above, it is much easier to arrange furniture when you have drawn a floor plan and when you use the layering process and place the furniture with this systematic approach in mind.

Expressing a Mood within a Room

When decorating a space, you will also want to make sure that you set a mood (ambience) for that space. Again, this will depend on your client's wishes and what they want to express. To determine this, you can ask your client the following questions:

- What kind of look do you want this room to have?

- What type of feeling do you want this room to have?

- What do you want the ambience (or mood) of this room to be?

There are many different types of moods an individual may wish to express in any one given space. For example, you may have one client who wishes to decorate a living room at their country home that expresses a rustic, casual, relaxing, cozy, warm, inviting mood and have another client in the city who wishes to decorate a living room and express a formal, elegant, classic, striking and sophisticated look. The mood that your client wishes expressed will be very personal to them.

When you are working to set a mood within a room, you need to take into consideration all of the room elements. For example, if you were hired to decorate a country home to express a rustic, casual, relaxing, cozy, warm, inviting mood, you would need to take into consideration the furnishings, flooring, walls, window coverings, lighting, fabrics, accessories, etc.

Following is a list of some of the kinds of items that could be included in a decorating plan for this type of scenario:

- Large comfortable upholstered furnishings

- Wooden furniture made from pine, logs or cedar

- Seating areas placed close together

- Wooden floors with a cozy area rug

- Fabric blinds or wooden shutters on the window

- Warm and natural colors on the walls and in fabrics

- Items influenced by nature such as birds nests, flowers, sea-shells

- Soft throws or quilts

- Soft, warm lighting

- Accessories such as baskets, candles, etc.

- Plants and fresh or dried flowers

As mentioned, the mood chosen by your client will be very personal to them. It is your job as a decorator to find out the mood your client wishes to express and then bring the items together to successfully express the mood.

3.5.11 Accessorize

Accessorizing is one of the keys to bringing the whole look together and one of the easiest ways to add personality to the room. However, accessorizing should only be done once everything else is in place, because if you try to accessorize before having the other layers in place, it is too difficult to know how things will balance out.

Start by adding artwork and mirrors, then add cushions/pillows, greenery and flowers, unique pieces, decorative table boxes, candles, etc.

Prior to heading to the stores to purchase any accessories for the space, take an inventory of what your client has available to use in the space. For example, your inventory could read:

- 1 6' palm tree

- 2 ledge plants

- 1 crystal vase

- Various silk flowers in whites and reds

- 1 large, 1 medium and 1 small gold decorative box

- Glass bottle collection (7 in total)

- 3 large gold and black floor candleholders plus 3 gold candles

- 2 medium sized candle holders

- Tuscany style painting (32" wide x 24" high)

- Scenic print in blues, yellow, rusts (18" wide x 24" high)

- 2 black velvet cushions (18" x 18")

- 2 gold striped satin cushions (14" x 14")

After taking the inventory of what your client has, take the time to determine what accessories are still wanted or required for the space being decorated. This way, when you are out at the stores, you can refer to both lists so that you can get the items required while making sure they will work with what is already in the room.

Hang Artwork

Use plenty of artwork. This helps to "finish off" a room and give it more color, personality and pizzazz. Most people do not have enough artwork within their homes.

When hanging artwork, if a piece is large enough to stand on its own, it should be placed alone on a wall for a more dramatic effect. However, if the artwork is not large enough to stand on its own, it is best to "group" artwork on a wall.

When grouping artwork, it is ideal to have similar frames or matting to coordinate pieces together. However, before hanging a grouping of artwork, it is best to experiment with the pieces on the floor and try various arrangements until you and your client find the most suitable arrangement. Additionally, you can experiment with wall arrangements by cutting out paper that is the same size and shape of each piece of artwork and then, with painter's tape, you can apply the paper to the wall to get an idea of where each piece of artwork in the grouping will hang.

When grouping artwork, the largest pieces should be kept at the bottom of the grouping to anchor the group. By experimenting with arrangements using the above techniques, this will save having nails hammered into the wall that may need to be moved if the original arrangement doesn't quite work.

Don't hang all artwork at the same level. A general rule of thumb is to place artwork approximately six to eight inches above a sofa or around eye level. However, ideally you should hang artwork at different levels.

An exception to this is when you are grouping a number of identically-sized items side by side. These items should be placed at the same level. Besides grouping artwork side by side, also stack artwork (in other words, place one piece above the other and so on). When grouping artwork, placing four to six pieces together can look fabulous.

Keep in mind that vertical arrangements draw the eye up and can add height to a room while horizontal arrangements can draw the eye across the room and make a room look wider. If your client has a large wall and a special, but not too large, piece of art that they want to showcase, you can always place the piece of art between two wall sconces.

A common mistake many people make is hanging artwork too high. Most artwork should be hung around eye level. Additionally, sometimes people hang artwork that is off scale and out of proportion for the particular wall or the area. For example, when hanging artwork over a sofa or love seat, group it or use a piece large enough to maintain balance and look proportional (such as a piece that is about two-thirds the size of the sofa or love seat). A small 12" by 10" piece of artwork would look totally out of proportion if hung on its own over top of a sofa.

Hang Mirrors

Mirrors are fantastic to use because they help to make a space look even larger than it is and open it up. The most important thing to take into consideration when hanging a mirror is what will be reflected back when you look into the mirror. It is ideal if a beautiful view, or an interesting piece or artwork are reflected back.

One of the biggest mistakes people make when hanging mirrors is hanging one over a fireplace mantel. This can work sometimes (if the mantel is low enough and the ceiling is high enough), however, most of the time, when individuals are sitting in a room and looking into a mirror over a fireplace mantel, what is reflected back is the ceiling, which is definitely not a point of interest. It is preferable to hang a unique and special piece of art over a fireplace mantel in such a case and hang the mirror opposite the fireplace.

If a mirror is too small to be placed on its own on a wall, then you can either group a number of mirrors together or hang items on each side of the mirror such as sconces or two pieces of artwork.

Place Cushions and Throws

Decorative cushions and pillows and throws are great accessories to use to bring color, texture and interest into a room. Cushions and pillows scattered throughout a room are in essence a form of decorative art.

Use cushions of different size, color, textures and patterns to add a whole new dimension to a room and to tie areas together. A modern way of displaying cushions is to make the top of the cushion inverted. Do this with down filled cushions by making a gentle karate chop motion in the middle of the top of the cushion. (This of course will not work with cushions made from stiff foam or polyester.)

On a sofa, you may want to place two matching decorative cushions on each side and a contrasting or complimenting cushion in the middle. A third matching cushion could also be placed on an armchair or on a love seat and an additional contrasting cushion could also be added to one of these items of furniture.

Throws look wonderful when draped over the side of an armchair or on a bench or settee or over the back of a sofa.

Add Plants and Flowers

Plants and flowers can bring warmth, color and freshness to a room. Use real plants and flowers wherever possible; however, silk plants and flowers are a good option for tall plant ledges or areas that don't get enough sunlight but cry out for a bit of color.

Many people feel that if they add more than one plant to a room, the room will look like a jungle. But that is not the case. Don't be afraid to include three or more plants in a large room. For example, in a large living room, you could include a six- or seven-foot-tall palm (silk palms look fabulous these days!), a six-foot ficus tree and a medium-sized plant in a nice urn or planter.

Silk or fresh flowers can be placed in crystal vases or decorative urns, vases or jugs to bring in more color and to brighten up the atmosphere of any space. Flowers can be placed in foyers, living rooms, dining rooms, kitchens, bathrooms, family rooms or any rooms that need more color and life added to them.

Place Unique Pieces

Add any unique items that the client wishes to keep in their newly decorated space such as heirlooms, sculptures, candleholders (with candles), decorative boxes, collectibles, books, etc. As mentioned previously, when displaying items, group those items together if there are a number of the same type of item.

After you have added all of the accessories to the space, you will have helped your client with adding their own sense of style and personality to the space and your client will have had the opportunity to include any items they love within the decorating scheme.

3.5.12 Evaluate the Decorating

After you have completed the decorating, it is time to step back and look at the end result. With a critical eye, go around from space to space (that you have decorated) and evaluate the decorating. You may want to do this first by yourself and then with your client. Some of the things to look for while evaluating are as follows:

- Does the space look fabulous?

- Is the space functional and can it be used in all ways desired?

- Do you get a good feel when looking at the space?

- Is there a sense of harmony and balance in the space?

- Does the space express the mood desired by your client?

- Are the design concepts of texture, pattern, line, form and scale properly incorporated?

- Does everything flow?

- Are their unimpeded traffic paths to move around within the space?

- Does anything need re-arranging or adjusting?

- Have you come within budget?

- Is your client happy with the end result?

At the end of the day, the most important thing is that your client answers yes to the last question and is happy with the end result. If your client is not fully satisfied, determine what further needs to be done and take the time to fix it.

After both you and your client are fully satisfied with the end result, you will know that you have successfully completed the decorating project at hand. Take the time to thank your client and then head home, pat yourself on the back and treat yourself for a job well done.

If your client is satisfied with your work and you have developed a good working relationship with them, they will most likely call on you again for any future business and recommend you to friends and colleagues.

More Tips from the Experts

Following are some additional tips from decorating experts:

- The most important tip is to create a space that is inviting and one that makes your client feel good and "at home." Remember that your client's home is their sanctuary.

- The three biggest (yet simplest) things that can be done to improve a home are: (1) use plenty of lighting (remember, lighting helps to set a mood), (2) use plenty of artwork, (3) use decorative cushions.

- Feel free to mix styles of furniture and different color woods and different types of fabrics and materials. Having the same type of material and matching woods throughout can be boring. Mixing different woods or combining stripes and plaids or checks and florals or satins with chenille can add interest and variety. However, as mentioned previously, you do need to anchor the varying patterns and textures together. For example, you can anchor a dark color in some of the fabrics and it can help to anchor some of the dark pieces of furniture in a room. Or, you can pick one color that unifies all the varying patterns and textures.

- Don't be afraid to use color. In fact, color is one of the cheapest and quickest ways to transform a room, whether it is on the walls or in your fabrics or in the accessories or artwork.

- When shopping for your client, make sure you keep their lifestyle and future in mind. For example, although cream colored linen rollback chairs may look fabulous in a dressed up kitchen, they won't work well for your clients if they have small children. Buy furnishings that your clients can own for a long time and that will work with their lifestyle.

- Place the furniture where it looks best. Try placing furniture at different angles to add some interest. It is not essential to place furniture parallel (or perpendicular) to the walls.

4. Getting Hired

Once you have developed your skills and knowledge of interior decorating, it's time to start getting paid for your talents!

While interior decorating is a glamorous career that attracts many people, the good news is that there is an increasing number of job opportunities. The U.S. Department of Labor has predicted that jobs for interior designers will increase by as much as 19 percent through the year 2018.

As an interior decorator you have many exciting career possibilities which involve either getting hired by an interior decorating company or starting your own interior decorating business. As you can see from the title, this chapter focuses on the first of these two options.

The chapter begins by taking a look at what "materials" can help you get hired for a job as an interior decorator. These materials include a portfolio, letters of recommendation, and your resume. We then take a look at what types of companies hire decorators, how to find job openings, and how to prepare for interviews. Throughout, you will receive advice on how to make a great impression on prospective employers.

4.1   Job-Hunting Materials

4.1.1   Your Portfolio

A portfolio is a collection of samples of your work, plus any other documents that can help show employers why they should hire you. A portfolio for an interior decorator may include the following:

- photographs of interiors you have decorated

- design boards (discussed below)

- certificates from any decorating programs you have taken

- letters of recommendation

- anything else that shows your skill as a decorator

A portfolio can help you stand out from other applicants. It offers an employer proof that you have the skills to do the job. Read on to find out how to get items for your portfolio, and how to put your portfolio together.

Photographs

As mentioned in the section on *"How to Get Experience"* in Chapter 2, try to arrange to have photographs taken of everything you decorate. While you won't include every photograph in your portfolio, it is a good idea to have as many photos as possible to choose from.

You do not need to hire a professional photographer (it could cost hundreds of dollars to hire a professional to shoot photos of a single room). A much less expensive alternative is to take photos yourself if you're handy with a camera, or get a friend or family member to take them for you. If you have someone else take photos for you, make sure they know the photos should be in color!

You may be able to get some ideas for your own photos by looking at portfolios of professional interior decorators and interior designers. Most decorators and designers with websites have an online portfolio of their work. Excellent examples can be found at the websites of

Visions Design Group (**www.visionsdesigngroup.com**), Nate Berkus (**www.nateberkus.com**), and Benjamin Noriega-Ortiz (**www.bnodesign. com**).

When selecting photographs of interiors you have decorated, remember that your portfolio should be a collection of your best work. Most employers do not have time to look through dozens of photographs, so it is better to have a few outstanding examples than many average examples. One suggested guideline is to choose 15-20 photographs of work you are really proud of. Also consider including "before" and "after" photos of interiors you have decorated because these can be particularly impressive to employers.

Once you have selected your photos, you can arrange them in a photo album, or get them blown up to 8" x 10" (check with your local one-hour photo outlet) and put them into a portfolio case or binder (see the section below on assembling your portfolio).

A few decorators also shoot video footage of rooms they have decorated, or put their photographs into a PowerPoint presentation. Employers do not expect you to do this, but if you are very comfortable with either of these technologies you can use them with your own portfolio.

Design Boards

A design board, also known as a presentation board, is a board used to show clients what you recommend for a decorating project. On this board you will paste:

- pictures of room elements (e.g. furniture, lights, accessories)

- samples of materials (e.g. fabrics, paint chips, carpet, flooring, wallpaper)

You do not need to include design boards in your portfolio, but they can certainly impress employers and help you get a job. If you don't have design boards from a real decorating project, you can produce sample design boards with pictures and materials you might use to decorate a room. See section 6.5.2 for information about how to create a design board.

Letters of Recommendation

The best letters of recommendation are those written by people you have done interior decorating work for. However, you can also include letters of recommendation from past employers, if the letters say good things about your abilities in areas that are important in the decorating business, such as interpersonal skills and organizational ability. You can also include thank you notes you have received.

As was emphasized in Chapter 2, every time you do a decorating project for someone – even a friend or family member (with a different last name from yours!) – ask for a letter of recommendation. Recommendation letters look particularly impressive if they are on letterhead, so ask for several copies on letterhead if possible.

> **TIP:** A recommendation letter should preferably not mention that you worked for free. You want to give the impression that your work has value, and an employer may assume the reason you received such a glowing recommendation is because you didn't charge anything. Remember, good work is good work no matter how much you were paid for it.

When you ask for a letter, keep in mind that many people are busy, so they are more likely to do what you ask if you can make it as easy as possible. To help get the kind of recommendation letter you want, and make the job easier on the person writing the letter, you could supply a list of points they might mention, for example:

- what you did (write it out for them—chances are, you remember exactly what you did more clearly than they might)

- how you got the work done ahead of schedule

- how you saved them money by finding the best suppliers

- how you got along well with everyone you worked with

- how you came up with many creative ideas

- how you listened and delivered exactly what they wanted

- how everyone has commented on how beautifully decorated the _____ is

Of course, all these things don't have to be included in a single letter! The specifics will depend on the particular job you did, but even a few glowing sentences can help you look good to employers.

What Else to Include

Your portfolio can include anything else that could impress someone who is considering hiring you. For example, if you received a certificate in decorating from an educational institution, or if you won a design award, put the actual certificate or award in your portfolio. If that's not possible, include photocopies or a photograph of the award.

Likewise, if you wrote an article about decorating that was published in a newspaper or magazine, you could include a clipping or photocopy of the published article. See Chapter 5 for information about how to write articles for publication, and other ways to establish your reputation as a decorating expert.

Putting It All Together

If you don't have design boards, you can put your portfolio items into a professional looking three-ring binder with plastic sheet covers to protect the pages. If you wish, you can mount your photographs and other portfolio materials onto thin cardboard. All of these are available from any office supplies store.

If your portfolio includes items such as design boards that won't fit into a binder, consider using a portfolio case, which you can buy at an art supply store (check the Yellow Pages). Portfolio cases come in a variety of sizes (e.g. 11" x 14", 14" x 17", 17" x 22") and cost from about $15 to over $150, depending on the size, material, and how fancy it is. However, employers are interested in what is inside of the case, so you don't need to spend a lot of money on the case itself.

In addition to preparing a portfolio to take with you to interviews, it's also a good idea to create an online portfolio (also known as a web portfolio). This is a selection of photos posted on a personal web page which employers can access at any time. Links to several online portfolios are included earlier in this section. See the next chapter for information about how to create a web page.

If you are conducting information interviews, as suggested in Chapter 2, it can be helpful to ask a professional interior decorator or interior designer for feedback on your portfolio.

4.1.2   Your Resume and Cover Letter

Here is the good news: Even if you have never been paid to decorate, you can write a powerful resume that can help you get an interior decorating job.

In order to do this, you will need to get some decorating experience using several of the methods suggested in Chapter 2. Even if the only homes you decorate are homes of friends and family members, you will still have decorating experience! The key is to present that experience in a way that is attractive to employers.

Employers are most concerned with the value you will bring to them as an employee. They want to know you have the specific skills necessary to do the job they are hiring for. They are not interested in reading about every previous job someone has had if those jobs are unrelated to the one being applied for. (If, like Stockwell Day, former leader of one of Canada's major political parties, you have held jobs such as logger, auctioneer, meat packer, youth counselor, deck hand, school administrator, and assistant pastor in addition to doing interior decorating, don't mention all those previous jobs on your resume!)

Some employers make a decision about a resume within seconds, so a resume containing too much irrelevant information could be rejected before the employer has even finished reading it. Therefore, instead of submitting a traditional resume focusing on each job you held and what you did, create a functional resume focusing on the skills and experience the employer is looking for.

Exactly what you will include on your resume depends on both the job you are applying for and your previous decorating experience. On the next page you will find a sample of a resume that could be used to apply for a position working as a decorator for a retail outlet. It assumes the person applying has some experience doing decorating work for charities and friends, as well as previous retail experience.

Sample Resume

Darleen Decor
4321 Main Street
Sunnyday, California
(123) 555-1212
decorator@abc.com

OBJECTIVE

- A position using my interior decorating and customer service skills.

INTERIOR DECORATOR

- Advised clients on: color, space planning, furniture styles, lighting, window coverings, flooring, art and accessories
- Purchased decorating materials
- Arranged and supervised installation of furniture and materials
- Coordinated multiple decorating projects at the same time, including two homes, an office, and a model home
- Recognized for completing decorating projects ahead of schedule and under budget

CUSTOMER SERVICE AND SALES

- Used effective listening skills to determine customer needs and recommend products
- Kept in touch with customers by phone to ensure satisfaction and repeat sales
- Received letters of recommendation from satisfied clients (copies available on request)
- Consistently exceeded sales targets by over 10 percent

WORK AND VOLUNTEER EXPERIENCE

- Self-employed Interior Decorator, Darlene's Decorating, 2010
- Homemaker, 2004-2009
- Humane Society, decorating for fundraising events, 2006-2009

EDUCATION

Completed courses on Color Theory and Understanding Antiques, Sunnyday College Continuing Education, 2009

PORTFOLIO AND REFERENCES AVAILABLE

Your own resume could include different categories. For example, if you are applying for an office job, it's a good idea to include computer programs you are familiar with, plus any previous office jobs you have held. Also include anything else related to decorating that you feel will help sell you to the employer, such as internships, certificates or awards you have earned, if you have created design boards, etc.

Other basic principles of preparing an effective resume are the same as for any job. For example, try to keep your resume to a single page unless you have extensive relevant experience. Also, you don't need to go back further than 10 years on your resume, since some employers may judge anything you learned before then to be outdated.

Something else to keep in mind is that you are applying for a job where appearance matters. Choose an attractive paper stock, lay it out nicely on the page, and make sure there are no typos. Ask someone else to look it over before you send it out.

You can find more advice about preparing a resume online at **www. FabJob.com/advice.html#resume**.

Cover Letter

If you are submitting your resume by mail, fax, or email, it is recommended that you include a cover letter. While it's okay to photocopy your resume, your cover letter should be personalized, and explain why you are a good candidate for the job.

To see what to do – and what not to do – in a cover letter, here are a couple of sample letters prepared in response to this ad:

INTERIOR DECORATOR

Regal Estates is seeking an interior decorator to work with new home buyers to help them choose paint and carpet colors, flooring, counter tops, etc. If you are customer service oriented and have previous decorating experience, please apply to Terry Smith at Regal Estates, 123 Main Street.

> ## Sample Letter 1
>
> Dear Sirs,
>
> I saw you're ad. This is the kind of job I've been looking for. I'm pretty sure I would enjoy it and it would be good experience for me. I've already sent out a bunch of resumes without much luck so I hope you'll hire me. As you can see I have everything your looking for. Its your loss if you don't hire me. Call me at 555-1234.
>
> *Andy Applicant*

In the cover letter above, Andy has done a number of things wrong. See how many of these mistakes you noticed:

- The letter is addressed to "Dear Sirs." Andy could make a better impression by addressing it by name to the person who will be reviewing resumes. If you don't know who to send your letter to, you can phone to ask the Human Resources department or address your letter "Attention: Human Resources Department." Since the person reading your letter may be a woman, avoid saying "Dear Sirs."

- It doesn't say which position is being applied for. Many companies advertise more than one position at a time.

- It has typographical and grammatical errors (for example, confusing "you're" with "your"). Proofread letters before sending them.

- The letter focuses on what Andy wants (to enjoy the job and get experience) instead of what the company wants. Employers want to know what value you will bring to them.

- The letter doesn't mention the company by name. Andy could make a much better impression by doing a little research in order to say something flattering about the company. (Find out what companies pride themselves on by checking their websites.)

- As you can imagine, saying something like "It's your loss if you don't hire me" does not make a good impression!

- By saying "I've already sent out a bunch of resumes without much luck" and "I hope you'll hire me," Andy sounds desperate. Employers may wonder if there's a good reason why no one else has hired Andy.

Employers would be more impressed with this letter:

Sample Letter 2

Attention: Terry Smith

I am writing to apply for the Interior Decorator position advertised in the *Saturday News*.

Regal Estates needs someone with previous decorating experience who is customer oriented. As my resume shows, I can bring you experience with interior decorating and assisting customers in choosing materials for their homes. I work to get repeat business for my employer, and have numerous letters of recommendation from satisfied customers.

It would be an honor to work with our city's #1 new home builder. I would like to arrange a meeting to discuss how I can be of service to Regal Estates and your customers. Please call me at 555-1234 to arrange a meeting at your convenience. I look forward to hearing from you and working with you.

Andy Applicant

Your own cover letter will of course depend on the position you are applying for, and the company you are applying to. It should also include your name and contact information at the top of the page.

4.2   Finding Job Openings

Several places may advertise jobs for interior decorators. If you're lucky, you may find a position in the classifieds of your local newspaper. However, as most decorating jobs are not advertised in the classifieds, it will usually take more effort to find job openings.

4.2.1   Advertised Positions

Job Websites

Although there are no online job boards specializing in interior decorating, several job sites include postings for interior decorators. For example, here's an excerpt from a Thomasville Home Furnishings ad found during a recent keyword search for "interior decorating" at Monster. com:

> "As a Thomasville sales associate you will be providing clients with home furnishing and decorating advice. You may even visit a client's home to help them furnish a room or their entire house."

Please note, jobs suitable for decorators are sometimes also listed under "interior design." Websites that sometimes have listings for interior decorating jobs include Careerbuilder.com, Yahoo! HotJobs.com and Monster.com.

Company Websites

Most companies advertise job openings at their websites. If there is no link for "jobs" or "careers" on the home page, click on the link for information about the company. That will usually take you to a page that includes a link to job postings. Section 4.3 of the guide includes contact information for some major employers.

4.2.2   Unadvertised Positions

The *Harvard Business Review* is reported to have said that almost 80 percent of jobs are not advertised in the classifieds. That figure may be even higher for a fab job like an interior decorator. In fact, it is rare to find ads for interior decorators placed by certain types of employers such as interior decorating or interior design firms. (It is much more common to find ads for interior designer positions.)

Even among the types of employers that usually do advertise for decorators, smaller companies may not have a website, and are unlikely to spend hundreds of dollars to post jobs at a site such as Monster.com. So how do these employers find employees?

Networking

Many employers find employees through word-of-mouth. When a small business owner needs a new employee, they will typically ask friends, business associates, and current employees if they know anyone who might be suitable for the job. In many cases, this is how they find the person for the job.

In section 6.1.2 you will find practical advice on how to network to find interior decorating clients. You can also use the advice in this part of the guide to help you meet and connect with people who can hire you – or recommend you to someone who can hire you – for a full-time or part-time decorating job.

Direct Contact

Even if you don't know anyone connected to a particular company, it may still be possible to get a job there by contacting the company directly. It rarely happens, but sometimes a manager will have just decided that they need a new person when they happen to receive a phone call or resume from someone who looks like they might be an ideal candidate for the job. Many employers would rather find someone this way than invest all the time and effort in advertising the job, screening resumes, and interviewing numerous candidates.

If you decide to make "cold" contact with employers (as opposed to the "warm" contacts that come through networking), it's a good idea to focus on specific types of employers. This will allow you to target your job search most effectively since it takes time to track down company owners' names, tailor your resume, and prepare personalized cover letters explaining why you want to work with that particular company.

If you decide to contact employers by phone, here are some tips:

- Always identify yourself. If you have been referred by someone else, mention that person's name as well.

- Ask to speak to the person in charge of hiring. Do your best to find out their name ahead of time so you can ask for them specifically.

- If the person you're trying to call isn't in, find out the best time to call back, rather than just leaving your name and number.

- When you get in touch with the person in charge of hiring, ask for an interview at a specific time, e.g., "Would Wednesday afternoon or perhaps Thursday morning work better for you?" This makes it easier on the other person and reduces the chance they'll say "I'll get back to you" and leave you waiting forever.

- If there are no openings at the current time, ask if you can call back in a few weeks to see if any positions have opened up.

- Speak clearly and smile. Your smile will carry over the phone.

The next section has information about the different types of companies that employ interior decorators so you can decide if you would like to target any of them.

4.3   Who Employs Interior Decorators

4.3.1   Retailers

The retail industry offers some excellent career opportunities for interior decorators. Retail is far ahead of any other industry in terms of the sheer number of jobs for decorators who want a steady paycheck.

While interior decorators may decorate the store they work in, the main focus of their job is selling the store's merchandise by helping customers choose products for their homes and businesses. To do this, a decorator/salesperson needs to ask questions to find out such things as the customer's needs and the preferred style, color scheme, space, budget, etc. The decorator/salesperson will then recommend suitable products to the customer and give the customer information about the recommended products.

As you can imagine, there are many types of companies that want to employ people with decorating talent, since someone who is skilled at their job can sell a lot of merchandise for their employer. Among the retailers that hire salespeople with interior decorating skills are:

- furniture stores

- department stores

- home improvement stores

- housewares stores

- decorating stores

- bed and bath stores

- paint stores

- stores that sell drapes or blinds

- lighting stores

- antiques dealers

- other stores that sell products used in home decorating

Depending on your interests and goals, working as a decorator/sales-person for any of these retailers may be a rewarding career in itself, or it may be a stepping-stone to another career in interior decorating.

For example, if you stay in retail you may move into a position such as buyer (someone who decides what merchandise the store will carry) or manager. Or you might use what you learn during your retail experi-ence to help you move into a job with a different type of employer, or start your own interior decorating business.

For your convenience, we have included a list of some of the major re-tailers that hire people with interior decorating skills, along with their website addresses. Many of these companies list store locations at their websites, and suggest that you apply directly to a store where you are interested in working. If you are interested in working at the compa-ny's head office, you can usually find corporate contact information as well.

If job information is posted on the website, read the job descriptions to find out which positions might relate to decorating, since the job title might be "sales associate" or something similar, and not include the word "decorator." (If there isn't a jobs link on the home page, you will usually be able to find employment information by clicking on the "About Us" link at the site.)

- *Bed Bath & Beyond*
  www.bedbathandbeyond.com

- *Bloomingdale's*
  www.bloomingdalesjobs.com/bloomingdales/index_flash.asp

- *Calico Corners*
  www.calicocorners.com

- *Chintz & Company (Canada)*
  www.chintz.com

- *Crate & Barrel*
  www.crateandbarrel.com

- *Domain Home Fashions*
  www.domain-home.com

- *Ethan Allen*
  www.ethanallen.com

- *Havertys*
  www.havertys.com

- *Home Depot*
  www.homedepot.com

- *Home Outfitters (Canada)*
  www.homeoutfitters.com/en

- *Kirkland's*
  www.kirklands.com

- *Linens 'N Things*
  www.lnt.com

- *Lowe's*
  www.lowes.com

- *Restoration Hardware*
  www.restorationhardware.com

In addition to the companies listed above, there are literally hundreds of other retail companies of all sizes that sell merchandise for the home. Check the local Yellow Pages under appropriate categories such as furniture, housewares, and even hardware.

4.3.2 Home Builders

Companies that build new houses or develop condominums may hire interior decorators for two types of work. The first type of work is decorating model homes (known as "show homes" in Canada or overseas, or "show suites" in the case of condominiums).

Every new home development has model homes that are beautifully decorated with furniture, linens, art, accessories, etc. Everything is color coordinated and positioned to make the home as attractive and comfortable as possible. The purpose is to sell the builder's houses or condominiums by making visitors feel this is a home they want to live in. This type of work may be done on contract by self-employed interior decorators (covered in Chapter 5) or by a decorator employed by the home builder.

In addition to decorating model homes, interior decorators may be hired by home builders to work with home buyers. Before construction on the home is completed, the decorator meets with new buyers to help them pick out the best combinations of flooring, carpeting, kitchen counter tops, etc.

Since many home buyers don't have the experience to know which combinations of colors, patterns, and materials will work best together, working with an interior decorator can help ensure they will be happy with their new home.

You can find home builders by checking the Yellow Pages or doing an online search. Some websites that list home builders in the U.S. and Canada are **www.homebuilders.com** and **www.home-builders.com** (note the hyphen).

4.3.3 Interior Decorating and Design Firms

Firms that may hire talented interior decorators to assist with their work include interior decorating firms, interior design firms, and architecture firms.

If you are hired as a decorator with an interior decorating firm, you may assist with all aspects of the company's work. If you are hired by an interior design or architecture firm, you may work as part of a team on residential or commercial building projects.

If you check your local Yellow Pages, you will likely find dozens of interior decorators, interior designers, and architects listed for your city. However, the few decorating jobs that open up with these firms are rarely advertised and are usually filled through networking. There are a couple of reasons these firms have relatively few opportunities for interior decorators (in comparison to the retail industry).

In the case of interior decorating firms, most are small businesses that manage to find just enough decorating work for the company's owners. Because of this, it is usually not a productive use of your time to repeatedly phone every company in the Yellow Pages trying to find a job. Instead, if you are eager to work with an interior decorating firm, you should focus your efforts on busy, growing companies that are more likely to need extra staff to handle all the work they have coming their way. These are typically the companies you will see mentioned in the local newspaper or hear about at networking events.

In the case of interior design and architecture firms, many prefer to have their decorating work done by interior designers who have particular academic credentials. That's because the owners of these firms have invested years in their own education, and often expect the people they hire to have done the same. However, there are exceptions. For example, one of the interior designers interviewed during the research for this guide owns a firm that has an interior decorator on staff.

The most effective way to break into a similar position is through networking. Section 6.1.2 has advice on networking techniques.

4.3.4   Other Employers

There are a variety of other companies that hire interior decorators. While these companies may have relatively few employment opportunities (for example, a national company may employ a single interior decorator), they are included here so you will know about your different career options. Remember, even if a company has only one job available, someone will get hired for it, and that someone could be you. You can find information and links to websites for national companies at **www.hoovers.com**. Companies that may hire interior decorators include:

Manufacturers

As you know, manufacturers are companies that make and sell products. While this may not seem like the type of company that would employ interior decorators, several types of manufacturers can use the services of a talented decorator, including:

- Furniture manufacturers

- Manufacturers of housewares (linens, glassware, etc.)

- Manufacturers of building materials

Manufacturers may hire interior decorators to assist in the marketing of their products. For example, one of the editors of this guide has a friend who worked as an interior decorator for Corning. Her job included decorating trade show booths. She also did decorating for photo shoots when the company was creating new advertising materials.

Since every company does some form of marketing, there may be an opportunity for you to help them sell their products by presenting them in as attractive a setting as possible.

Hotel and Restaurant Chains

If you have ever stayed at a luxury hotel, you almost certainly entered a gorgeous lobby – possibly decorated with antiques – and spent the night in a room that was as attractive as it was comfortable. Someone had to choose the furnishings, wall coverings, and other elements for those interiors.

Decorators are needed for new hotel and restaurant chains, as well as existing facilities. While a chain may hire an interior designer, or a single restaurant may use a self-employed interior decorator, full-time jobs for decorators are sometimes available with hotel and restaurant chains.

4.4 Interviews

Interviews for interior decorating jobs are much like interviews for other jobs. With that in mind, there are several specific tips that can help you make an excellent impression in an interview.

4.4.1 What Employers Are Looking For

Employers are looking for someone who will do an excellent job. But they are also seeking someone with certain character and personality traits. Here is how Lynn Donaldson, president of Lynn Donaldson and Associates Design & Contracting in Calgary, Alberta, described it:

> "The first things I look for are personality, character and work ethic. An employee can always be taught work skills, but they can't always be taught how to care for people, be polite and use common courtesy."

According to Susan Mielke, of Susan J. Mielke Designs, the two things that will help a beginner have the best opportunity of getting hired at a decorating firm are "A great, personable attitude, and a great portfolio!"

Attitude

Earlier you got some good advice on preparing a portfolio. Now let's take a look at the other part of Susan's equation—a great attitude.

Your attitude is being evaluated from the moment you first walk into the building, or even earlier, when you first speak on the telephone with anyone from the company. Anyone you encounter in the lobby, the elevator, the washroom, or the reception area may have input into whether or not you are hired. We have conducted hundreds of employment interviews, and after many of them we have asked the receptionist what she thought of the person we had just interviewed. We wanted to know if the applicant treated the receptionist with as much friendliness and respect as she treated us.

During the interview itself, try to be as outgoing and enthusiastic as possible. Of course, this isn't always easy because interviews can make people nervous, and nervous people tend to smile less, and act more stiff and formal than they normally would. However, as an interior decorator, you will be working with many people who are important clients. The employer wants to see that you are comfortable even in a potentially uncomfortable interpersonal situation like an interview.

If you tend to be stiff and uncomfortable during an interview, it is time to perform. Act how you would if you were not nervous. This may feel unnatural at first, but behaving as if you are not nervous can actually make you start to feel that way as well. It can also help to do some role plays (practice interviews) with a friend before you go to the interview.

Be positive as well as enthusiastic. Avoid saying anything negative, especially about former employers. Focus on what value you would bring to the company as an employee and not on what you want to get from the job. For example, don't discuss how much vacation time you want or bring up salary until the employer does.

Also avoid saying anything negative about yourself, which some applicants do by sounding as if they are desperate for a job. Before the interview, remind yourself how much you have to offer an employer, and that there are many opportunities for you. Believe that if this particular job doesn't work out, there is something better out there for you.

Within 24 hours after the interview, write a thank you letter to the person who interviewed you and anyone else who may have been helpful to you, such as the interviewer's assistant. Thank the interviewer for their time, give any additional information that you feel will help you get the job, and say how enthusiastic you are about the possibility of working with their company.

You can send a thank you letter by email, but you will make an even better impression if you deliver it in person.

Above all, you want the interviewer and the other people you meet to think: "What a nice person! It would be great to have someone like that working here."

Appearance

Interior decorating is a visual business, so it's not surprising that part of what you will be judged on is your appearance.

Barbara Moses, Ph.D., best-selling author of *Career Intelligence*, advises applicants to think about what the interviewer might be wearing, and to match the style. She says:

> "Effective presentation as a job candidate means showing that you understand the culture in which you would be operating and that you would readily fit in."

If possible, visit the business before the interview so you can see how people are dressed. If that's not possible, ask the assistant of the person you are going to meet with about the company's dress code. If you have no information to go on, choose standard interview attire, such as a navy suit, but with a subtle twist. Use your clothing to show that you are creative and have a good eye. A man might wear a tie with an interesting pattern while a woman might wear an accessory such as an unusual pin or another striking piece of jewelry. Whatever you choose should say something about you and your style.

4.4.2   Questions to Expect

You can expect to be asked standard interview questions such as the following. It's a good idea to prepare some answers before the interview.

- Why do you want to work for our company?

- What are you doing now?

- What kind of position are you looking for?

- What did you like most about your last job? What did you like least? Why?

- What experience do you have with _____? (Depending on the company, they may want to know your experience with decorating, selling, customer service, working in teams, juggling many projects at once, etc.)

- What are your strengths? What are your weaknesses?

- What do you want to be doing in five years?

- What are your salary expectations?

- Do you have any questions for us?

In order to ask good questions and give an effective answer to "Why do you want to work here?" you will need to learn something about the company before the interview. Make sure you visit their website or stop by the office to pick up any promotional brochures.

Also be prepared to answer behavioral questions. These are questions that ask you about an experience you had in the past, and require you to answer with a specific real-life example. For instance, the interviewer might say, "Tell me about a time you experienced conflict with a co-worker. What happened, and how was it resolved?"

The interviewer will not be satisfied with a hypothetical answer about what you would do in such a situation. They want to hear about an actual time you experienced conflict. The purpose is not to see if you have ever had a conflict (they expect that you have); the purpose is to see how well you resolve difficult situations, and, if something did not work out in the past, what you learned from it.

The interviewer will likely also ask to see your portfolio. If they do not ask, you can offer to show it to them, and explain the different pieces as the interviewer is looking at them if anything requires an explanation.

You can find some more advice on preparing for an interview and answering interview questions online at **www.FabJob.com/advice.html# interviews**, or at Rita Sue Siegal Resources (**www.ritasue.com/resources/ tools/interview.html**).

4.4.3   Discussing Salary

If an employer is interested in hiring you, they will bring up the issue of salary. (As mentioned above, you should not be the first one to bring up salary if you want to make a good impression on the interviewer.)

To maximize your salary, try to get the employer to state a figure first. If you are the first one to mention a specific salary figure, and it's lower than the one the employer had in mind, you risk getting hired for less than they might have been willing to pay you. Therefore, if they ask your salary expectations, try turning the question back to them by saying something like "It depends on exactly what I would be doing. What is the salary range for this position?"

It's a good idea to have a sense of how much you should be getting paid before the issue comes up during an interview. One figure that has been reported as a starting salary for entry level interior decorators is $10 per hour, with commissions starting at six percent for those working with retailers that pay commission. In addition to a base salary and commission, decorators working for retailers, wholesalers (companies that sell to retailers) or manufacturers may earn substantial discounts on merchandise. If you want to work in positions involving sales or retail, you can find average salaries at **www.salary.com**.

However, Salary.com does not list information specifically about interior decorating salaries, and salaries for interior decorators vary widely depending on geographic area and type of employer. For example, a job with a small interior decorating firm in North Dakota will probably pay you less than a job with a large retailer in New York City. To get information about typical salaries in your community, connect with people in the decorating industry using the techniques described in this guide, such as informational interviews (see Chapter 2), mentoring, and networking (see Chapter 6).

In many cases, you may be able to negotiate a better salary or better benefits than the employer's initial offer. If the employer isn't flexible on salary, they may be able to offer higher commissions, or be willing to negotiate vacation or overtime. While effective negotiations can lead to a higher salary, if you really want an unlimited potential for income, then you should consider being self-employed. In the next chapter you will learn how to start your own interior decorating business.

Interior Decorator Success Story

Frederick Udey used talent and determination to break into a fab job as an interior decorator. His story may give you some ideas to help you get started in this fab job.

Fred has been decorating interiors since he was a teenager. He started out with his family home, then moved on to helping his older sisters decorate when they moved into homes of their own. Word spread about Fred's talents and he started getting calls to decorate other houses and home businesses. Someone might call Fred and say, "I just bought a new sectional. I love it, but I didn't realize it would be so big in my home." As Fred describes it, "They needed somebody with the instincts to say 'If you do this and this and this, it would work'."

To pay the bills, he took a full-time job hanging wallpaper for a woman who sold wall coverings. "The money was great!" he says, but his heart was in decorating. To further develop his skills, he took continuing education courses on topics such as color and space, and volunteered to decorate model homes for charity raffles for the local children's hospital.

Through word of mouth Fred heard that a new home improvement store was opening in town and that they were looking for decorators. The building was still under construction, with no power, when he showed up with his resume. Scores of applicants for all types of jobs came by while he was there. The person taking applications told people they could leave a resume or wait for an interview. Fred chose to wait for more than two hours. After a 40-minute interview, he was hired as a full-time decorator.

He has been with international retailer RONA (**www.rona.ca**), for the past seven years and worked his way up to a position as buyer. As a decorator for the store, he designed "fake room vignettes" — displays that look like a room in a home. He also appeared numerous times on a local television breakfast show talking about interior decorating topics ranging from color to countertops.

Fred loves his fab job and the freedom it gives him to continue doing freelance interior decorating for a variety of clients, including restaurants, bars, offices, boutique stores, and homes. He was one of the experts interviewed for this book and generously shares advice on topics ranging from getting decorating experience to working with clients.

5. Starting Your Own Business

As a self-employed interior decorator you can enjoy freedom and the potential for much higher income than you might earn as an employee. If you dream of having your own decorating business, the information in this chapter will help you get started. It covers:

- What you need to get started

- Information about interior decorating franchises

- How to set up your office

- How much to charge for your services

- How to get clients

- Working with suppliers

In the next chapter you will find step-by-step advice on how to work with clients and make your new business a success.

5.1 Getting Started

Before you can get to the fun part of having your own interior decorating business (doing the decorating!) there are a number of not so fun, but very important, matters to be handled. Before we get into the details of what needs to be done, here are some resources that can help you get started.

5.1.1 Where to Get Help

If you decide to buy an interior decorating franchise (covered in section 5.2), the company will likely provide you with the training you need to start your business. However, franchises are expensive, so here are some sources of free advice to help you do it yourself.

SCORE

The Service Corps of Retired Executives has volunteers throughout the U.S. who donate time to mentor small businesses free of charge. Visit their website at **www.score.org** for helpful information or call 800-634-0245 to find the nearest SCORE counseling location.

Small Business Administration

The SBA is an excellent source of free information for anyone starting a business in the U.S. To learn about SBA programs and services, visit their website at **www.sbaonline.sba.gov** or call the SBA Small Business Answer Desk at 800-U-ASK-SBA (800-827-5722).

U.S. Chamber of Commerce Small Business Nation

The U.S. Chamber of Commerce website offers free information on preparing a business plan, incorporating, choosing your office location, and other aspects of starting and running a business. Visit their website at **www.uschambersmallbusinessnation.com/toolkits/tools/start-up** or phone 1-800-638-6582.

Canada Business Services for Entrepreneurs

You will find a wide range of information at this site, including step-by-step instructions to guide you through starting your new business. Visit **www.canadabusiness.ca/eng/125**.

Nolo.com

Nolo is a publisher of plain English legal information, books, software, forms and a comprehensive website. Their website has an online resource center at **www.nolo.com** which offers free advice on a variety of small business matters. Click on "Business, LLCs & Corporations."

5.1.2   Creating a Business Plan

Business planning involves putting on paper all the plans you have for your business, including:

- the services you will provide

- who your customers are

- who your competitors are

- where you will get your supplies

- what you will charge for your services

- how you will advertise and market your services

- how much money you will need to get started

If you enjoy being spontaneous, you may be thinking you'd prefer not to do much advance planning. However, if you are seeking financing for your business from a bank or other lender, they will expect to see a business plan that shows you have a viable business idea with an excellent chance for success. Even if you don't need financing, putting ideas on paper will give you a "road map" of where you want to go with your business and how you are going to get there.

While you are working on your business plan, you may start to question some of your previous ideas. You may come up with ideas that are even better, or decide to make some changes to ensure you have a greater chance of success.

A business plan can also help you avoid costly surprises. If you are considering whether to leave a secure job to start your own business, a business plan can help you determine the resources you will need to start your business and decide when the timing is best for you to get started.

As previously mentioned, the SBA offers an extensive selection of information on most business management topics. Online, they offer business plan advice at **www.sba.gov/smallbusinessplanner/plan/write abusinessplan**. This information is also available in print form in the "Resource Directory for Small Business Management." For a free copy contact the nearest SBA office, which you can find listed in the U.S. Government section of your telephone directory.

5.1.3 Choosing a Business Name

Your business name can communicate the focus of your business, and may help attract the types of clients you want. For example, if you wish to attract wealthy clients who want their homes to be lavishly decorated, a name like Elegant Interiors (used by an interior design firm in California) might be more suitable than Simple Surroundings.

In most jurisdictions, if you operate under anything other than your own name, you are required to file for a fictitious name. It's usually just a short form to fill out and a small filing fee that you pay to your state or provincial government.

Before registering a fictitious name, you will need to make sure it does not belong to anyone else. If someone else has trademarked the name you are using, you may be forced to stop using the name and possibly have to pay the owner damages.

Search the federal trademark database to determine whether a name has already been registered with the U.S. Patent and Trademark Office (PTO). Online you can go to the PTO's Trademark Electronic Business Center and choose "Search."

- *General Information Services Division*
  Website: **www.uspto.gov/main/trademarks.htm**
  Phone: 1-800-786-9199

Canadians can find information and search a database of existing trademarks through the Canadian Intellectual Property Office.

- *Canadian Intellectual Property Office (CIPO)*

  Website: **www.cipo.ic.gc.ca/eic/site/cipointernet-internetopic. nsf/eng/Home**

  Phone: 866-997-1936

Most small businesses do not bother to trademark their names because it can be costly and time-consuming. However, if your company name is truly unique, you might want to consider it. You can try doing it yourself, or hire a lawyer specializing in "intellectual property" to do it for you.

5.1.4 Legal Matters

Your Business Legal Structure

Your business structure affects the cost of starting your business, your taxes, and your liability (responsibility) for any debts of the business. There are several different legal forms a business can have.

Sole Proprietorship

If you want to run the business yourself, without incorporating, your business will be known as a "sole proprietorship." This is the least expensive way to start your own business. It is also the easiest because it requires less paperwork and you can report your business income on your personal tax return. One drawback to this type of business is that you are personally liable for any debts of the business.

Partnership

If you want to go into business with someone else, the easiest and least expensive way to do this is by forming a partnership. Legally, you would both be responsible for any debts of the company.

Corporation

Whether you are working alone or with partners, if you want a more formal legal structure for your business, you can incorporate. Incorporation can protect you from personal liability and may make your business appear more professional to some clients. However, it usually costs several hundred dollars and there are many rules and regulations involved with this type of business structure (among other require-ments, corporations must file articles of incorporation, hold regular meetings, and keep records of those meetings). Many new business owners consult with an attorney before incorporating.

Limited Liability Company

A Limited Liability Company is a newer type of business legal struc-ture in the U.S. It is a combination of a partnership and corporation, and is considered to have some of the best attributes of both, including limited personal liability.

The resources at the start of this chapter have further information on business structures. Excellent advice is also offered at the Intuit MyCor-poration website at **www.mycorporation.com/business-formations/ incorporate.jsp**.

Working with a Partner

Beyond any legal issues, before going into business with a part-ner you should spend many hours talking about how you will work together, including:

- what each of you will be responsible for

- how you will make decisions on a day-to-day basis

- what percentage of the business each of you will own

- how you see the business developing in the future

- what you expect from each other

During your discussions you can learn if there are any areas where you need to compromise. For example, one of you may want to have an interior decorating business as a fun part-time job, while the other wants to work full-time and eventually build a business that will employ a dozen or more people. You can avoid future misunderstandings by putting the points you have agreed on into a written "partnership agreement" that covers any possibility you can think of (including one of you leaving the business at some point in the future).

Business Licenses

You can find information about getting a city business license from your city hall. You may also be required to have a county or state license so be sure to check with regulatory agencies in your area to determine what you'll need. Check the resources in the first part of this section or see the SBA's licensing webpage at **www.sba.gov/smallbusinessplanner/start/ getlicensesandpermits**. For a list of links to state business license offices websites visit **www.business.gov/register/licenses-and-permits**.

5.1.5 Taxes

You may be wondering why you need to think about taxes when you are just starting up your business. Certainly you don't have to pay taxes until you start making money. However, it may be advantageous to register with the government as soon as you can, and it is wise to plan ahead.

Tax Returns

If your business is a sole proprietorship or partnership in the United States, you will file a schedule C with your personal tax returns. You'll also have to file a form to determine the amount you owe on your social security.

When you fill out your tax return, you will need to include either your Social Security Number or an Employer Identification Number (EIN). A number of business owners recommend filling out an SS-4 Form to obtain an EIN even if your business is a sole proprietorship. Your corporate clients will need this for their records as will your suppliers to set up wholesale accounts. An EIN is also required if your company is incorporated, if you have employees, or if you plan to sell interior decorating products.

Taxes on Product Sales

In most jurisdictions, if you buy supplies at wholesale prices then resell them to your clients for a higher price, you will need to collect sales tax from your clients and turn it over to the appropriate city, county, state, and/or country. In order to collect sales tax, you must be registered with, or have a sales tax license from, each level of government you collect taxes for.

TIP: You do not need to obtain a sales tax license if your clients simply reimburse you the actual purchase price for any materials you buy for them.

To find out which taxes apply in your jurisdiction, check the resources below and consult with an accountant.

Resources

For tax information, forms and publications, see the resources at the start of this chapter or contact your government tax authority. Check your local phone directory for an office near you, call their national office, or visit their website.

The U.S. Internal Revenue Service (IRS) can be reached at 1-800-829-4933 or online at **www.irs.gov**. In Canada, you can get information from the Canada Revenue Agency at **www.cra-arc.gc.ca/tx/bsnss/menu-eng. html** or by calling 1-800-959-5525.

5.2 Franchises

If you are eager to start your own interior decorating business, but concerned about how much work is involved in getting everything set up, you may want to consider franchising.

5.2.1 What is Franchising?

Franchising happens when an established company allows someone to run a local business using the same company name, logo, products, services, marketing and business systems. The original company is known as the "franchisor" and the company that is granted the right to run its business the same way as the franchisor is known as the "franchisee."

You have probably bought products and services from many franchisees. For example, if you have ever bought lunch at McDonald's, Kentucky Fried Chicken, Burger King, or Wendy's Restaurants, you were buying from a franchise.

Pros and Cons of Franchising

People who choose to franchise – rather than start their own business from scratch – often do so because they want to minimize their risk. They see the franchise as a proven business that already has name recognition among the public. (Although there is less name recognition for interior decorating franchises than for fast food franchises!) By working with an established system, franchisees hope to avoid costly mistakes and make a profit more quickly.

Franchises are also good for people who want support. Franchisors typically provide training to help franchisees start, market, and run their new business. The franchisee may receive assistance with everything from obtaining supplies to setting up record keeping systems. Many franchisors are continously working to develop better systems and products, and you can take advantage of those developments.

It is important to keep in mind that a franchisee does not own any of the trademarks or business systems. Also, a franchisee must run their business according to the terms of their agreement with the franchisor. For example, the franchisee may not be permitted to offer a sales promotion or use a supplier that has not been authorized by the franchisor.

While some people appreciate having such guidelines to follow, if you are an independent person who enjoys taking risks and being spontaneous, you might find owning a franchise to be too restrictive. Since someone else is ultimately "in charge" you may be wondering how having a franchise is different than being an employee. In fact, there are significant differences. For example, you have more freedom than an employee (e.g., you might choose your own working hours). And you could ultimately earn a lot more money than an employee.

On the other hand, franchisees must pay thousands of dollars up front for the opportunity to work with the business, and there is the possibility that the franchise will not be financially successful. Many websites on the topic of franchising claim more than a 90 percent long-term success rate for franchisees. However, the Business Link website (see resources below) cites a study reported in the Wall Street Journal which found a 35 percent failure rate for franchises. Your own success will depend on a variety of factors including your geographic location and the particular franchise you become involved with.

TIP: If you are considering franchising, do your homework and gather all the information you need to make an informed decision. What you receive for your investment varies from franchise to franchise, so make sure you know exactly what you will be buying and that any claims are substantiated. Before signing a contract, it is also wise to consult with people you trust to give you unbiased and sound advice, perhaps your accountant or attorney.

5.2.2   Interior Decorating Franchises

There are numerous franchises that touch on some aspect of home improvement or decor. For example, there are franchises to sell window blinds, frame art, or open a furniture store. In this section we focus on several franchises that involve interior decorating skills. You can find other franchises by doing a search at the International Franchise Association website at **www.franchise.org**.

Costs

Estimated start-up costs for an interior decorating franchise range from $19,000 to $195,000. (The higher figure is to open a retail store in a major market area.) The initial investment typically includes two components, payment of a franchise fee and other startup costs.

Entrepreneur Magazine describes a franchise fee as a one-time charge paid to the franchisor "for the privilege of using the business concept, attending their training program, and learning the entire business." Other start-up costs may include the products and services you will actually need to run the business, such as supplies, stationery, advertising, etc. For excellent advice on franchises, visit the magazine's site at **www.entrepreneur.com/franchises/index.html**.

A franchise fee might be $12,000 with an additional $18,000 required for other start-up costs. Or it might be $24,000 with an additional $6,000 required for other start-up costs. There are a variety of factors involved in determining the initial investment, including:

• the geographic area you will be working in

- the nature of your business (will you have a retail store, a studio, or travel to customers in a company van?)

- the particular company you franchise with

In addition to your initial investment, you can expect to pay the franchisor ongoing royalties. These royalties typically range from seven to 11 percent of your sales; the exact amount will depend on the company you franchise with.

Franchisors

The companies listed here are provided only for your information. They are not recommendations. Only you can decide which franchise, if any, will be best for you. Also note that contact information can change, so visit the company websites for current information.

Deck the Walls

Website:	**www.dtwfraninfo.com**
Phone:	866-719-8200
Fax:	877-832-6694
Email:	**ddahl@fcibiz.com**
About:	Custom artwork and framing design franchisor. Provider of wall decor for home and office, prints, and custom framing.

Decor&You

Website:	**http://decorandyou.com/pages/ franchise-information.php**
Phone:	800-477-3326 or 203-264-3500
Email:	**info@decorandyou.com**
About:	Franchisees consult with customers about color, fabric, texture, lighting, furnishings, flooring, wall and window coverings. They identify decorating goals and create a customized "Decor Plan" to change the look of kitchens, bedrooms, offices and more.

Decorating Den Interiors

Website:	**www.decoratingden.com**
Phone:	410-822-9001
About:	Established in 1969, Decorating Den now has more than 700 franchisees who work out of custom-designed vans, bringing drapery, furniture, carpet and wall covering samples to the client's home or office. There the franchisee helps the customer select everything from window treatments to furniture to artwork.

5.3   Setting Up Your Business

If you decide to franchise, your franchisor will assist you in setting up your business. However, if you are like most people who start an interior decorating business, you will be doing it on your own.

To help you get your business up and running, this section offers advice on:

- Location

- Telephone

- Equipment and supplies

- Insurance

- Employees

- Finances

5.3.1   Location

The first thing you will need is a place to work. Your choices include working from home or renting space. Many interior decorators choose to work from home when they start their businesses, because it saves on the cost of an office. After all, unlike many other types of business owners, you won't be expecting your clients to come to you – you will usually be going to their homes or businesses.

Identify Your Needs

Although clients may not come to your office very often, you will need to ensure you have enough space to carry out your business. Ask yourself if you will need any of the following. (If you're not sure, return to this section after you have read through the entire guide.)

- Storage space for materials to be used in decorating

- Space for construction

- Space for employees

- Retail space if you decide to open a store

When it comes to construction space, most decorators will only need an area to create design boards (the samples you show to clients). However, a few decorators enjoy actually creating some of the materials they use to decorate homes, for example, sewing curtains.

Working from Home

There are many benefits to working from home. For example, you don't have to commute to an office, you can take breaks whenever you want, you can spend more time with your family, etc. Another important benefit is that you are allowed to deduct from your income tax a percentage of your mortgage interest and property tax (or your rent) along with a similar share of some utilities and maintenance.

TIP: The IRS has a form and publication to help you learn how to compute the calculation and file the deduction. See section 5.1.5 (*"Taxes"*) for more information on where to get forms.

If office space is expensive in your area and you have enough room to work from home, your financial breaks can really add up. Before you decide, however, be sure your local zoning laws allow you to have a home-based business in your neighborhood. Zoning laws are often regulated by a city or county's planning department. To contact the department, look up "zoning" or "planning" in the government section of your phone book.

To help you focus on business, and keep other family members from intruding on your workspace, try to find at least an entire room to use for your office. (Having a separate room also makes it easier to calculate your tax deduction.) You could work from a spare bedroom, a den, a basement, or any other area that can be kept separate from the rest of the house.

Set regular office hours when the rest of the family knows you're working and not to be interrupted unless there's an emergency. (And train your family to know what you mean by "emergency" – a house on fire is an emergency; needing to know where the cookies are is not.)

Once you have chosen your space, decorate it as beautifully as you would a client's office. After all, you may have the odd client dropping by, and your office is an opportunity to showcase your work. Plus, it's tax deductible! (Remember to make your workspace functional with as large a desktop as possible, and a comfortable chair.)

Renting Space

While a home office works well for many interior decorators, others prefer to rent a separate space. If you find it challenging to stay motivated, or tend to get easily distracted when you're at home, an office may be just what you need to help you focus on business.

A separate space also creates a better impression if you plan to have people visit you. If you want a place to meet with clients and contractors, or work with employees, you might want to consider getting an office outside your home. If you plan to be a retailer of decorating materials, you will almost certainly need to rent a store or studio.

If you simply need office space, look for a place that is convenient to get to from your home, and that gives you quick access to any services you may need. Such services might include your bank, suppliers of decorating materials, even a good coffee shop! If you want to retail materials to the public, the most important consideration is your customers. Will your business be the kind that customers will seek out? Or do you need to be in a high traffic area such as a mall? Pick an area that suits your needs and fits your budget.

If you want the appearance of a professional office space, but cost is an issue, consider shared office space in a business center or executive suite. These facilities are typically furnished offices that provide you with receptionist and mail services. They may also offer photocopiers, fax machines, Internet access, and conference rooms that you can use for client meetings. Check the Yellow Pages under "office space" or do a Google search for your city and "shared office space," "business center" or "executive suite."

For good advice on what to consider before renting space, visit **www. nolo.com**. (Click on "Business, LLCs & Corporations," then "Business Name, Location & Licenses," then "Your Business Space & Commercial Lease.")

5.3.2   Telephones

You'll notice this section is titled "Telephone**s**" rather than simply "Telephone." That's because many interior decorators have more than one phone. For many business owners, the basics are: a business line, a fax line, and a cell phone. If you are on the Internet a lot, you may also want a separate line to connect to the Internet. If you have employees, you may want phone lines for them as well. Here is some information to help you decide what is best for you – and how to best use the lines you have.

Your Business Line

Your telephone should always be answered professionally with the name of your business.

If you work at home, it's a good idea to have a separate telephone line that is off limits to the rest of the family. If a client's call is answered by a family member saying "hello," you will likely be taken less seriously by the client. If a child answers your phone, you will almost certainly lose credibility in the eyes of the client. This kind of telephone answering can cost you much more than a separate phone line ever would!

A true business line will cost a little more than a residential line but you will be listed under your business name in the white pages and under directory assistance (which makes it easy for clients to find you) and you can receive a free listing in the Yellow Pages under "Interior Decorators."

If you want to ensure your phone is answered at all times during business hours, you can hire someone to answer it for you. It's actually not a good idea to always be personally available to answer the phone. A client may assume that a successful interior decorator would be out decorating, not sitting by the phone.

> **TIP:** Don't hire an answering service that only takes messages. These are the type of services that say in response to callers' questions: "I don't know, I'm just the answering service." This is frustrating to callers and can create a poor impression.

If you decide to use someone to answer your calls, it is better to hire an individual, possibly working from home, who can answer callers' questions and act as a public relations person for you. See the information below for hiring employees or contractors.

A less expensive option to hiring someone to answer your calls is to use voice mail. Voice mail is widely accepted in business communication. For example, if you call the direct line of a corporate executive, you will probably get voice mail if you don't connect with the executive. If you do opt for voice mail, consider leaving your pager or cell phone number for callers who may have an urgent need to reach you.

Additional Phones

It's wise to have a separate line for faxes. A potential client may not be impressed to hear you say, "Please wait a few minutes before sending that fax because I have to switch on the machine" (it suggests you are just a beginner working from home).

If there will be more than one person in the office or you expect a moderate to heavy amount of incoming calls, you should consider buying a two-line phone and getting a roll-over line. Your local phone company can set-up the service.

You should also get a cell phone as soon as possible. As a successful interior decorator, you can expect to spend a lot of time away from your office visiting clients in their homes and offices. You may also have to travel to suppliers to pick up materials. Any time you are away from the office, you risk missing a call from someone who wants to hire you. A cell phone enables you to check messages on your voice mail and return calls as soon as possible. You should be able to get a cell phone from the company that provides your business line—or even pick one up at your local shopping mall.

Of course you would not take a call when you are with a client for the same reason it's not a good idea to have call waiting on your business line—you want the person you are speaking with to feel that they are important to you, which will not happen if you interrupt your conversation to speak with someone else. So keep your cell phone on vibrate mode instead of ring.

5.3.3   Equipment and Supplies

In addition to telephones, you will need a variety of office equipment and supplies for your business. The initial cost of these items can come as a bit of a surprise to new business owners. However, once your office is stocked up, your ongoing expenses should be minimal.

Check with your local office supply stores to find out about sales. The sales reps who work there can also be of assistance when it comes to getting help putting together everything you need for your office. Chances are these retailers have stores in your community, but you can also order what you need by phone and online.

- *Staples*
  www.staples.com

- *Office Depot*
  www.officedepot.com

- *OfficeMax*
  www.officemax.com

Supplies

Of course you will need the supplies any business needs, including pens and pencils, paper, stapler, clips, Post-Its, scissors, tape, Liquid Paper, file trays, etc. Additional supplies you will likely need for your decorating business include magazine holders (you'll end up with a ton of magazines), a utility knife, graph paper, tape measure, rulers and supplies to create design boards and a portfolio (see those sections of the guide for details).

Computer and Software

In addition to the computer, it's a good idea to get a printer, something to back up your files (such as a Flash drive or CD-RW), and a digital camera (or a regular camera and scanner) to take and send electronic photos of events you have planned.

Many computers already have the basic software needed to run a business. Some versions of Microsoft Office come with a whole suite of small business tools. You may also want to get a bookkeeping program such as Quicken or Quickbooks as well as a database program to keep track of your clients. The MS Office Small Business Suite has one, or you can buy a database program such as ACT! or Filemaker Pro. The staff at a computer store or your office supplies store can give you more information about specific programs and help you decide which ones are best for you.

A design program is not an essential piece of software, but you may find it useful. A design program such as Better Homes and Gardens Interior Designer ($79) lets you decorate interiors on your computer (arranging furniture and other room elements, applying color to walls, changing flooring, etc.). You can then print out the finished design to show clients.

There are also a variety of low cost ($9.95 - $29.95) design programs available at a site such as Amazon.com with fewer features. However, as mentioned above, a design program is not essential. Even though you can create impressive designs on your computer with a design program, you may prefer to sketch them by hand (as described in Chapter

3), or use a system like Home Furniture Planner that lets you plan by rearranging vinyl stickers. See **www.homefurnitureplanner.com** for details.

Photocopier

This used to be considered optional equipment for small businesses. But today, when you can get a unit that is a combination photocopier, fax machine, scanner, printer, and telephone for a few hundred dollars, you should consider getting one. You are unlikely to need dozens of photocopies; you might need to make a copy or two of an agreement from time to time, and if you have the equipment right there, you won't have to go all the way to Kinko's to do it.

And remember, time is money, especially when you have a lot to do and a lot on your mind. This business is fun, so keep excess stress as far away as you can — consider buying one of these things.

Calculator

A good desktop calculator or adding machine can make your job easier. One that makes it easy to calculate percentages would be nice. A credit-card sized calculator is nice to have in your briefcase, too, for working out charges on the spot.

You might even want to consider getting a small calculator that prints. These actually do come sized to fit into a briefcase, and having a paper tape of your calculations might come in handy later when you need an answer to a cost question for a client.

File Cabinet

You'll need to organize and store information you receive from vendors and keep files for each client and event. Lateral filing cabinets (which store files from side to side, rather than front to back, and look like a bureau drawer) are terrific. They are easy to use and more attractive, usually, than the standard metal two- or four-drawer variety, but they are expensive.

Furniture

The office supply retailers mentioned above offer good prices on new office furniture. And locally, you can probably find a used or discount office furniture store. But, especially since you are in a creative business, you might want to consider the home office furniture sold by two trendy lifestyle stores, Pier One and Ikea.

Pier One has stores everywhere. Ikea has fewer, but they do have a great catalog – both paper and online – and they ship. Of the two, Ikea offers more in the way of home office furniture, and it's inexpensive. You can get a computer desk, chair and lamp for under $150, and it will be stylish in a Scandinavian modern way.

Pier One doesn't have office suites, but it does have occasional pieces that can be useful in home offices, from chairs (like inexpensive director's chairs to use as guest chairs) to entertainment centers and wardrobes you might find useful for your purposes.

5.3.4   Insurance

Once you have equipped your office, you should protect what you have. However, insurance is one thing many small business owners would rather not worry about. It may seem like something that costs you time and money, but doesn't contribute to your business. In fact, having insurance could save your business one day.

Types of Insurance

Liability Insurance

This type of insurance protects you in case you make a mistake or have a misunderstanding with a client. For example, if you thought a client asked you to dispose of something that turned out to be a valuable heirloom.

Property Insurance

This insurance covers losses to your personal property from damage or theft. If your business will be located in your home, you're most likely already covered with homeowner's insurance. However, it's a good idea to update your plan to provide coverage for office equipment and other items that aren't included in a standard plan.

Because a lot of what you produce is "intellectual property," you might want to inquire as to how the insurance company you are considering regards paper; bills, invoices, designs, plans you've discussed with a client and written out, etc. You may be able to add a rider to your policy to cover the cost of reconstructing these things if something happens to your office.

Life and Disability Insurance

If you provide a portion of your family's income, then you need to carry life insurance and disability insurance to make certain they are cared for if something happens to you. If you become sick or otherwise disabled for an extended period, your business could be in jeopardy. Disability insurance would provide at least a portion of your income while you're not able to be working.

Car Insurance

Be sure to ask your broker about your auto insurance if you'll be using your personal vehicle on company business.

Health Insurance

If you live in the United States and aren't covered under a spouse's health plan, you'll need to consider your health insurance options. You can compare health insurance quotes at **www.ehealthinsurance.com** which offers plans from over 150 insurance companies nationwide.

> **TIP:** Some insurance companies offer discount pricing for members of particular organizations. When you are looking for organizations to join, whether your local Chamber of Commerce or a national association, check to see if discounted health insurance is one of the member benefits.

Canadians have most of their health care expenses covered by the Canadian government. For expenses that are not covered (such as dental care, eyeglasses, prescription drugs, etc.) self-employed professionals may get tax benefits from setting up their own private health care plan.

Puhl Employee Benefits (**www.puhlemployeebenefits.com**) is an example of the type of financial planning company that can help you set up your own private health care plan.

More Information

The Small Business Administration has an excellent insurance and risk management guide for small businesses available online at **www.sba. gov/tools/resourcelibrary/publications/serv_pub_mplan.html** (scroll down to #17).

5.3.5   Employees

You may be working on your own when you first start your business, but at some point you could decide to hire people to work with you. For example, you might hire an office assistant, other decorators, or someone to help market your firm.

> **TIP:**   When you hire "contractors" (businesses or self-employed individuals) to do work such as painting, installing flooring, wallpapering, tiling, etc. they are not considered to be employees. Section 5.5 has tips on working with contractors.

The other people who work for your company may be either employees or contractors. For example, if the person you hire to do your marketing has their own business providing marketing services to a variety of clients, they may be considered a "contractor" rather than an employee. Hiring contractors instead of employees could save you a tremendous amount of money and paperwork. Excellent advice on hiring both employees and contractors can be found at the Nolo.com website at **www. nolo.com**. (Click on *"Employment Law & HR,"* then *"Human Resources."*)

If you decide to hire employees, you will need to check with the IRS as well as your local department of labor to find out all the rules and regulations required as an employer. There may be numerous state and federal rules and regulations that apply to you, including: health and safety regulations, Workers' Compensation, minimum wage, unemployment insurance, etc. You can find additional information through the resources listed at the start of this chapter.

Canadian employers must also register with the government and comply with federal and provincial laws. For information on becoming an employer in Canada, visit **www.canadabusiness.ca/eng/85**.

5.4   Financial Matters

5.4.1   Start-Up Funding

Depending on how you set up your business, the cost of starting your interior decorating firm might range from almost nothing to thousands of dollars. Obviously, your start-up expenses will be much higher if you decide to rent space and buy equipment.

You will also need to consider your "working capital" requirements. This is the money you will need for the day-to-day operation of your interior decorating firm. If you are buying materials to decorate a client's home you can ask for a deposit (see section 5.4.2 on *"Setting Your Fees"*). But other expenses will come out of your pocket before you get your first client—such as business cards, telephone, etc.

Many entrepreneurs are optimistic about how much money they will earn from their business, and how quickly they will earn it. While you may be tremendously successful right from the start and exceed your own expectations, it is wise to be prepared for the possiblity it may take longer than expected until your business is earning enough to support you.

A standard rule of thumb is to have six months' living expenses set aside beyond your start-up costs. Or you might consider remaining at your current job and working part-time on your decorating business until it is established.

Depending on the start-up costs you calculate in your business plan, you may find you have all the money you need to get started in your savings account (or available to spend on your credit cards). If your own resources won't cover all the things you would like to do with your interior decorating firm, you will need to look for financing.

One place to look for financing is from family members. They may be willing to invest in your company or give you a loan to help you get started. To avoid any misunderstandings, it's wise to get any agreements in writing even with family members.

If you decide to approach a bank for a business loan, be prepared. Write a loan proposal that includes detailed information about your business, how much money you want to borrow, what you plan to do with the money, and so on.

Advice about financing can be found at the SBA and Nolo sites given at the start of this chapter. Also look into the Small Business Administration business assistance programs. The SBA has a Loan Guarantee Program that provides loans to small businesses. Contact your local SBA office or check out **www.sba.gov/services/financialassistance/ index.html**.

5.4.2   Setting Your Fees

Before meeting with your first paying client, you will need to decide how much you are going to charge for your services. The question is almost certain to come up, possibly even before your first meeting, so you will need to be prepared with an answer.

Fees can vary tremendously from one decorator to another. Here are ways interior decorators may charge for their services:

- Initial Consultation Fee
- Hourly Fee
- Flat Fee
- Cost-Plus

Initial Consultation Fee

When it comes to charging for an initial consultation with a prospective client, most interior decorators are like lawyers and other professionals—they offer a free initial consultation. In most cases, this first meeting is simply an opportunity to learn more about what the client needs and explain how your services can benefit them. You will not be doing any actual decorating in this meeting.

However, if a client calls and says they want to hire you to start decorating right away, you can certainly charge an hourly fee at the very first meeting (see below). In addition, some decorators whose services are in demand will charge an initial consultation fee (such as $100 per hour for a one- to two-hour consultation) to ensure they spend their time only with people who are serious about going ahead with decorating.

Hourly Fee

An hourly fee is a common way for interior decorators to charge for their services, especially for home decorating projects. A few decorators who are in great demand to work on wealthy people's homes command fees of hundreds of dollars per hour. Most interior decorators charge fees ranging from $25 to $125 per hour.

You do not have to start at $25 per hour. In fact, you may want to charge a higher fee (such as $40 to $60 per hour) when you start because it may actually make certain clients more likely to work with you. Many professionals believe "you get what you pay for" so they may assume a decorator who charges $50 per hour is more experienced or does better work than one who charges $25 per hour.

On the other hand, renters or homeowners in some communities may not be willing to spend as much as business owners or homeowners in upscale communities. Thus, consider your target markets when deciding what fee to charge. And remember that you can change your fee in the future.

If you charge by the hour, you could also charge for your travel time. However, many decorators do not charge for local travel, or charge a lower fee for travel time (e.g. if their hourly fee is $50 per hour they might charge $25 per hour for travel).

Flat Fee

Some clients may want to know up front what the total cost will be for your services. These clients prefer to pay a "flat fee" rather than an hourly fee so they know the cost will not go above a certain amount.

Most interior decorators do not work on a flat fee basis, unless they are doing a small job. For example, if a job involves rearranging a client's existing furniture in their living room, you might estimate that would take you two hours, and charge a flat fee based on your estimate. The more experience you acquire, the easier it will be to determine a flat fee for a particular job.

Decorators may charge a flat fee when doing advance planning work, such as design boards or concept plans, for their "intellectual property" or ideas. If you draw up concept plans (much like a landscape designer would do) and illustrate possible furniture placement, color schemes or renovation ideas you may want to charge the client to "buy" your ideas. The client is then free to shop the plan around or to pull the plan together themselves. If the client decides to use your services the cost of the plan is included in your total agreed fee whereas, if the client decides not to proceed with your plan, they will own the ideas.

Instead of offering a flat fee to clients who want to know an overall cost for the decorating services, most decorators will give a "ballpark estimate." For example, they might say they expect a particular project will take them about 10 to 15 hours. If a project ends up taking longer than expected, for example if the client asks you to do some additional work after you have started, you can then advise the client that it will be above and beyond the original estimate.

Cost-Plus

Cost-plus is a commonly used method for charging clients who will need to purchase furniture or materials for their decorating project. As you will see in section 5.5.4, because you are an interior decorator, you will be able to buy products from suppliers at wholesale prices (typically at a discount of 20-40 percent percent below the regular retail price). You can then charge the client a service charge such as 20-30 percent above your cost.

In some cases, even after paying your "commission," your client's cost will be less than they would have paid to buy the same item at a retail store.

As an alternative to cost-plus, some decorators act as retailers. This involves buying products at wholesale prices, then reselling them to clients at or near the manufacturers' suggested retail prices. If you are considering this method, make sure you consult with your accountant to find out how to properly collect retail sales tax in your jurisdiction.

You can also charge a markup for work done by subcontractors you hire to do painting, wallpapering, installation of flooring or countertops, etc. For example, your markup might be 15 percent on top of the subcontractors' charges.

TIP: You are not limited to choosing just one of the above methods. You can combine them if you wish. Depending on the project, you might decide to charge both an hourly fee and cost-plus, or a flat fee and cost-plus.

Getting Paid

One of the good things about being an interior decorator is that you do not have to wait until the end of the project to start getting paid. At the end of your initial consultation, if the client wants to go ahead, you can either ask the client for a retainer (a deposit) for work you will be doing to select materials, prepare design boards, and develop a detailed cost estimate. Or you can arrange to have the client pay a fee (e.g. $100 per room) at the meeting where you present the design boards.

Once the client has approved your decorating plan and cost estimates, have the client sign a contract or letter of agreement that sets out a payment schedule, with your final payment due upon completion of the project. (See section 6.5.4 to learn how to prepare a contract.)

When entering into a contract with your client you will normally want to ask for a retainer (money in advance of doing the project) ranging anywhere from 25 to 50 percent of what the anticipated total cost of the project will be. At the least, you should arrange to have the client give you a deposit to cover at least the costs of any materials you need to buy. Normally the project is paid for as it progresses and as new items are purchased. By the end of the project, there should only be a nominal amount owed by your client.

TIP: To protect yourself, don't pay for materials out of your own pocket. Buy materials only after you receive a deposit from the client.

5.4.3   Keeping Track of Your Money

There are a variety of resources available to help you keep track of your business income and expenses.

Financial Institution

The first of these resources is a financial institution – bank, trust company, or credit union – where you will open your business checking account. You can shop around to find a financial institution that is supportive of small business, or use the same one that you use for your personal banking. In addition to your checking account, a financial institution may provide you with:

- a corporate credit card you can use to make purchases for your business

- a line of credit in case you want to pay up front for some materials before you get paid by a client

- a merchant credit card account if you are planning to retail products (this enables you to accept credit card payments from your customers)

Bookkeeping System

Your bookkeeping system is a record of your expenses and income. To keep track of your expenses, you will need to keep copies of all receipts. This can sometimes be a challenge for new business owners who might have a habit of tossing out receipts for small items (or not asking for receipts in the first place). However, you are likely to have numerous small expenses related to your business, and these can add up over time.

The cup of coffee you buy for a prospective client, the latest issue of a decorating magazine, the mileage you travel to a client's house, the pack of paper you pick up at the office supply store—these and many other expenses should be accounted for so you can minimize your taxes. And, of course, knowing exactly where your money is going will help you plan better and cut back on any unnecessary expenses. So make it a habit to ask for a receipt for every business expense.

If you have the time, you can do your own bookkeeping. As mentioned in the section on software, programs such as Quicken or QuickBooks can make the job much easier for you. These programs can also be used to prepare invoices. **Quicken.com** offers some good advice to help you with managing your finances and developing your business.

If you find yourself so busy with decorating work that you don't have time to do your own bookkeeping, consider hiring a part-time book-keeper on a contract basis to do your bookkeeping for you. Depending on how busy you are, it may take the bookkeeper a few hours per week to get your books up-to-date and balance them with your bank state-ments. You can find a bookkeeper through word-of-mouth or check the Yellow Pages.

Financial Experts

Just as people will hire an expert (you!) to decorate their homes, you may want to hire experts to assist with your finances. An accountant or tax advisor can be expensive (e.g. you might pay $100 per hour com-pared to the $20 per hour you might pay a bookkeeper). However, their advice could possibly save you hundreds or even thousands of dol-lars at tax time. If you're not able to find an accountant or tax advisor through word-of-mouth, you can try the Yellow Pages.

5.5 Working with Suppliers and Contractors

As an interior decorator you will likely need to buy products from a variety of suppliers and use the services of a variety of contractors. Sup-pliers are companies that supply the products you need to decorate. They include retailers and wholesalers of furniture, wall coverings, flooring, fabrics, etc.

Contractors are businesses or self-employed individuals who do work such as renovations, painting, wallpapering, laying carpet, installing flooring, re-upholstery, etc. Many interior decorators have a core of con-tractors (or subcontractors) they can call when they need work done.

Savvy decorators and designers use wholesalers as much as possible for products. If your client wants to use a particular store because they hold a credit card from that retailer or the store has a "don't pay for 12 months" deal happening that's fine. However, you should research all possible sources of wholesale products in your area before taking on your first client. Ask renovators or building contractors in your area where they get their supplies and also do a little legwork to find these outlets.

5.5.1   How to Find Suppliers and Contractors

Many suppliers and contractors can be found through word-of-mouth. For personal recommendations, check with friends, family members, other decorators, contractors, or retailers.

If you don't have a personal recommendation, you can find suppliers through the Yellow Pages, online through websites such as **www.interior decorating.com** or **www.interiormall.com**, or try the following:

Accessories	You can find accessories at art stores, furniture stores, department stores, flower shops, specialty gift stores and antique shops. Additionally, The Bombay Company, Pier 1 Imports, and Bowring and Winners (in Canada) have an excellent selection of unique home accessories.
Area Rugs	You can find area rugs at furniture stores, home improvement stores or even at auctions and garage sales. To find stores specializing in area rugs, check your Yellow Pages under "Carpets & Area Rugs" or "Rug & Carpet Dealers".
Carpentry	Check the Yellow Pages under "Carpenters".
Fabrics	To find a good fabric store, ask a friend who sews for recommendations or check in the Yellow Pages under "Fabric Shops," "Fabrics," or "Textiles." To sew cushions and fabrics, look under "Seamstresses" or "Sewing Contractors."

Flooring	You can find various flooring options at home hardware stores such as Home Depot, Lowe's, Rona (in Canada), Homebase or B&Q (in England). To find a flooring supplier in your area, look in the Yellow Pages under the appropriate category: *"Carpet & Rug Dealers," "Floors Materials," "Hardwood," "Laminated Wood," "Tile Contractors & Dealers,"* or *"Vinyl Floor Coverings."*
Furniture	To find furniture stores in your area check the Yellow Pages under *"Furniture Dealers."* To find out how to shop at and find wholesale furniture outlets, design centers and showrooms in your area, refer to section 5.5.4.
Household Repairs	Check the Yellow Pages under *"Contractors—General," "Home Repair & Maintenance,"* or *"Handyman Service."*
Light Fixtures	You can find light fixtures at home improvement stores or look for lighting stores in the Yellow Pages under *"Lighting."* For light fixture installations check the Yellow Pages under *"Electricians."*
Moldings	Moldings can be purchased at home improvement stores, however, the selection is much greater at a molding supply store. One of the more well known manufacturers of moldings is Balmer Architectural Moldings. You can see some of the molding options and locate a dealer at **www.balmer.com**.
Painting	To find a paint supplier in your area check at your local home improvement store or look in the Yellow Pages under "Paint Dealers." To find a painter, check the Yellow Pages under "Painting Contractors." For faux finishes, look for painting contractors in the Yellow Pages who advertise them.

Renovations	Check the Yellow Pages under "Renovations & Home Improvements" or "Building Contractors."
Re-Upholstery	Check the Yellow Pages under "Upholsterers."
Walls	To find suppliers of wall coverings check the Yellow Pages under "Wall Coverings" or "Wall Papers & Wall Coverings." You can find contractors in the Yellow Pages under "Drywall Contractors" or "Wall Coverings—Contractors." You can also find a professional wallpaper installer (a member of the National Guild of Professional Paperhangers) at **www.ngpp.org/find_paperhanger.php**.
Window Coverings	Check at your local home improvement store or in the Yellow Pages under "Blinds," "Draperies," "Shutters" or "Window Shades." One well-established and popular manufacturer of blinds shades, sheers and shutters is Hunter Douglas. You can find out about their products at: **www.hunterdouglas.com**.

5.5.2 Tips for Working with Contractors

You are ultimately responsible for how well contractors do their work, so you will need to find people you can depend on to do the job right, by the agreed upon deadline, for the agreed upon price.

To help you choose contractors, make appointments to meet either by phone or in person. Most contractors are often busy but if you let them know when you first contact them that you have a decorating business and would like to meet with them (or talk with them) to find out about their services and fees with the possibility of hiring them for future decorating projects, they are more likely to take the time to discuss what they can offer.

Remember, time is money for these contractors so make sure you are prepared in advance with a list of questions to ask. For example, you may want to ask exactly what services they provide (do they drywall, sand, paint, do carpentry work, do repairs, do electrical work, etc.), and find out their hourly rate or how their rates work.

What Is a Contractor?

There are a number of important differences between contractors and employees.

- You may train employees. Contractors received training elsewhere.

- Employees work only for you. Contractors may have their own clients and work for other interior decorating or interior design firms.

- Employees are paid on a regular basis. Contractors are paid per project.

- Employees work for a certain amount of hours, while contracted workers may set their own hours, as long as they get the job done.

- Employees can be fired or quit. Contractors can't be fired in the usual way while they are working under contract. You may decide to have them stop working on a project, but you will be obliged to pay them according to your contractual agreement unless you are able to renegotiate the contract or successfully sue them if you are unhappy with their work. (Of course that would only be in extreme cases; it is best to avoid lawsuits altogether!)

Also ask their normal availability. Will they fit you in on weekends if they have regular project work throughout the week? What will happen to your project if another project they are working on ends up taking more time than expected?

You need to know that you can depend on the contractor, and that they will be willing to work overtime if necessary to keep their agreements with you. (Unfortunately, some busy contractors consider deadlines to be "suggestions" rather than requirements.)

As the interior decorator it will be your job to supervise them and ensure they get the job done. Remember your name (not the contractors) is on the line if you bring in a contractor to do any renovations or repair work and they don't come through in a timely or professional manner or within cost. So look for someone reliable, and have at least one back-up for each job.

Wherever possible, get agreements (e.g. for costs, delivery dates, services to be provided) in writing. And make sure that your contractors (or you, if you are doing the work yourself) hold liability insurance, which covers both them and you in the event that the client's property is damaged, or if the work is not satisfactory for some reason.

Before working with a contractor, check their references. It is also advisable to contact the Better Business Bureau to find out if any complaints have been lodged against the contractor or their company. Look them up in your local phone directory or locate a BBB anywhere in the U.S. or Canada at **www.bbb.org**.

By establishing a relationship with contractors, you may be able to negotiate a discount on their services. Chapter 2 has some good resources for developing the interpersonal skills that will help you deal with subcontractors.

5.5.3   Buying from Retailers

As described earlier in this guide, clients may expect you to shop for and buy a variety of items to be used in decorating, such as furnishings, area rugs, accessories, lamps, window coverings, etc. The information that follows gives advice on buying from retailers. In the next section, you will discover how to buy from wholesalers. While the information focuses on buying furnishings, many of the tips can also be used when purchasing other room elements.

Floor Model or Special Order

Ordering In Furniture

The good news about "ordering in" (or making a "special order") is that you are rarely limited to the items shown on the floor of the furniture show room. Almost all furniture stores keep catalogues of additional furnishings that can be ordered in. Often furniture stores carry or can order in a number of different lines of furniture and all you need to do is ask a salesperson if you can review their catalogs to see what other pieces of furniture can be ordered in.

Although you often won't be able to take a piece of furniture home to your client right away, you will be able to order in furnishings and select the textures, patterns and colors to get the decorating look you and your client are after.

If you find a style of sofa, chair, ottoman, etc., that will work great for your client, ask what upholstery options there are for that piece of furniture. With any fine furniture, there is normally a number of upholstery options. Additionally, with some pieces of furniture, you may even have options with respect to the color of wood and sometimes even to the shape of legs, etc. Make sure you find out all the options available before making a decision.

If you are ordering in a piece of furniture, find out how long it will take to get the piece in. It can sometimes take anywhere between eight to 16 weeks to order certain furniture items.

Floor Models

While many furniture stores display furniture items that can be ordered in, they often will not sell their floor models unless they are ready to clear out the item (either to provide for more space in the store, because the furniture line is being discontinued, or because the store has decided not to carry the product any longer). On the other hand, there are some specialty and boutique furniture stores that will sell their product line directly off the floor.

If you are allowed to purchase a floor model from a standard furniture store, normally they are trying to clear out the item or are selling an item "as is" due to some defect (possibly scratches or some form of wear from being used as a display model in their store). Buying an item that is being cleared out or buying an "as is" item may be a great way to get a bargain for your client. However, you should thoroughly check over the item of furniture and speak with a sales representative directly to determine exactly why the item is being cleared out or sold "as is."

If you are buying a floor model (especially an "as is" floor model) then you will normally be able to purchase the item at an amount discounted anywhere between 10-75 percent off the price.

Often "as is" means that the item is no longer like new and may contain some scratches, chips or other flaws. One of the decorators who contributed to this guide has found numerous bargains for her clients at stores selling "as is" products that have very slight defects (which the clients are made aware of) that can be fixed up by a furniture crayon without anyone ever noticing that there was ever a scratch on the item. One thing to make note of is that not all "as is" items have minor defects. Sometimes the items may have major defects and you won't be doing your client a favor to select one of these types of items for their home even if it will save them a lot of money.

Another thing to keep in mind is that often warranties are not offered on "as is" items, and depending on the store, they may or may not allow returns. However, if a store has a policy that all sales are final and no returns are allowed once the item is removed from the store, often you can work around this by talking directly with the manager of the store and asking if they would kindly allow you to buy the item on approval (i.e. your approval or your client's approval).

In this type of situation, you are normally required to pay for the item up front and are then allowed one to three days to take it to your client's place where you can determine whether it is a good "fit" for the decorating plan. If it isn't, you are then allowed to return the product for a full refund.

If you are given a special concession by the manager to do this, make sure that you have them write directly on to your receipt that the item can be returned for a full refund (within whatever time is allotted) and then have the manager sign the receipt.

Specialty Furniture Stores

You may find that in your area there are a number of smaller specialty or boutique furniture stores or chain retail home décor stores (such as The Bombay Company, Pier 1 Imports, or Bowring in Canada) that offer a variety of home merchandise including items of furniture. Many specialty furniture stores will sell their product line directly off the floor and some have a small supply of items in stock at the back of the store. In specialty and boutique stores, when items are sold off the floor, they are normally sold at full price.

Depending on the store's policy, you may or may not be allowed to return the item for a refund. This is something you should clarify before taking the item out of the store.

> **TIP:** Some retailers offer a small discount on all your purchases (not just "as is" items). Kirkland's, for example, says "as a design professional, you can receive a 10 percent discount on all client-related purchases."

Returns and Refunds

Return and refund polices vary from one furniture store to the next and can be as strict as no returns/refunds allowed whatsoever to having 30 days (and on rare occasions even longer) for you and your client to decide whether you are satisfied with the furniture after the item has been delivered.

Before any furniture item is ordered or purchased, find out the store's policies on returns and refunds. Even if you and your client think that the item will be perfect with the other items in the room, sometimes an item can look quite different in your client's home from what it looked like in the showroom because of different lighting, carpeting, furnishings, etc.

Additionally, although your client might be incredibly enthusiastic about a particular piece of furniture while you are at the furniture store, they might not feel the same way about it later on. Therefore, it is helpful to either know that an item is nonrefundable or to have a plan in place to return an item if it does not work or is not wanted once delivered to your client's home.

If an item is special ordered (where you have selected the upholstery and/or wood color, etc.) chances are you will not be able to return the product once it is delivered to your client. However, some stores will allow returns if you pay a restocking fee. A restocking fee is normally a percentage of the original purchase price that is paid to the store to take back the item for a refund. An average restocking fee is 10-15 percent (but they can even range from as little as 5 percent up to 25 percent).

As an example, if your client had custom ordered a sofa for $2,000 and after a number of days they decided that it wasn't right for them, in a situation where there was a 10 percent restocking fee on refunds, your client could then return the sofa and receive $1,800 back. In essence, they will have paid the furniture store $200 as a restocking fee to cover the store's cost of ordering the product in plus the fact that they now have to keep the product on their floor until it is sold to another individual.

Some stores will only give store credits on allowed returns (and no cash back) to ensure that the money your client paid out for the original piece of furniture stays with the store. However, your client will then have an option to select a different piece of furniture from that store that may work better for their situation.

If a full refund is allowed on the return of an item, this means that your client will receive the full amount back for the item purchased. But they will not receive back any delivery charges to get the product to them in the first place and you or your client will be responsible for ensuring that the product is returned to the store at your client's expense.

Although some stores will allow a form of refund on special order items, keep in mind that the vast majority of furniture stores have a policy that once you special order a piece of furniture, the item is yours and there are no options to return it.

Warranties

Another thing you will need to find out about when selecting furniture are any warranties offered on the merchandise. Warranties, when provided, are normally a form of insurance that your client will get some or all of their money back if there are any defects with the furniture. Wear of a product over time is rarely ever part of a furniture warranty.

When purchasing furniture, make sure that both you and your client are fully aware of what is being warrantied and how long the warranty is good for. One year is the norm for any defects except, as mentioned previously, "as is" items are normally not covered under warranty. Keep in mind that often a warranty will only cover certain parts of a piece of furniture and not the entire piece of furniture.

For example, on a recliner, the components for reclining the chair might be covered under warranty for life, however, this might mean that only parts are covered and labor to fix a broken recliner isn't covered. Additionally, the warranty might state that the consumer is responsible for paying the cost of shipping the product back to the manufacturer to fix any defects.

Make sure you read all information and that your client is happy with what is being offered before proceeding with any purchases.

5.5.4   Buying Wholesale

In most cases, you can get substantial discounts by shopping in showrooms and other places, such as trade shows, that are restricted to "professionals only" or "trade only" (that includes you!). By shopping at these places you will pay wholesale prices that are typically 20-50 percent below the regular retail price. As mentioned in the section on setting your fees, you can either pass the savings on to your clients, or mark the price back up to retail and keep the difference.

Pros and Cons

Once you know the ropes, purchasing supplies wholesale is a great way for interior decorators to keep their costs down. You will also have the advantage of seeing the latest styles of furniture and designs before they are available to retail consumers, or have access to home furnishings that are not available to the general public at all. Your clients will be impressed by your style savvy.

Shopping wholesale does have some challenges, but armed with the knowledge of them ahead of time, they shouldn't be a problem to you. For instance, rarely can you bring your purchases home the same day. If your client needs something right away, you may have to settle for retail that time around, or investigate the possibility of purchasing floor models.

Many times you will not be able to purchase using your credit card at wholesale establishments, so you will need to have funds readily available to cover your purchases with a check. (Cash is also not always accepted.) It is also becoming common business practice for some wholesalers or showrooms to require you to have a business bank account. This will be further proof that you are a professional and not simply someone off the street who wants discounted materials.

Most manufacturers will ask you to pay COD or as shipped until you have established yourself with them. Some wholesalers will only allow payment through check or cash when extending you a discount as they don't want to incur the extra cost when a client uses credit cards. They may ask for industry references, which shouldn't be too hard to find once you spend a bit of time getting known to the community. They will probably ask you to set up an account with them to start purchasing goods but you won't have to prove you have already made money as a decorator to do this unless you are asking for credit.

Your purchases will not be able to be returned, whether the item is custom made or not, unless you have made arrangements to do so with the seller.

You will need to make shipping arrangements for your purchases, including someone to help you carry heavy furniture when it arrives. You will also need to be able to transport the furniture to your clients' homes.

You will not have many of the "luxuries" of retail shopping when you purchase direct from the supplier, such as sales staff who fawn over you, or being able to bring all your friends to get their opinions. You might not even be able to have access to a bathroom.

Finally, every once in a while you will run into suppliers who, despite you doing everything right, do not want to deal with interior decorators, for any number of reasons. They may have minimum purchase requirements that are beyond your client's needs, they may restrict their materials to interior designers only, or they may have a set circle of purchasers that keep them in business.

If this happens, don't take it personally; it is the nature of the industry. There will be many other suppliers who will be happy to do business with you, and the money you save purchasing in this way is, in the end, worth the occasional snubbing.

What You Need to Purchase Wholesale

To get admitted to a showroom, design center, or trade show and purchase items at wholesale prices, or even to order wholesale items by mail or phone, you will need to show evidence that you are a professional interior decorator. In the U.S. this requires three things: a general business license, a resale number, and business cards.

General Business License

Call your city hall to get the location of your local Occupational License Office, where you will purchase a home occupational license. This is a license to work from home.

You will need to fill out your business name and phone number, and give some details on the nature of your business. Most questions on the form are designed to detect and deter people who will be a nuisance or a risk to their neighbors, and will not apply to you.

This license should cost you about $100, and will be valid for one year. You will provide a photocopy of your license (not the original, or you might lose it!) upon entrance to wholesale shopping establishments.

Resale Number

Also known as a tax number, a resale permit, or a sales tax permit, you are required to show this number on a certificate (again, use a photocopy) when you want to shop wholesale. You will not pay sales tax at the point of purchase, but will file your purchases with the state or county and mail them a check.

This application should also be available at the Occupational License Office, but you will register it with either the county or the state, depending on where you live. Again, you will have to fill out a short form with information about the nature of your business. There is usually no charge to register, and the certificate will be mailed out to you within a few weeks.

Either quarterly or monthly, you will fill out a form that lists the total retail dollar amount (not wholesale amount) of the merchandise you purchased during the relevant period of time, calculate the tax owed, and mail in a check. File these forms on time, or you risk being assessed some hefty fines and interest on the amount owing.

It is very important to note that the tax is on the resale value, not the wholesale price. When you shop for wholesale items, you will want to make a habit of noting the retail price. If there is no retail price listed where you purchase the item, you can assume to double the wholesale price to get the retail.

In turn, you will also collect the sales tax from your clients, so you won't be out the money unless you sell to your clients at a marked down price. In some states and provinces you will also be eligible for a vendor's compensation (commission), which means that you can keep a very small percentage of the tax you collect as payment for being a "government agent." When you purchase items wholesale, you may also be asked to fill out a blanket certificate of resale by the seller. This simply means that you understand the situation and agree to pay the sales tax on the items you purchase.

In Canada, the process is quite similar. You will want to contact your provincial Department of Finance to apply for a vendor's license or permit for the purpose of collecting provincial sales tax (applicable in most provinces). Also, businesses with revenue exceeding $30,000 must register with the Canada Customs and Revenue Agency for a business number in order to collect the Goods and Services Tax.

Business Cards

You will present these cards when you shop wholesale, as further proof of your credentials. Standard business cards will do. See section 6.1.3 for tips on business cards.

Ways to Buy Wholesale

Wholesale Design Centers

Many large cities in the U.S. such as Boston, Dallas, Houston, New York, and San Diego have large design centers that are open to trade buyers like you.

Once you register at the front desk, you are free to explore within the center, which is a grouping of showrooms. If you plan to bring your client with you, they should register as such. Prices should be marked on items in wholesale codes that only you (and not your client) will be able to decipher. There is usually no admission charge at a design center.

Although most showrooms within the center will allow you to browse, some will require you to be accompanied by a salesperson. Design centers are becoming more public-friendly, and may have days you can enter without your credentials. Be aware, though, that the deep discounts rarely apply on these occasions.

As you start networking with other professionals in your industry, you will hear about a variety of suppliers in your community. In the meantime, you can check out Design Centers Across North America at **www.i-d-d.com/interior_design_centers.htm**.

Factory Showrooms/Outlets

These are not retailers you see at malls that call themselves "factory outlets" (but actually offer little or no discount), but are true outlets or showrooms located by the manufacturer's factory that feature their products exclusively. There are factory outlets for hundreds of furniture brands, including Drexel-Heritage, La-Z-Boy, Thomasville, and many others.

With smaller factories you may find that no outlet or showroom exists, but you can arrange a meeting with a salesperson to look at samples, place orders, or purchase the older sample items. In this setting, it is very important that you respect the supplier's time and environment since you are not their major source of income and could potentially be a nuisance.

Again, a call to ask if they work with decorators will point you in the right direction. If they require you to be a "stocking dealer," this means they require a considerable minimum purchase. If you are still set on one of their items, ask them to refer you to one of their distributors (where you will likely have to pay a mark-up fee).

There are other opportunities to buy from a manufacturer by visiting either an "Agent Showroom" (one which will carry one line predominately but also many other items and lines) or the manufacturer's "Corporate Showroom". The Corporate Showroom will not necessarily be in the same city as the headquarters but often will be. If you decide to become an accredited Interior Decorator by taking classes at a local institution, chances are that somewhere in the curriculum there will be an opportunity for showroom visits. You may also be given a list of showrooms or wholesalers that work with decorating professionals in your area.

If you are nowhere near the factory you want to purchase direct from, but know the item you want, they sometimes will allow you to place an order by phone. You will pay in advance and supply your credentials, and the product will be shipped to you.

You can find manufacturers, many of which are located in North Carolina, at **Hoovers.com**. A helpful resource is *The Furniture Factory Outlet Guide*, by Kimberly Causey. It has addresses, phone numbers, and detailed reviews of what types of furniture each outlet has available.

Trade Shows

Wholesale trade shows happen at different times of the year in a variety of locations. While some trade shows cover all types of home furnishings, others focus on certain elements such as fabrics or window coverings. You can pick and choose what suits your needs.

Admission is sometimes charged to get into these shows, and a few have prior purchasing requirements, but most should be free and accessible to decorators with credentials, which you will show when you enter. Guests are sometimes welcome as well, although they will not be authorized to buy. The common discount at these shows is 50 percent off retail, although wholesale will usually be the marked price.

You may find trade shows to be the perfect opportunity to network within your industry, as they often have social events in conjunction with the day-to-day buying and selling. Some will also offer seminars on business and design topics that may be of interest to you, but be sure to pre-register for these.

As mentioned above, you can find out about a variety of upcoming events, including trade shows, at the American Society of Interior Designers website at **www.asid.org/Events+Calendar.htm**.

Calculating Your Discount

Although the cryptic numbers on sales tags are a mystery to most, there are really only three basic types of codes that are used in wholesale showrooms. You may question why these codes exist in the first place, until the first time you bring a client with you and they clearly see your mark-up. In other words, they are for your benefit.

The 5/10 Code

When samples have tags that look like fractions, such as 50/35 or 60/55, this is known as the 5/10 code. To determine the wholesale cost, you subtract $5 from the first number in the fraction, and ten cents from the second number. So for example, an item that was tagged 80/60 would cost you $75.50. When dealing with furniture, the price is per unit; with fabric, it will be per yard or meter.

Straight Discounts

If you do see actual prices rather than codes, and you are in an environment that allows decorators to bring clients with them, those prices are retail. Discreetly ask a salesperson what the decorator discount is (usually quoted in percents) then calculate the price based on that. If you are told the discount is "keystone," this is industry lingo for a 50 percent discount.

Compound Discounts

This type of discount is most often found when dealing with hard window treatment showrooms, and carries with it a deeper discount. The items will be tagged retail, and you will be told that your discount is a fraction, for example 50/20, or 50/50.

To calculate what you will pay, you deduct each percentage in order from the amount. For example, to figure out a 50/20 compound discount on an item tagged $200, deduct 50 percent from 200 (200-100=100) and 20 percent from the remaining 100 (100-20=80). Thus, a 50/20 compound discount price on a $200 retail item would be $80.

Wholesale vs. Retail Shopping

Conducting yourself like a professional is extremely important to building relationships with suppliers, or even getting in the door in the first place. You will want to wear business dress and be prepared to ask the right (and not the wrong) questions.

There are enough differences between shopping wholesale and shopping retail that you will want to review this section carefully before you make your first shopping trip so you don't make any first-time gaffes that could endanger your future relationship with that supplier.

Don't: Ask the salesperson for advice on decorating. If you are truly a professional decorator, you don't need anyone else's input on how to decorate. Your client has hired you for your ideas and vision, so use them.

Don't: Ask to use the washroom, or leave the showroom area. Unless you are at a trade show or a design center, you may not be in a commercial building. Taking you to the bathroom would require leading you past private areas of the showroom or building, something competitive manufacturers take very seriously. Respect their privacy.

Don't: Bring along more than one person to shop with you. This person should be identified as your co-worker or partner–preferably with business cards that state this– or as your client. Shopping with a gaggle of friends to whom you promised discounts brands you as someone who is unprofessional, and may even prevent you being admitted. Children are also not accepted when you are shopping wholesale.

Don't: Try to find a central checkout. There won't be one. When you are ready to buy, let a salesperson know, and they will place the order and arrange for shipment.

Don't: Take pictures of showrooms. Home furnishing design and manufacturing is a competitive business, and they don't appreciate their innovations being photographed. Your camera may be confiscated. If you need to let a client see an item before you buy it, you can often get swatches or samples, or better yet, try out the sample item "on memo" (loan) for a few days. Just make sure you keep it to a few days.

Don't: Sit on furniture on display, or bring food or drinks into a showroom. These samples are costly to replace, and salespeople won't appreciate wear and tear or damage.

Arranging for Shipment

When you buy home furnishings wholesale, you will rarely be purchasing an item that you can bring home the same day. As a rule, you will pay in advance and wait to have the item shipped to you. If the item is custom made or out of stock, this may take from six to eight weeks.

The shipping fees will normally be included in your purchase price, but ask the salesperson if you are unsure and get an estimate of the charges if they are paid upon delivery. Larger items will likely arrive by truck from the factory, and the shipping fees will be yours. You will have to be home to receive these items when they are delivered, and unfortunately, you will only get a "window of time," not an exact time.

You will need help to unload large items, as well, as this is not the job of the truck driver—they're paid to drive the truck. You may also have to assemble some furniture that was disassembled for shipping. Smaller items will likely arrive by UPS and can be left with neighbors if you make prior arrangements. Be sure to note any obvious damage to the shipping box or item on the delivery form when you sign, and inspect the item carefully.

It does happen that items are damaged in delivery. If you have not purchased shipping insurance, the delivery company will only pay you a portion of the item's value, based on its weight. Purchasing insurance will cover the true value of the item if it is damaged in shipping, but not if the manufacturer packaged it improperly. In that case, you want to deal with the shipper directly.

But you should also be aware that some jurisdictions won't allow delivery trucks of a certain size or shipments of a certain frequency to be delivered to your home-based business address. When applying for your business license, ask what the regulations are regarding receiving shipments to your home address. You may have to make other shipping arrangements if you will be in violation of local regulations.

6. Working with Clients

This chapter of the guide provides information on what is involved in each stage of working with clients, including:

- finding clients

- telephone inquiries

- client consultations

- preparing a decorating plan, budget and contract

- presenting the decorating plan

The first stage is finding clients. Most interior decorators use a variety of methods to find clients including networking with prospective clients, referrals, advertising, and publicity. These and other marketing techniques are discussed in section 6.1.

Once someone is interested in using your decorating services, your first discussion about the project will likely take place over the telephone. Because people do not buy decorating services over the phone, your purpose during the initial phone call will be to arrange a face-to-face meeting. This is covered in section 6.2.

After that, you will meet your prospective client in person at their home (or the place to be decorated) for an initial client consultation. Client consultations are meetings with new clients and prospective clients that serve two main purposes: (1) to find out what the client wants, and (2) to sell your services. Sections 6.3 explains what happens during an initial consultation and gives advice on everything from what to wear to what to say.

Depending on the scope of a project, you may meet with your client a couple of times before you begin decorating. After your first meeting, you may be hired to prepare a decorating plan and you may need to meet with your client a second time (a second client consultation) to get more information about their wants and style preferences, to measure the space, and to assess the area to be decorated. You'll learn what information to gather in section 6.4.

Then you'll prepare everything you need to get the client to agree to go ahead with the decorating project. In section 6.5 you'll discover how to prepare a:

- decorating plan, including floor plan and written proposal
- design board
- project budget
- contract

Finally, as described in section 6.6, you will meet with your client again to present the decorating plan and budget and get approval to proceed with the decorating project.

6.1 Finding Clients

"I love what you've done with your home! Who decorated it?"

"My decorator is [your name]. I'm delighted with the job s/he did."

"May I have your decorator's phone number? I'd love to have my home done too."

This is an example of the way many decorators find most of their clients—through word-of-mouth. Someone who has been thinking of getting their home redecorated visits a friend whose home was recently decorated, and the conversation naturally turns to "who did it?" As you probably know from personal experience, a recommendation from a friend is perhaps the most powerful form of advertising that exists.

But don't despair if you want to sell your decorating services to a market you have no previous experience with (for example, if you want to work with the wealthy, but haven't yet decorated any multi-millionaires' homes). In this section of the guide you will find a variety of ideas to help you attract clients. And once you have done a great job for those first few clients, you can start attracting more through word-of-mouth.

6.1.1   Choose Your Target Markets

Before you start trying to sell your services to prospective clients, you should decide which types of clients you want to decorate for. These are your "target" markets.

It can be tempting for a new decorator to say something like "I want to decorate for anyone who'll pay me!" Avoid the temptation. It is costly and time-consuming to try to market your business to "everyone" and the truth is that some people will be more interested than others in the services you have to offer. In fact, people are more likely to hire you if they see you as an expert who specializes in what they need.

When you are just starting out, of course you might take whatever business comes your way. However, you can focus your marketing efforts on the target markets you most want to work with. Once you start getting more business, you may be able to give up work you find less rewarding, and spend your time on decorating projects you find most rewarding.

Here are some types of clients you might consider targeting:

Homeowners

People who own their own homes are an obvious market for interior decorators. A recent American Express Retail Index study found over

30 percent of homeowners were planning several home improvement projects within the next year.

However, there are many different types of homes. "Homes" may include houses, apartment condominiums, townhouses, cottages, estates, recreational vehicles, "manufactured homes" (also known as "trailers"), and even yachts. There are also many different types of homeowners you might target, such as new home buyers, the rich, married professionals, etc.

Any of these groups might want to hire someone for a major redecorating project. Or you might target people who simply want their furniture rearranged. You could also specialize in redecorating particular rooms, such as kitchens, bathrooms, or home offices. (You could even target renters instead of homeowners.) As you can see, there are many different areas you can focus on if you want to work with homeowners. Spend some time deciding which markets appeal to you most.

Home Builders

Companies that build new houses or develop condominums often hire interior decorators on contract to decorate model homes. As mentioned in Chapter 4, every new home development has model homes that are beautifully decorated with furniture, linens, art, etc. Everything is color coordinated and arranged to make the home as attractive and comfortable as possible. The purpose is to sell houses or condominiums by making visitors feel this is a home they want to live in.

The builder may have a warehouse full of furnishings for you to choose from, or they may give you a budget to go and buy what you need. If you decide you would like to work with home builders, you can narrow your market down further by focusing on either houses or condominiums (apartments or townhouses).

Businesses

There are many businesses that might want to use the services of an interior decorating firm—from doctors' offices to car dealerships. However, some types of businesses are more likely than others to use a professional decorator. They include:

- advertising agencies

- art galleries

- bed and breakfasts

- boutique stores

- corporate head offices

- hotels

- investment firms

- law firms

- museum stores

- public relations firms

- restaurants

- spas

In addition to the businesses listed above, you might find work decorating for a wide variety of other types of businesses. You can narrow down your market by focusing on businesses that attract upscale clients. So instead of targeting "doctors offices" you could target plastic surgeons. And instead of targeting "car dealerships" you could focus on luxury car dealerships.

As you get more experience you may decide to go after new target markets, or your business may naturally evolve to focus on particular types of clients. However, starting with some specific target markets in mind can help you focus your marketing efforts most efficiently—saving you both time and money.

6.1.2 Networking

Once you know who you want to work with, you can start "networking" with them. This is where it really pays to have clearly defined your target markets. You simply do not have the time to network with "everyone" who might possibly ever have a need for an interior decorator.

There are different definitions of networking, but a particularly useful definition is the one given in the *American Heritage Dictionary of the English Language*: "To interact or engage in informal communication with others for mutual assistance or support."

As you will see from this definition, two keys to networking are that it is "informal" and "mutual." This type of networking does not involve making cold calls to strangers, or trying to arrange meetings so you can talk someone into buying something. Instead, it involves meeting and interacting with people informally at social and business events.

While some of the people you meet may have an immediate need for an interior decorator (or know someone who does), in many cases you are laying the foundation work for future business. As mentioned in the section on relationship building in Chapter 2, people do business with people they like. By establishing relationships through networking, you can be the one people think of when they need a decorator.

Who to Network With

In addition to networking with prospective clients, you may also be able to get a tremendous amount of business by networking with professionals who do business with your prospective clients. Anyone who works in a field related to home products or services may occasionally have people ask them if they know any interior decorators.

By establishing relationships with these professionals, you can be the one they recommend when someone asks if they know a good decorator. Of course, they will expect you to do the same and recommend them whenever you're asked if you know anyone who offers the service or product they are selling.

Depending on who you have identified as your target markets, any of the following may come into contact with your prospective clients:

- real estate agents
- architects
- antiques dealers

- artists

- art dealers

- home renovators (contractors, carpenters, painters, etc.)

- owners of businesses that sell home furnishings, fabrics, etc.

There are many other types of professionals who might be able to recommend you to their clients or customers. You may even get referrals from other interior decorators who are too busy with other projects, or aren't interested in working on a particular job.

Where to Network

Network wherever you expect to find prospective clients or professionals who might refer you to prospective clients. This section offers a variety of ideas but of course you don't have the resources to do all of them. So choose a few to begin with, based on your target markets. If the first ones you try don't turn out to be great networking opportunities, scratch them off your list and try something else.

Trade Shows

The industry trade shows mentioned in section 2.3.1 are an excellent way to learn about interior decorating and design. They can also be an excellent opportunity to network with other people in the industry. Debbie Travis, best-selling author and star of television's *Debbie Travis' Painted House,* says although she doesn't have time to chat with beginning decorators who phone her, "If I bump into you at the design show, it's a chance to schmooze."

Attend Openings

When a museum or art gallery has a new exhibit, they will hold an "opening" which may attract a crowd of wealthy and cultured people— exactly the type of people who hire interior decorators. An opening usually combines a social event, such as a wine and cheese reception, with an opportunity for people to view the exhibit. For the museum or gallery, these events can be an excellent opportunity to make sales, attract donations, or simply get the word out about their new exhibit. Some museums and galleries hold openings throughout the year.

There is usually no cost or obligation to attend. In some cases, getting invited to these events can be as simple as phoning and asking to be put on the mailing list.

Another possibility is to visit local art galleries that are also dealers (retailers) and speak with the owner or manager. Explain that you are an interior decorator whose clients may be interested in purchasing art. Ask to be put on their mailing list and notified of upcoming events.

Get Involved with Charities

Many wealthy and professional people attend charitable fund-raising events such as fashion shows, teas, luncheons, dinners, etc. Attending these events yourself is one way to start connecting with the wealthy, but it can be very expensive. (Since they are "fundraisers," getting into each event might cost you $100 or more!) Plus, there may not be much time to meet and mingle with other attendees.

You will have a much greater opportunity to connect with people and support a good cause by volunteering to help with the event. As a volunteer you may work closely with the type of people you want to attract as clients. Many wealthy people don't just make financial donations—they also donate their time to charities, and are actively involved in fund-raising and event planning.

Volunteer for activities that will bring you into contact with these people. In other words, leave the envelope stuffing to other volunteers and focus on helping out with events. In addition to serving on committees, see if you can volunteer the services of your interior decorating firm to handle decorations for the event.

This is a wonderful opportunity not only to meet people, but to get the name of your firm in front of every person who attends the event! Most organizations publish a brochure or booklet to give to each attendee. This usually contains information about the event along with a list of suppliers—including the name of the company that supplied decorating services.

If you are chosen to handle decorations (if the charity is prominent you may need to be involved with the organization for a while before being given this responsibility), you may be expected to get donations of materials from suppliers.

However, many suppliers want to attract wealthy clients and you can explain how this will give them an opportunity for greater exposure.

> **TIP:** As mentioned in Chapter 2, some charities hold fundraisers in which a dream home is raffled off. This is another excellent opportunity for you to volunteer your decorating services.

So which charities do your target markets get involved with? If you have read *Town & Country* magazine or the social column of a local newspaper, you have probably seen photos of wealthy people at charitable events. The rich typically are involved in arts organizations, including:

- ballet
- theater
- symphony
- opera
- visual arts

Many are also involved in health causes, such as organizations that work to find cures for AIDS or Breast Cancer. Others are involved with political campaigns. (Although technically not a "charity," political campaigns do fund-raising events where you can meet prospective clients.)

To volunteer, simply phone up the organizations in your community that interest you. You may be able to find them through word-of-mouth or listed in the Yellow Pages under a category such as "Societies" or "Charitable Organizations."

Local Associations

One of the best ways to network is by joining an association that prospective clients and other professionals belong to. Some examples include:

- service clubs (such as Rotary Club or Kiwanis Club)

- business organizations (such as the chamber of commerce)

- networking clubs (such as Business Network International)

- clubs that attract the wealthy (e.g. golf, polo, yacht, country clubs)

- industry associations (for example, you might be permitted to join a homebuilders' association as an "associate member")

Other organizations you could get involved with include cultural organizations and churches. You will probably find scores of oranizations in your community that you could get involved with. So get involved with those that interest you personally, as well as those that could lead to business.

Membership fees may vary from $20 to hundreds or even thousands of dollars (the latter if you want to join an exclusive country club or private golf club). The more expensive clubs usually require current members to introduce you and put you up for membership, so you may have to join some less exclusive clubs in order to meet people who might also belong to the more expensive clubs. Many less exclusive clubs will let you attend a few times for a nominal fee so you can decide if you really want to join.

You can find organizations by asking your friends and colleagues what they are involved in. You can also find them in your local telephone directory or online. A couple to look into are Executive Woman International at **www.executivewomen.org** and the National Association of Female Executives at **www.nafe.com**. Also check out your local chamber of commerce. For the U.S. Chamber of Commerce Directory visit **www.uschamber.com/chambers/directory**. For the Canadian Chamber of Commerce Directory visit **www.chamber.ca/index.php/en/links/C57**.

While membership in any organization can potentially be valuable, simply attending "networking" functions is not the only way to make an impact on prospective clients. To make the most out of your membership in an association, there are several things you can do to raise your profile, including:

- Serve on a committee

- Write articles for the association newsletter

- Do volunteer work such as offering to decorate for events

- Run for election to the Executive Committee

The more involved you are in an association, the more likely you are to connect with prospective clients or professionals who can refer you to clients.

6.1.3   Marketing Tools

Once you start networking, you'll need a website and printed materials for prospective clients.

Printed Materials

Your printed materials include business cards, stationery (such as letterhead, envelopes, and mailing labels), and other marketing materials such as brochures.

If you have a computer with a high quality laser or ink jet printer, you may be able to inexpensively print professional looking materials from your own computer. Free templates for all the print materials you are likely to need in your business can be found online. HP offers templates for a variety of programs at **www.hp.com/sbso/productivity/office**. For example, you can create a matching set of stationery (business cards, letterhead, envelopes) in MS Word. The site includes free online classes and how-to guides to help you design your own marketing materials. Another excellent resource is the Microsoft Office Online Templates Homepage at **http://office.microsoft.com/en-us/templates**.

As an alternative to printing materials yourself, consider using a company that provides printing services. Beautiful stationery can help show prospective clients you have a good eye and can make their interiors look beautiful, too. Consider using textured papers, raised printing, and a professional design. Your printed materials can be easily designed, paid for and delivered without leaving home. Here are links to some printers that provide services for small businesses:

- *FedEx Kinko's*
  www.fedex.com/us/officeprint/onlineprint

- *Acecomp Plus – Printing Solutions*
  www.acecomp.com/printing.asp

- *The Paper Mill Store*
  www.thepapermillstore.com

- *VistaPrint*
  www.vistaprint.com

While the resources listed above can help with all your printing needs, here is some advice about two types of materials that are particularly important for marketing purposes – business cards and brochures.

Business Cards

The first thing on your list of marketing tools is your business cards. This is one item that you can't do without as an interior decorator. The basic information to list on your business cards includes:

- Your name

- Your title (such as President or Interior Decorator)

- Your company name

- Your contact information (phone numbers, email address, fax number)

- Your web address

In addition, consider including the following items to promote you and your decorating services.

- Professional memberships and certifications (see section 6.3.5)

- Your specializations and services offered

- Company logo

- Your mailing address

Keep business cards the standard size, 2 x 3 ½ inches, and if possible, invest in a sturdy card that has a good weight and feel to it. If your budget is limited, a good source for high quality low-cost cards (currently $19.99 per 250 cards) is VistaPrint at **www.vistaprint.com**. Visit their site to see a wide variety of designs you can consider.

Brochures

You will have many opportunities to give out your business card. In fact, you should get in the habit of giving it to almost everyone you meet. But there are also times to give out brochures.

For example, when you give a presentation at a networking meeting or when people seem particularly interested in your services. You should also provide some to the companies with whom you do a lot of business. Your major suppliers should have some, in case someone asks them if they know an interior decorator they could recommend.

Your brochure will contain your company name and contact information, including your web address. It can also include some of the information you have on your website, such as:

- Before and after photographs of interiors you have decorated

- Benefits of hiring you (see section 6.3.5 for ideas)

- A list of the services you provide

- A photograph of you

- Some testimonials from satisfied customers

Your brochure can be folded in three, with printing on both sides of the sheet, or you can simply print a one-page flyer which you could also pin up on bulletin boards. If you are printing only a few copies of your brochure, you may be able to find nice paper at your local office supply store which you can run through your PC's printer.

If you aren't able to produce brochures on your home computer, or if you need hundreds of brochures (for example, if you are participating in a trade show), it may be faster and cheaper for you to have your brochures professionally printed. Check the Yellow Pages under "Printers," or use the printing services of your local office supply store.

TIP: Spell-check and grammar check everything. Also check your phone number, email address, and other contact information carefully to make sure clients can reach you.

When you decide you do need professionally printed brochures, check the Yellow Pages under "Printers" or use quick-printer services such as FedEx Office or Minuteman Press, or even the printing services of your local office supply store.

Website

A website is an excellent marketing tool for an interior decorator. Although it probably won't generate much business itself (people are not likely to search for an interior decorator online), your website can complement your other marketing efforts. When someone who is looking for an interior decorator sees your web address on your business card, in a Yellow Pages ad, or elsewhere, they can visit your website 24 hours a day to learn more about your services.

Most interior decorators use their websites as a place to showcase their best work. You can create an online portfolio with before and after pictures (or even just the after pictures) of places you have decorated. Section 4.1.1 explains how to get photographs for a portfolio and includes links to several examples of decorators' online portfolios.

However, webpages with lots of large photos (which best show your decorating skills) can be incredibly slow to load unless someone is using a high-speed Internet connection. Therefore, many interior decorators use "thumbnail" photos—small photos people can click on to see a larger photo.

You can get some ideas for your own website by looking at what other decorators and interior designers have done with their sites. To find websites of interior decorators and interior designers in your own community, check their Yellow Pages ads for their web address or do an online search.

Designing Your Website

Clients will judge the quality of your business and services by what they see on your site. If you don't have the time or expertise to design a polished website yourself, you can have a professional web developer build and maintain your site. There is no shortage of web designers, so consult your local phone directory or search online for one in your area. If you are already experienced at creating web pages, or learn quickly, you can design your website yourself using a program such as Adobe Dreamweaver or a free program like SeaMonkey (available at **www.seamonkey-project.org**). You may also use the website development tools offered by domain and hosting companies, described below.

Getting a Domain Name

To present a professional image and make your web address easier for clients to remember, consider getting your own domain name, such as www.yourbusinessname.com. There are a number of sites where you can search for and register a domain name. One web host we have found that provides good service for a low cost is **www. godaddy.com**. Microsoft also offers a quick search for domain name availability using their sign-up feature at **http://smallbusiness.officelive. com**. (They'll also help you to set up a free website for your business.) If your preferred domain name is available, but you're not yet ready with your website, you can also "park" your domain. This means that you register the domain so that someone else does not take it before you're up and running with your business website. You then park the domain with your web host.

Finding a Host

Once you register your domain, you will need to find a place to "host" it. You can host it with the same company where you've registered the name. For example, if you register a domain name through GoDaddy, you might use their hosting services to put your website online. You may also be able to put up free web pages through your Internet Service Provider (the company that gives you access to the Internet). However, if you want to use your own domain name, you'll likely need to pay for hosting. Yahoo! also offers a popular low-cost web hosting service at **http://smallbusiness.yahoo.com/webhosting**. You can find a wide variety of other companies that provide hosting services by doing an online search. Before choosing a web host, read the article about web hosting scams at **www.loriswebs.com/internethostingscams.html** to help you avoid hosting problems.

Promoting Your Site

No matter how much you spend on creating your website, if people don't know it exists, it won't help your business. Make certain you list your site on all your business forms, cards, and brochures. Encourage people to visit your site by mentioning it as often as you can, for example, whenever you write an article, give a presentation, or are interviewed by the media.

Make sure people can find your website by getting it into the search engines and listing it with industry websites. While some sites and search engines charge a fee to guarantee that your website will be included in their directory, you can submit your website for free to Google at **www.google.com/submityourcontent**. Once you're on Google, your site is likely to be found by other search engines as well.

Your web hosting company may offer a search engine submission service for an additional fee. You can find information about "optimizing" your website, to help it rank higher on search engines, at the Search Engine Watch website at **http://searchenginewatch.com** and at Google's Webmaster Help Center at **www.google.com/support/webmasters**.

6.1.4   Advertising

While word-of-mouth and networking can be particularly effective ways to get business for your interior decorating firm, you may also be able to attract some clients through advertising.

Yellow Pages

You have probably used the Yellow Pages many times. But before you buy an ad for your own business, you should carefully investigate the costs compared to the potential return. Many new business owners find a Yellow Pages ad does not "make the phone ring off the hook" with buyers. If someone does respond to your ad, they may be "shopping around" so you must be prepared to invest time as well as advertising dollars if you use this method of advertising.

To minimize your risk, you might want to consider starting with a small display ad, such as a 1/8 page ad. If you can get your hands on a previous year's edition of your local Yellow Pages, compare the ads for interior decorators from year to year. If you notice other decorators have increased or decreased the size of their ads, this can give you an indication of what might work for you. Also, if you are doing information interviews (as suggested in Chapter 2) you can ask decorators about how well their Yellow Pages ads are working for them.

Take a look at the ads in the interior decorating category of your current Yellow Pages for ideas. One thing you will probably notice is that most decorators indicate their specialties and target markets. While you wouldn't say "specializing in rich people's homes," you might say something like "specializing in fine homes."

You can either design the ad yourself, have the Yellow Pages design it for you, or hire a designer. Contact your local Yellow Pages to speak with a sales rep. Check the print version of your phone book for contact information.

Magazines

Magazine advertising can be expensive, and may not generate the results you want unless you do it repeatedly. It has been estimated that many people need to see an advertisement three to seven times before they buy.

If you choose to buy advertising, it will probably be most cost effective to place ads in small local magazines read by your target markets. Look into magazines focusing on the arts and lifestyles, or targeted to upscale readers, the gay community, home buyers, etc. The publications you advertise in will usually design your ad for an additional cost, and give you a copy of the ad to run in other publications. However, you will get much better results if you can get free publicity in those publications, instead of paying for advertising.

6.1.5   Media Publicity

The "media" are magazines, newspapers, radio, and television. When a business gets positive coverage in a magazine article, newspaper story, radio or television talk show, it can result in a lot of new business. Here are some ways interior decorators can get publicity.

Photo Features

Many decorating magazines publish photo features showcasing the work of interior decorators and interior designers. While there is tremendous competition to get into national magazines, as a beginning interior decorator you may be able to have your work featured in a local magazine, or the homes section of your local newspaper.

If this opportunity interests you, study several issues of the magazines or newspapers you're interested in to get a sense of the types of features they do. Many features focus on something unique or how a particular decorating challenge was overcome. If you followed the advice in Chapter 2 and have already decorated some interiors, consider what was special about those particular decorating projects. If it's something that might interest readers of the magazine or newspaper, and it's a topic that has not been covered in the last few issues, you can propose a story to the editor.

Most magazines and newspapers publish contact information for their editors. Newspapers may have dozens of editors, so make sure you target your submission to the appropriate one. (Our local newspaper has both a "Homes" editor and a "HomeStyle" editor, but only the latter publishes decorating features.) Find out the editor's name, and send a brief letter by email, fax, or snail mail saying what the decorating project is, what's unique about it, and why it would be a great idea for a story (i.e. why it would be interesting to readers).

While it is not necessary to submit photographs to a daily newspaper editor (most newspapers have their own photographers), photographs may help attract the editor's attention. They might also be published in a smaller publication that doesn't have a photographer on staff.

If you send photos, put them in an attractive two-pocket folder with your business card and a cover letter about the decorating project. Then follow up a week later with a phone call.

Write a Column

One of the best ways to establish yourself as an expert is to write a column for a newspaper, magazine, or newsletter. While most large daily newspapers already have decorating columns, there may be an opportunity to write for smaller newspapers or local magazines that reach your target audience.

There are many possible topics you could write on—how to make a small space appear larger, decorating for the holiday season, decorating tips to help sell a home, etc.

The length and frequency of your column will depend on the publication. You might produce a weekly 500 word column for a local newspaper, or a monthly 1,000 word column for a newsletter or magazine.

Or you might write a single article to start with. For example, perhaps you could write an article on how to decorate a nursery for a parenting magazine, or how to merge two households for a wedding magazine. Make sure your article provides valuable information to the publication's readers. Articles that sound like an ad for your services are not likely to get published.

Once you have written your first column or article, phone the editor to ask if they would be interested in seeing it. If so, they will probably ask you to email it. If they want to publish it, they may offer to pay you. However, even if they don't pay, you should consider letting them publish it in return for including a brief bio and your contact information at the end of the article or column.

Online Publicity

As well as offering articles to print publications, consider offering them to online publications. A popular site you can use to distribute your articles is EzineArticles at **www.ezinearticles.com**. Once your articles are posted at EzineArticles, they may be published at a variety of websites and ezines (email newsletters).

You could publish your own blog, using a site such as Blogger (**www. blogger.com**) or WordPress.com (**www.wordpress.com**). However, it can take a while to build up an audience for a blog, and ongoing work to make regular updates. If you don't have time to devote to maintaining your own blog while doing everything else required to build your business, you may be able to get articles you write into other people's blogs by distributing them through EzineArticles.

If you do have a good chunk of time to devote to online marketing, you can also use social networking sites such as Facebook (**www.facebook.com**) and LinkedIn (**www.linkedin.com**), do micro-blogging (brief updates) at Twitter (**www.twitter.com**), create videos to post at YouTube (**www.youtube.com**), and create pages for sites such as Squidoo (**www.squidoo.com**), among other online marketing activities. Many entrepreneurs find the number of online "social media" sites overwhelming. If you want to learn more about how to use them, consider subscribing to the free Publicity Hound newsletter at **www.publicityhound.com**.

Even if you decide not to use online social media, you can nevertheless market your business online using methods discussed earlier in this chapter, such as building a website, doing online advertising, and publishing an email newsletter.

Television and Radio Talk Shows

Phone local radio and TV shows to let them know you are available to provide decorating advice to their viewers or listeners. Shows that might be appropriate include morning shows and afternoon talk shows. The person to contact is the producer of each show.

The producer will probably ask you to send them some information, so be prepared to email or fax a few paragraphs about yourself, along with a list of frequently asked questions. These are questions their audience would likely be interested in knowing the answer to, such as "How can I make a small space look larger?" or whatever you find people asking your advice about. Television is a visual medium, so it's also a good idea to suggest some things they could shoot you doing, either in their studio or elsewhere.

6.1.6   Teaching and Speaking

Teach Classes

Teaching continuing education classes is a great way to earn extra money, establish your reputation, and meet prospective clients. The first step is to review the current catalog of courses offered by local colleges and other organizations that provide continuing education courses in your community. Call and ask for a print catalog if they do not have one at their website.

Once you have reviewed their current list of courses, come up with some ideas for new decorating courses. (They already have instructors for any courses that are in their catalog.) To find out how to apply to teach the course, call the organization and ask to speak with whoever hires continuing education instructors. An example of what to expect is at the Colorado Free University website at **www.freeu.com/teach.html**. At the time of writing they were actively seeking teachers for a variety of courses including a course on "One Day Decorating Ideas."

Give a Speech

Even if you don't join a networking organization, you may still be able to connect with their members and get new business by being a speaker at a breakfast meeting, luncheon, or workshop.

The topic can be any aspect of decorating that their members would be interested in. Depending on the organization, it could be anything from "Decorating tips to help sell your home" to "Using Feng Shui to help your business prosper." Whatever you find friends asking your advice about is probably something that many people would like to learn about.

Let people know that you are available to speak on decorating topics. This is a tremendously popular subject for many people, so chances are that many organizations would love to hear you talk. Contact the local organizations mentioned above and ask friends and acquaintances if they belong to any groups that have presentations from speakers.

While you probably will not be paid for your presentations, it can be an excellent opportunity to promote your business. Your company name may be published in the organization's newsletter, it will be mentioned by the person who introduces you, you can distribute business cards and brochures, and you will be able to mingle with attendees before and after your presentation. (You may get a free breakfast or lunch too!)

If you give a good talk and offer useful advice, you will be seen as an expert. As long as there are people in the audience who need decorating services, this can be an excellent way to attract clients.

6.1.7 Other Ideas

Keep your eyes open for every opportunity to promote your services. For starters, review the suggestions in section 2.5 on *"How to Get Experience."* Many of those ideas are good not only for getting experience, they also are an excellent way to network and build word-of-mouth for your decorating business.

Other Markets

As mentioned earlier, when you are starting out you may want to consider doing all kinds of decorating work even if it isn't always for your target markets. For example, you might want to consider decorating for home builders just because it can lead to other work. Many model homes have a placard posted with the decorator's name and phone number, so you may get business from visitors to the model home.

Home Shows

Home shows were mentioned in Chapter 2. As well as being a good source of information about decorating, they can be a good way to showcase your work to prospective clients by creating room "vignettes" (i.e. decorating a fake room). Contact your local convention center to ask for a schedule of upcoming events. Then contact the home show's organizer and find out how you can participate.

Retailers and Design Centers

Some retailers will allow you to leave promotional information (brochures, business cards) which they will pass on to customers who are looking for an interior decorator. If you have a design center in your city (such as the Washington Design Center in Washington, D.C.) you may be able to leave a copy of your portfolio for prospective clients to look through.

6.2 Telephone Inquiries

Your first contact with a prospective client may be a telephone inquiry. It is for this reason that it is most important your telephone is always answered in a professional, friendly voice with your company name.

Most telephone inquiries will come from people searching for information on what services you provide and how much you charge. However, if you simply give them the information on the phone, you are unlikely to hear from them again. People do not generally buy decorating services on the telephone. They are much more likely to hire you if you set up a face-to-face meeting to discuss your services.

So how can you keep someone on the phone and convince them to meet with you? By gently taking control of the conversation and keeping your answers concise and focused on what a valuable service interior decorators (and more particularly you) provide to clients. Your conversation could go something like this:

CLIENT: Hello, I'm looking for some information on how much you charge to do interior decorating.

YOU: Thank you for calling. My name is: _____. May I get your name?

CLIENT: Candice Client.

YOU: Would you prefer if I called you Candice or Ms. Client?

CLIENT: Call me Candice.

YOU: Well, Candice, our company has many excellent packages available depending on the number of services the client prefers we handle but we can also design a package especially for you. We are experts at negotiating and securing fair prices from our suppliers and pass the savings on to you. Our services range from shopping for furniture and accessories, to furniture re-arrangement in a particular room, to developing a decorating plan for a number of rooms in your house including supervising contract renovations required and start at $150. Have you had a chance to see our portfolio or any information on our company's services?

CLIENT: No. I just got your number from the phone book and thought I'd call. I'm not sure I know exactly what I want done or what an interior decorator can do for me.

| YOU: | Candice, I'm not sure what other interior decorators would tell you, but I can tell you my goal is to create and implement a beautiful and unique decorating plan that will be suitable for your needs and in a price range that will work for you. I offer a free one hour initial consultation and I'd be pleased to meet with you to take the mystery out of what services I can provide you and to discuss options with you. I have Tuesday, Thursday and Friday open. Which day would be good for you? |

If Candice Client decides she'd rather see written information, you can refer her to your website. If she wants to receive information by mail, and you have a brochure, mail it at once. Make absolutely certain you spell her name correctly, repeat the address back to confirm it, and ask for her phone number for follow-up purposes.

Mail your materials in an appropriately sized envelope (don't squish them in) and make sure you use the correct postage. Send a cover letter thanking her for her interest in your company and tell her you will follow up within a couple of weeks. Call in a couple of weeks to ensure she received the materials and ask to arrange a meeting.

So, what happens when the client says yes to a meeting?

6.3 Initial Client Consultation

The purpose of your initial client consultation is to learn as much as possible about your client and what they want so you can show them how hiring you will help them achieve their decorating goals.

6.3.1 Where and When to Meet

The best place to meet is the place the client is considering having decorated. This will give you an opportunity to see what you will be working with. However, it may not always be possible to see it during your first meeting. For example, someone may be interested in having you decorate a summer cottage located miles out of town, or a company may want their boardroom redecorated, but it might be in use at the time of your first meeting.

Be flexible and meet wherever the client wants to meet, unless they want to meet at your "office," and you work from home. Unless your home is a mansion, the client may perceive that your work is a "hobby" or that you don't need to be paid as much as someone working from an office. You could explain that you should meet at the client's premises to get a greater feel for their "corporate culture" or needs.

> **TIP:** Plan to meet your clients at a quiet time of day when there will be no distractions such as ringing phones, meals to be prepared, children to be looked after, etc. Let your client know in advance that your initial meeting with them will be much more productive if you can have some uninterrupted time with them so you can assess their needs.

6.3.2 What to Bring to the Meeting

It is highly likely that the initial meeting with your prospective client(s) will take place away from your home or office (most likely at the place to be decorated) and for this reason, you need to come well-prepared.

Here are some items an organized interior decorator can bring to an initial client consultation:

- Your decorating kit (see *"Tools of the Trade"* in section 3.1)

- A list of questions to find out what the client wants (see Sample Client Decorating Questionnaire below)

- A notepad and pen to make notes

- Your portfolio

- References from past clients (friends or family included)

- Your business cards

- Your brochure if you have one

- Catalogs and brochures from preferred suppliers

- Price list for sample packages (e.g. preparation of decorating plan, re-arrangement of furnishings in one room, hourly rates for shopping, complete redecorating package, etc.)

- Master budget form (a sample is included later in this chapter)

- A calculator

- A calendar or date book

- A blank contract (a sample is included later in this chapter)

Although this initial consultation may be seen as only an opportunity for the client to assess whether they would like to hire an interior decorator or not, it is a good idea to come prepared to write up a contract, at least a contract to do up a decorating plan (more about this later), in case the client decides right there and then that they wish to proceed.

6.3.3   What to Wear

While a consultation with a potential client is not exactly a job interview with a major corporation where you would wear a dark business suit or similar attire, it is nonetheless a business meeting and appropriate clothing is called for. On the other hand, interior decorators are usually creative people with a flair for fashion and the latest trends. So how do you dress? Somewhere in the middle.

Remember your mother's advice: You only get one chance to make a first impression and yours should say professional, forward thinking and creative. Women may wear colored suits, either pant or skirt sets, or separates that are well put together. Possibilities include:

- Dress with matching suit jacket (solids are best)

- Skirt (no minis!) and matching suit jacket

- Bright but solid colored pant suit

- Skirt or pants with complementary colored jacket

- Anything black (except jeans)

- For creativity add a funky piece of jewelry, fashionable scarf or dynamite handbag

For men the best choice is business casual (no jeans or khakis), which could include:

- Slacks with a matching solid colored sweater

- Suit jacket and pants — no tie

- Slacks and matching knitted turtleneck sweater

- Suit pants or dress slacks with solid color shirt and tie, but no jacket

For both men and women: shoes should be absolutely spotless, in good repair (no cracked heels or broken shoe laces) and scuff-free.

6.3.4   Questions to Identify What the Client Wants

During the initial meeting with your prospective client, your main focus will be on identifying what the client wants and determining the scope of work to be performed. This is something referred to as identifying the "client's needs." However, most people make buying decisions based on their wants rather than their needs. (After all, no one needs to buy Coca-Cola or McDonald's hamburgers.)

When you first get together with your prospective client, let them know that you will want to sit down with them first to get to know them a little better and to discuss their decorating desires in general. After that, tell them you would appreciate taking a tour of their home (or the specific rooms to be decorated) so that you can see the layout, get a feel for their home, look over the rooms or specific spaces to be decorated and to discuss, in general, what they want.

Of course during this consultation you will also be focused on trying to sell your services, but interestingly enough, the best way to sell your services is to develop a rapport with your client and focus on what the client wants. Many people who are trying to sell something make the mistake of thinking they should do most of the talking. You probably know from personal experience how well these kinds of sales pitches have worked on you. If you are like most people, you are more likely to buy when someone carefully listens to what you want, then makes a recommendation based on what you have said.

The key to identifying the client's wants is to ask questions. The client should be doing most of the talking in your meeting while you listen and take notes. The particular questions you ask will depend upon the type of client, but you can start with questions from the sample questionnaire on the next page.

As the client is answering questions, you can ask any follow-up questions that occur to you, and explain how decorating can help them achieve what they want. For example, after the client tells you what they dislike or want to change, you can describe how decorating will help them have the home they want.

Client Decorating Questionnaire

A questionnaire can help you narrow down your client's decorating needs and wants, determine the scope of work to be performed and identify your client's likes and dislikes. You can ask questions during your meeting. If time is limited, leave a questionnaire with the client to fill out later. (Ask them to fax or email their responses to you.)

A sample client decorating questionnaire begins on the next page. The questionnaire is for home decorating and includes a variety of questions that may or may not be appropriate depending on the scope of the job you are requested to do. For example, if a customer is hiring you to decorate only one room (for instance, the dining room), some of the questions can be removed from the questionnaire, such as questions relating to reading and having a home office, etc. However, if a client is hiring you to help decorate their whole home, you may decide to leave all the questions in. Feel free to use this questionnaire as a starting point and adjust it to fit your needs.

Likewise, if the client is a business you can simply adapt many of the questions. (For example, instead of asking "How many people live in your home?" you would ask "How many people work in your office?") You can also ask who comes to the office (e.g. the public, clients, suppliers, investors, etc.) and what message they want to communicate to people who visit the office.

Sample Client Decorating Questionnaire

1. What is your purpose for hiring an Interior Decorator (for example, is it to make your home look more beautiful or to make your home more functional or both)?

2. Do you own or rent your home? (This is important to know because if the home is rented, there may be limitations on what can or cannot be done in the home with respect to painting, changing light fixtures and window coverings, etc.)

3. How long do you plan to stay in your current home?

4. How many people live in your home?

5. Do you have or plan to have any children?

6. What are the ages of the children you have?

7. Which rooms do you want to have decorated?

8. What are you hoping to do with the rooms to be decorated?

9. What do you want to use each of the rooms for? (For example, you may want your living room to be a formal place that you only use when entertaining, or you may want to use it for entertaining, watching television and reading, etc.)

10. How important is comfort to you compared to having things look more aesthetically pleasing?

11. Do you like to kick your feet back and even put your feet on the furniture?

12. What rooms in your house do you really "live" in and spend a lot of (awake) time in?

13. Do you do or plan to do much entertaining in your home?

14. Do you plan to have formal dinner parties or informal gatherings?

15. Where would you prefer to do most of your entertaining (e.g. in the living room or dining room, or in the family room or kitchen, or in another room all together)?

16. How do you feel about clutter in your home? Is it acceptable to have some or should everything be put away in its place?

17. Is organization and are organizational systems important to you?

18. Do you like to keep children's toys contained in a play area (instead of spread throughout the house)?

19. Do you or your partner (and/or kids) read very much?

20. Where would you like to read?

21. Do you or your partner or kids enjoy crafts or have special hobbies? Do you need a separate space for this?

22. Do you need a home office? Does anyone work at home? (If so, please specify what kind of workspace is required.)

23. Where do you eat most of your meals?

24. Is the lighting in your room(s) acceptable?

25. What type of flooring do you prefer (for example, carpet, wood, laminate, vinyl or tiles)?

26. What do you prefer for window coverings (for example, blinds, drapes, curtains, shades, shutters, decorative sconces with scarves, etc.)?

27. What are your color preferences?

28. What is your preferred decorating style (e.g. Country, Modern, Victorian, etc.)?

29. What do you want to keep?

30. What do you want to get rid of?

31. What type of mood do you want to express in each of the spaces to be decorated?

32. What type of look and feel do you want in each of the rooms to be decorated?

6.3.5   Selling Your Services

As mentioned above, the most important key to selling your services is to listen to what the client wants and explain how you can provide it for them. Even so, many clients will want some evidence that you are a skilled interior decorator.

An excellent way to establish your professionalism with a client is by joining a professional association. For example, you may be eligible to advertise yourself as a member of the Designer/Decorator Society of America, or a Member, Interior Design Society. A list of professional organizations is included on the next page.

You can also demonstrate your skills by showing the client a portfolio containing photographs of your previous decorating work. Portfolios are covered in detail in section 4.1.1 of this guide. Your portfolio should also include sample design boards, which are covered in section 6.5.2 of this guide. Even if this will be your first paid job, you can show the client boards from previous unpaid decorating work. (Of course you should avoid mentioning to the client that you were not paid!)

It is also a good idea to provide the client with copies of your letters of recommendation, or the names and telephone numbers of references. Once again, these can be people you did unpaid decorating for. However you should make sure you have their permission to give out their phone numbers to prospective clients, and ask them to avoid mentioning that you were not paid, if possible.

Explain to the client the benefits of using your services. For example, depending on what the client wants, if you work entirely on an hourly fee basis, you might explain how the discounts you are able to get for the client on furniture and materials will more than cover the costs of your services. Or if you work on a cost-plus basis, you can explain how there will be no charge for your services beyond the cost of materials, and that the cost for those materials will be no more than they would spend if they did it themselves.

You can also explain how your services will save them time and help them avoid costly mistakes.

Professional Associations

Canadian Decorators' Association (CDECA)

Graduates of college decorating programs are eligible to join CDE-CA (**www.cdeca.com**) for $300 (Canadian funds), which allows you to use the designation "Member of CDECA." Students at recognized colleges may join for $120.

Certified Interior Decorators International (CID)

To join CID as a professional member, you must have completed a study course in Interior Design and Decoration, and provide proof of employment. Students may join as associate members. Benefits include use of the CID designation, a newsletter, discounts on books, seminars and materials, and a referral service. Membership costs $295 per year ($150 for students). Visit **www.cidinternational. org**.

Decorators' Alliance of North America (DANA)

When you become a member of DANA (**www.decoratorsalliance. com**), you'll receive a number of benefits, including free monthly continuing education courses, a quarterly newsletter, and a listing in the online directory. You will also have the opportunity to take an exam to become a Certified Professional Decorator (CPD). Membership is $184 per year, or $459 for the first year's membership plus the CPD Certification Manual and Exam.

Interior Design Society (IDS)

As a member of IDS (**www.interiordesignsociety.org**), you can receive such benefits as a referral service, publications, educational materials, programs and services for the residential interior design trade. Although professional membership is limited to interior designers, interior decorators may join as Affiliate Members for a $175 annual fee.

International Interior Design Association (IIDA)

Membership in the IIDA (**www.iida.org**) is available at three levels: affiliate, associate or professional. Professional membership requires a degree or diploma in interior design and proof of certification by the National Council for Interior Design Qualification (NCIDQ), while associate members meet the NCIDQ educational requirements but have not yet completed the NCIDQ exam. Affiliate members represent related design disciplines such as lighting designers, photographers, etc., and require submission of a business card. Affiliate and professional memberships cost $455 per year; associate memberships cost $260. Student memberships are also available for $50.

6.3.6 Next Steps

After you have discussed with your client their general decorating wants and needs, you and your client will have a better idea of what is desired moving forward. If it appears that there will be a good fit between you and the client, this would be an ideal time to ask the client when they would like to get started.

Assuming they want to go ahead with having you decorate, explain that the next step is for you to develop a decorating plan for them. This will involve meeting with the client a second time (unless you have kept your schedule open and both you and the client are wanting to start that day) to:

- Measure the space

- Find out more specifically what the client wants

- Find out more about their likes and dislikes

- Assess what is staying and what needs to be changed

Let the client know that after the second meeting (or after that meeting if you decide to go ahead that day), you will then need to prepare the decorating plan and this will include:

- Selecting materials

- Creating room plans and design boards

- Preparing a detailed estimate of costs (a project budget)

After you describe what you will do for the client, tell them the fee to prepare the decorating plan, and either get a retainer or have them agree to pay for the decorating plan the next time you meet. Before you leave, determine a date that will work for both you and your client to get together again and make sure you write down the details in your day timer. If your client does not give you a retainer at your first meeting, fax or email them a letter of understanding when you return to the office.

This is a brief letter outlining what you have agreed upon, including what you will do to prepare the decorating plan, the fee to prepare it, and when payment is due. A sample appears below.

Sample Letter of Understanding

July 29, 2011

Dear Carla Client,

It was a pleasure to meet with you today. I am excited about the opportunity to decorate your living room.

As discussed, I am pleased to go ahead with preparing a decorating plan for your consideration. This will involve measuring your living room, selecting materials, designing a room plan and design board, and preparing a proposed budget. As we agreed, the cost to prepare the decorating plan for your living room is $150.00, payable at our meeting on August 3, 2011.

I look forward to working with you on this exciting project.

Best wishes,
Darla Decorator

6.4 Second Client Consultation

At your second client consultation, your purpose is to gather further information to put together a decorating plan. Given this you will need to meet at your client's home (or the place to be decorated).

At this second meeting (or at the end of your first meeting, if you decide to continue on then), you will need to:

1. Get a clearer picture as to what the client specifically wants done

2. Measure the space to be decorated and any items of furniture staying

3. Perform a general assessment

Although you will have certain tasks to attend to, don't forget to take the time to continue to build a rapport with your client. Ask them how they are doing and whether they have had any additional ideas since you last met and give them an opportunity to talk about their decorating wishes.

6.4.1   Identify the Client's Specific Needs

At this second client consultation, make sure you get the completed Client Decorating Questionnaire back from your client. It is preferable to ask for this near the beginning of your meeting so that you don't forget to get it. If your client hasn't yet completed it, it will give them enough time to complete it before you leave.

Just in case your client has misplaced the questionnaire, make sure that you have an extra one on hand that your client can fill out while you are attending to other things such as measuring and/or assessing the rooms to be decorated. To get a clearer picture of what your client wants, you will need to find out more about:

- your client's personal style

- your client's general likes and dislikes

- desired functionality for each room

- items to keep and items to get rid of

- your client's budget and priorities

Client's Personal Style

One of the first steps is to find out your client's personal style. What are their style preferences for their home:

- modern/contemporary, traditional/classic or eclectic

- bold or subdued

- lots of color or neutral earthy tones

- simplistic or collector of lots of "things"

Also, does your client have a preference for a particular historical period style (such as Neoclassical, Georgian, Art Deco, or Victorian)? Do they have a preference for a particular regional style (such as Southwestern, Oriental or French Country)? Or do they prefer an Eclectic look?

It is important to note that if you are decorating for a couple, each person may have conflicting styles they prefer. If this is the case, you may need to discuss with your clients the possibility of selecting a style that both will be happy with but may not necessarily be the first preference of either (possibly an Eclectic style will work best). After all, both individuals need to feel "at home" and happy in their newly decorated home.

Once you find out all the answers to the above style preferences for your client, you will then be in a better position to help them with their decorating plan.

General Likes and Dislikes

Another way to find out more about your client's personal style, particularly their likes and dislikes, is to have them look at photos in a few interior decorating magazines with pages you have previously bookmarked for the purpose. Preparing these in advance will save you time and prevent clients from being distracted by ads and other articles. (You can find a selection of different decorating magazines to choose from in section 2.3.3 of this guide.) Alternatively, you could show them some decorating books, for example, window fashion books to gauge your client's preferences.

In addition to the above, it would also be helpful to find out some more decorating specifics to help you set out a plan for decorating your client's home, such as:

- what their favorite piece of furniture is and why

- what their least favorite piece of furniture is and why

- types of accessories they like (and don't like)

- what their favorite accessory is and why

- what their least favorite accessory is and why

- fabric and pattern preferences (have them tell you both their likes and dislikes)

- the style of furniture they like best (e.g. big cushy furniture or elegant formal furniture)

- color scheme preferences and which colors they absolutely don't want in their home

What you are working towards is finding out what types of items and colors your client likes most so that you can include these in your decorating plan and so that your client will ultimately be happy with the end result.

Desired Functionality for Each Room

After you have determined your client's personal style and found out a bit more about their likes and dislikes, take the time to go on a more detailed tour of your client's home (particularly the specific rooms to be decorated) to get a more in-depth feel for the home and to find out what the client wants to use each room for.

Begin by asking "What will this room be used for?" If they give you an ambiguous answer such as "relaxing in" or "resting in," you will need to dig deeper. Some additional questions you could ask are:

- Do you want to watch television in this room?

- Do you want an area for reading in this room?

- Do you want to have a games area in this room?

- Do you want to eat in this room?

- Do you want to work in this room?

- Do you want a study area in this room?

- Do you want to be able to do any hobbies in this room?

- Will anyone be sleeping in this room?

- Do you want to entertain in this room? If you do plan on entertaining in this room, how many people on average will you entertain in this room each time?

After you find out the answers to the above questions, you can then plan to decorate the room so that all desired functions can be met in the room.

Items to Keep and Items to Get Rid Of

The next step is to find out what items of furniture will be part of the new decorating plan. Find out from your client which items of furniture (and accessories) they absolutely love, which items give them the most pleasure, which items they could do without, which items they no longer like or would prefer to get rid of and also find out what they no longer have a use for. Besides taking notes, it will be helpful to take photos of the items that are staying, for your decorating plan.

Your Client's Budget

The next item to discuss with your client is their budget. What you will need to find out is the total amount they have budgeted to pay for both your services and any new furnishings, window and wall coverings, accessories, etc. and to find out their priorities.

Chances are your client will have a limited amount of funds to work from. Once you know what the limit is, and you know what your client's decorating wants are, then you can get an idea of what types of plans to make for decorating. You can also make plans to prepare a project budget for discussion with them at the next client meeting. More information about budgeting is in section 6.5.3.

6.4.2   Get Measurements

While meeting with your client for the second time, it is important to take the time to accurately measure each of the rooms to be decorated so that you can make a floor plan and later a decorating plan.

As explained in section 3.5.1, you will need to ensure that you measure and record the dimensions of all parts of the room, including walls, doors, windows, closets, any openings such as archways, electrical outlets, locations of switches, and any other items and/or permanent fixtures in the room. Ensure that you not only measure the width of each room but also find out and record the height of each wall.

These measurements will come in handy for your decorating plan and will give you an idea of how much room you have to work with, and how much paint, flooring, fabrics and/or other materials you will require. In addition to measuring the space to be decorated, also measure any furniture items and larger accessories that will stay in the room.

6.4.3   Assess the Room(s) to be Decorated

While touring your client's home and looking over the areas to be decorated, take the time to jot down notes from your observations to help you with making your decorating plan. Some things you might want to note are:

- Do any repairs need to be done in the room (such as patching a crack in the ceiling or in a wall)?

- What are the wall coverings (paint, wallpaper, faux finish, etc.)?

- Will the walls need to be painted?

- Is there a pre-determined color within the room that the client wishes to keep in the room (whether on the walls, carpet, etc.) which you will need to incorporate in the decorating plan?

- What type of flooring is there (e.g. carpet, tile, hardwood, vinyl, cork, area rugs) and what color is it?

- Will the flooring need to be replaced?

- Will moldings, casings, baseboards, or trims need to be replaced or added?

- Does the room have sufficient light or will new light fixtures need to be installed?

- Are there any architectural elements within the room that should be noted (such as columns, archways, high ceilings, etc.)?

- What are the window coverings (e.g. drapes, blinds, shades, shutters, etc.) and what color are they?

- Will the window coverings need to be replaced?

- Are there any built in cabinets or shelving within the room or would it make sense to add any? If there are any, what color is the wood?

- Is there a pre-determined focal point within the room (such as a fireplace or an amazing view)?

- Are there enough electrical outlets?

- What items will be staying (such as furnishings, an area rug, accessories, lamps, etc. that your client already has and loves and wishes to keep in the room)?

- Where would the largest piece of furniture go within the room?

- How much wall space is there for artwork, mirrors, etc.?

After you have found out all of the information above, both you and your client will have a better idea of what is wanted moving forward and you will be in a much better position to go away and draw up a decorating plan which can be reviewed by your client the next time you get together. Before you leave, determine a date that will work for both you and your client to get together to go over the decorating plan and proposed budget and make sure you write down the details in your day timer.

6.5   Preparing for your Follow-up Meeting

There are a few things you will need to prepare before meeting with your client the next time including:

1.   Preparing a decorating plan

2.   Preparing a project budget

3.   Preparing your form of contract

6.5.1   Prepare a Decorating Plan

After meeting with your client(s) and discussing and determining their wants and needs, the next step is to prepare a decorating plan for the decorating project. Ideally, at your second consultation, you will have compiled relevant information such as the measurements/dimensions of each room to be decorated, where the doors and window are located, measurements of pieces of furniture that will be staying, color and fabric preferences, etc.

After you have compiled all of the information, then it is ideal to map out a decorating plan and include: (1) a floor plan, (2) a written proposal, and (3) a design board (covered in the next section).

> **TIP:**   Some decorators find it beneficial to prepare a second, less expensive, decorating plan to show their clients, so their clients have alternatives to choose from.

Prepare a Floor Plan

After you have obtained all of the measurements and dimensions of the room and pieces staying within the room, you will then be able to draw a floor plan (see detailed information for drawing a floor plan earlier in this guide). It is ideal to draw the floor plan at a scale of 1/24, which would equate to 1/2" (drawing) for each one foot (within the room). You can either draw the floor plan on graph paper or use a scale ruler and draw it on white paper.

On the floor plan, you will want to show the measurements of the room, and where any doors, windows, fixtures (including fireplaces) or openings are. Additionally, you should draw in the furnishings (including both furnishings that are staying and furnishings to be bought), plants, etc. to give your client something to look at to visualize the desired result for the room.

Prepare a Written Proposal

In addition to having a floor plan and design board, it is also useful to prepare a written proposal that sets out in writing what you plan to do within the room (some of these items can be visualized in the floor plan or on the design board, however, others need to be specifically mentioned to get the full plan across to your client). The written proposal could be as simple as the one shown on the following page (or you can make it more elaborate if you like).

6.5.2   How to Prepare a Design Board

A design board, also known as a presentation board, is a board onto which you have pasted pictures and samples of materials to show clients what you recommend for a decorating project. You will prepare a separate design board for each room you decorate.

If you attend a decorating program at an educational institution, they will likely teach you how to make design boards. If you are a self-taught decorator, you can create your own design boards using a format that looks good to you.

What to Put on the Boards

Once you have decided on the color scheme and materials you would like to propose to the client, gather the following items for your board:

Materials

These are samples of all the materials you intend to use in the room, including samples of: upholstery and drapery fabrics, wallpaper, carpet, flooring, paint chips, etc. You can get samples of these materials from suppliers such as showrooms or home hardware stores.

TIP: Section 3.1, *Tools of the Trade,* has helpful suggestions on where to get samples.

Room Elements

These are pictures of the different elements you are proposing for the room, including: furniture, lights, window coverings, accessories, etc. You can take photos of any existing items the client wants to use. To illustrate new items, you can either draw them to scale, or cut pictures out of magazines. Use a ruler and an X-ACTO Knife (available at any office supply store) to cut out pictures. Avoid using scissors because it is extremely difficult to make cuts that are completely straight with scissors.

Sample Proposal to Decorate Living Room

- Repair crack in wall

- Have new accent light fixture installed over fireplace

- Paint wall camel color (paint chip No. 3753 as shown on design board)

- Add crown molding 6" wide

- Replace area rug with one in taupe, camel, gold and black

- Rearrange furniture and make fireplace the focal point

- Remove oversized chair

- Add extra seating area (purchase two occasional chairs in gold tones and occasional table)

- Purchase additional floor lamp or table lamp

- Have five cushions made (two in gold, two in black and one small gold/red cushion with fabric shown on design board)

- Purchase accessories (such as candle holders, candles, vase and artwork); pick up gold and black tones with a hint of red

- Change window coverings (make drapes with fabric shown on design board)

- Add plants and flowers (where appropriate)

Making the Boards

You will be putting your samples onto picture matting or heavy poster board, which you can buy from an art supply store. (Check the Yellow Pages.) Your board can be white, black, or another color that you feel looks best with your samples. The size can be 14″ x 17″, 15″ x 20″, or any size that allows you to effectively display the materials.

You can arrange the samples on a board in a way that looks most attractive to you. While you can use glue to attach your samples, using double-sided tape can help you avoid any bumps caused by glue. To give your pictures the appearance of depth, you could mount them on foam core before attaching them to the board.

There is no single way to produce design boards. The finished boards will be a reflection of your personal creativity and decorating skills. You will show the design boards to the client for their approval, and make any adjustments based on their feedback.

The color section of this book has a sample design board showing decorating materials for several different rooms. That design board has labels indicating what materials would be used in each area (see sample below). You can decide how much detail to include on your own labels. For your own design boards you may wish to create labels that simply indicate beside each material what it will be used for (e.g. flooring, wall color, etc.).

Sample Design Board Label

LOUNGE	
Furniture Fabrics by Kravet: • Pattern 18764 Colour 9 • Pattern 16815 Colour 4 **Window Treatments by Kravet:** • Pattern 20244 Colour 324 • Pattern 8486 Colour 909	**Wall Colour by C2 of Walls Alive:** • #3079 Kazoo • Faux Finish (base Kazoo) • #1329 Hot Tamale & #4080 Wasabi **Counter Top for Eating Bar:** • Arborite #P-971 CA Renoir de nice

6.5.3 Prepare a Project Budget

The next step is to prepare a detailed project budget. The project budget will break down the costs for:

- all furnishings, accessories and materials

- any contractors fees

- any installation or delivery charges

- your fee

This budget will not only be helpful for your client so that they can see a breakdown of the costs to implement the decorating plan, but it will also be a useful tool for you to use while implementing the plan.

To prepare a realistic budget you will need to be familiar with the cost of different repairs, contractors' fees, decorating items such as paint, wallpaper, and window coverings, furnishings, artwork, accessories, etc. If you don't have prior experience and/or knowledge of the cost of various items or services in your local area, you will need to do some research. Ways to research costs include: meeting with contractors; visiting home improvement stores, showrooms, and furniture stores; and reviewing catalogs.

Talk with Contractors

As mentioned in section 5.5.1, you can find contractors through recommendations or the Yellow Pages. Phone or meet with at least a couple of each type of contractor to find out how much they charge for the services you will need. Let them know that you have a decorating business and would like to talk with them about their services and fees with the possibility of hiring them for future decorating projects.

Visit Home Improvement Stores

Another way to perform research about costs is to go to your local home improvement store such as Home Depot, Lowe's, Rona (previously Revy) or Home Hardware in Canada, Homebase or B&Q in the U.K. Plan to visit at a slow time, such as the middle of the day on a Wednesday (weekday mornings and any time on weekends are bad times to do research because these are often their busiest times).

Spend some time talking to the salespeople in the various departments and pick up as many brochures, pamphlets and pricing booklets or other information that you can. You can find out information about pricing for flooring, wall treatments, window coverings, cabinets, countertops, wood products, lighting and a number of other areas all in one visit. Additionally, ask about delivery charges while you are there.

While you are at the home improvement store, also take the time to find out if they offer discounts to tradespeople. Many stores do offer a minimal discount (between five percent and 10 percent on certain items) to professional contractors; however, sometimes they will extend this to interior decorators. You might need to bring in your business license and a business card and register with the store but it will pay off in the end with savings on future purchases.

Visit Showrooms

A great way to perform research and to find out costs of various room elements is to visit some of the many showrooms for lighting, flooring (including carpeting), window coverings, kitchens and bathrooms, etc. You can find these showrooms by looking in your Yellow Pages. For example, if you wish to visit a lighting showroom, look under "Lighting Fixtures" in your Yellow Pages.

Again, make a plan to visit at a slow time of day so that you can get the salesperson's full attention. Remember to pick up catalogs and pricing information. Also find out whether most products are kept in store or whether they will have to be ordered in, and, if so, what the timing is to get in the different products. And find out about any installation and delivery costs. Additionally, don't forget to ask about what types of discounts they provide to interior decorators and find out how to register to get discounts.

Besides showrooms that are open to the general public, if you live in a large city, you may also have access to wholesale distributor showrooms, factory showrooms/outlets, and wholesale design centers. See section 5.5.4 of this guide to find out how you can get into these types of showrooms and to learn more information about getting decorator discounts.

Visit Furniture Stores

Familiarize yourself with as many furniture stores as you can in your area, including everything from fine furniture stores (such as Ethan Allen) to more casual stores (such as Ikea and Pottery Barn) to small boutique furniture stores and even check out any consignment furniture stores that carry quality furniture.

Pick up catalogs, brochures and pricing lists and get familiar with what each place has "in store." However, don't forget to ask about what additional furniture lines they can order in and make sure to look over the in-store catalogs. Most stores only carry a small fraction of items that can be ordered in because of their limitation of floor space.

Make sure you ask about fabric choices, delivery charges and how long it takes to order in certain furniture lines. Additionally, find out what discount is available to interior decorators and find out how to register to obtain that discount when you shop at the furniture store in the future. After visiting your local furniture stores, you will have a good idea of what stores carry (or can get in) and the types of prices (and discounts available) for various furnishings.

Although most fine furniture stores will offer discounts to interior decorators, not all furniture stores will. Additionally, most stores that do offer discounts will not give any further discount on clearance or already marked down items.

As mentioned previously, if you live in a large city, you may also have access to wholesale distributor showrooms, factory showrooms/outlets, and wholesale design centers where you will be able to get a much greater discount (up to as much as 50 percent off of furnishings) and it will make more sense to shop at these wholesale places than at retail furniture stores for furnishings.

If there are any furniture manufacturers in your area, you might want to contact them or visit them in person to obtain catalogs and price lists. Establishing a relationship with manufacturers in your area will help you to stay on top of their new product lines, styles and fabrics and current prices. Find these in the Yellow Pages under: Furniture Designers Wholesale and Furniture Dealers & Custom Builders.

Another way to obtain prices during the budget process once you're established is to fax a simple Request for Quote (RFQ) to suppliers. Most suppliers will be happy to give you a quote once they are familiar with you and your business. You should send an RFQ to at least 3 suppliers (if you can find that many that carry the products you're looking for) before finalizing a budget. See section 5.5.4 of this guide to learn where you can find wholesale outlets and how you can register at them to get decorator discounts.

Review Catalogs

Another way to obtain pricing information is to get mail-order catalogs sent to you. You can obtain these from a number of different companies that sell a variety of home items such as furnishings, accessories, window coverings, bedding, etc. Although some companies charge a nominal fee, most of the companies offer their catalogs for free. Some of the companies you may wish to order a catalog from are:

- *Crate & Barrel*
  Phone 1-800-967-6696 or visit **www.crateandbarrel.com**

- *Ethan Allen*
  This catalog costs $25.00. Phone 1-888-324-3571 or visit **www.ethanallen.com**

- *Ikea*
  www.ikea.com

- *Laura Ashley*
  Phone (803) 396-7744 or visit **www.lauraashley-usa.com**

- *Pottery Barn*
  Phone 1-888-779-5176 or visit **www.potterybarn.com**

- *Sears*
  Phone 1-800-366-3125 to order a specific "Showcase" catalog or visit **www.sears.com** to order the general catalog

- *Spiegel*

  Although Spiegel offers fashion, jewelry, electronics, etc., they have a wonderful selection of items for the home. There are two catalogs that might be of interest to U.S. residents. The first is a free online catalog titled "Home." The second is the "Big Book" that lists all items currently available and costs $5. Phone 1-800-345-4500 or visit **www.spiegel.com**

Make sure you find out the delivery times and costs from any company you plan to do future phone-in/mail-in orders with. Additionally, when contacting the companies to obtain a catalog, ask if they offer discounts to interior decorators (many don't).

As mentioned, it will be beneficial to have completed some research prior to even taking on your first decorating project so that once you do start decorating, you will have a broader knowledge of the places you can go to get things, the anticipated costs (including any delivery and/ or set-up charges), any discounts you will be eligible to receive and the anticipated time to get certain products ordered in.

It is suggested that you put together an expandable file folder with separate folders or covered plastic storage box (for storing larger catalogs) for each type of store, service and product. Include in the particular folder any catalogs and pricing information, any discount information, and anything else that might be helpful to you for preparing a budget when you do decide to use a certain store or service. The pricing information that you obtain from your research will be invaluable in helping you prepare a specific budget for the project to be completed.

After you have finished your budget research, take the time to develop a budget for the project on hand. First make note of any items to be purchased, any renovations or repairs to be undertaken, and anything else that may have a cost or price tag associated with it. After that, take the time to budget what each item will cost.

On the next few pages you will find a sample all-inclusive budget form. This form sets out numerous items that may be required for a full decorating job of a home. If you are hired to decorate only a specific room, a number of these items would not apply, so feel free to modify the budget form for your individual needs.

Sample Budget Form

Flooring

Carpet	$	Tiler's wages	$
Carpet Installation	$	Area Rugs	$
Wood Floors	$	Linoleum/Vinyl	$
Contractor's Wages	$	Flooring Installation	$
Tile/Stone	$	Miscellaneous	$

Walls and Ceiling (and in between)

Paint	$	Casings/Moldings	$
Painter's Wages	$	Contractor's Wages	$
Wall Coverings	$	New Doors/Knobs	$
Other Wall Treatments	$	Miscellaneous	$

Window Coverings

Drapes	$	Scarves	$
Blinds	$	Valances	$
Shades	$	Curtain Rods/Hardware	$
Shutters	$	Contractor's Wages	$
Window Sconces	$	Miscellaneous	$

Lighting

Light Fixtures	$	Wall Sconces	$
Electrician's Wages	$	Lamp Shades	$
Floor Lamps	$	Switches/Dimmers	$
Table Lamps	$	Miscellaneous	$

Furnishings (and extras, where applicable)

Living Room

Sofa(s)	$	Bench	$
Loveseat(s)	$	Armoire	$
Armchair(s)	$	Settee	$
Occasional Chair(s)	$	Chaise Lounge	$
Ottoman	$	Wall Shelving	$
Cocktail Table	$	Bookshelves	$
End Table(s)	$	Piano	$
Sofa Table	$	Chest	$
Games Table	$	Footstool	$
Occasional Table(s)	$	Miscellaneous	$
Consul Table	$		

Family Room

Sofa(s)	$	Occasional Table(s)	$
Loveseat(s)	$	Armoire	$
Large Chair(s)	$	Entertainment Center	$
Occasional Chair(s)	$	Stereo Stand	$
Ottoman	$	Games Table	$
Cocktail Table	$	Wall Shelving	$
End Table(s)	$	Bookshelves	$
Sofa Table	$	Miscellaneous	$

Games Room

Sofa(s)	$	Games Table	$
Loveseat(s)	$	Pool Table	$
Large Chair(s)	$	Bar	$
Occasional Chair(s)	$	Bar Stools	$
End Table(s)	$	Miscellaneous	$
Occasional Table(s)	$		

Kitchen				
Kitchen Table	$		Island	$
Kitchen Chairs	$		Cupboards	$
China Cabinet	$		Countertops	$
Buffet/Hutch	$		Appliances	$
Bar Stools	$		Hanging Pot Racks	$
Phone Table/Desk	$		Miscellaneous	$
Bedroom(s)				
Bed Frame	$		Armchairs	$
Mattress/Boxspring	$		Occasional Table(s)	$
Headboard	$		Occasional Chair(s)	$
Footboard	$		Ottoman	$
Bedside Tables	$		Chest	$
Dresser	$		Vanity	$
Wardrobe	$		Crib	$
Armoire	$		Change Table	$
Chest of Drawers	$		Rocking Chair	$
Bench	$		Shelving/Book Cases	$
Settee	$		Desk	$
Chaise Lounge	$		Toy Chest	$
Sofa	$		Miscellaneous	$
Loveseat	$			
Dining Room				
Dining Room Table	$		Buffet/Hutch	$
Dining Room Chairs	$		Consul	$
China Cabinet	$		Miscellaneous	$
Home Office				
Desk	$		Bookshelves	$
Office Chair	$		Filing Cabinet(s)	$

Armchairs	$	Printer Stand	$
Sofa	$	Occasional Table(s)	$
Loveseat	$	Occasional Chair(s)	$
Coffee Table	$	Storage Cabinets	$
Library Table	$	Miscellaneous	$
Bathroom(s)			
Vanity	$	Sink(s)	$
Chair	$	Bathtub/Shower	$
Cupboards	$	Toilet	$
Countertop	$	Miscellaneous	$
Miscellaneous			
Storage Units	$	Exercise Equipment	$
Accessories			
Cushions/Pillows	$	Mirror(s)	$
Plants	$	Throw Blankets	$
Artwork	$	Sculptures	$
Wall Hangings	$	Unique Pieces	$
Decorative Sconces	$	Clocks	$
Vases	$	Decorative Boxes	$
Silk Flowers	$	Screens	$
Candleholders	$	Miscellaneous	$
Candles	$		

Miscellaneous			
Decorator's Fees	$	Cording/Tassels	$
Plumber	$	Bedding	$
Heating Contractor	$	Delivery Charges	$
Re-upholstering	$	Setup Charges	$
Slip Covers	$	Miscellaneous	$
Fabric	$		

6.5.4   Prepare a Contract

The next step is to prepare a contract to present to your client at your next meeting. The contract is a document specifying your fees and the services you will provide. It helps avoid misunderstandings, and can protect you and help you get paid if the client later changes their mind. Your contract can include the following:

- Your name and company name
- The client's name
- Description of the services being provided
- When the decorating services are to be performed
- Fees, including payment terms, deposits, and reimbursement of expenses
- Cancellation policy
- Signature lines for you and the client

This section includes two sample contracts. The first is a sample "engagement letter" you might use with an individual client such as homeowner. You could ask your clients to sign it at your initial meeting, or have them return it to you later.

The second is a services agreement which you could adapt for use with a corporate client. It covers a number of additional areas, such as a product/service liability disclaimer so that you won't be held responsible for defects in items you buy or services you subcontract for your clients. After both originals are signed, you can keep one for your records and give one to your client for their records.

While you will want to design your own form of contract or have an attorney draft one for you, these samples can get you started. You can adapt these contracts to fit your needs. Before using any contract, make sure you have it reviewed by your lawyer.

Sample Engagement Letter

(On Your Letterhead)

[Insert name of Client]
[Insert address of Client]

[Date]

Dear *[Name of client]*,

As promised, I have set out below a description of the services that *[your name/company]* will provide to you.

I will provide the following services:

[Insert description of the services, such as consultations with the client, arranging for contractors, shopping for furnishings, etc.]

My fee for the services performed will be as follows:

[Insert rates, amount of deposit, etc.]

If you agree that the foregoing fairly sets out your understanding of our agreement, please sign a copy of this letter in the space indicated below, and return it to me at *[insert address, fax number or email address]*.

Yours sincerely,

[Name]

Agreed and Accepted:

_____

[Insert name of client]

_____

Date

Standard Services Agreement

THIS AGREEMENT is made this *[date]* day of *[month]*, 20__.

BETWEEN
[insert name of your client] (the "Client"); and *[insert your name or your company's name]* (the "Interior Decorator"), collectively referred to as the "Parties."

1.1 Services

The Interior Decorator shall provide the following services ("Services") to the Client in accordance with the terms and conditions of this Agreement: *[Insert the name of the decorating package, if applicable, and describe the services you are to provide].*

1.2 Delivery of the Services

The Interior Decorator shall provide the Services at the following site(s): *[insert details here].*

The Interior Decorator agrees to provide the following Services at the specific dates set out below: *[insert dates here]*

EXAMPLE: Client Consultation July 12, 2011 to measure and assess space; Follow-up Client Consultation July 17, 2011 to present the decorating plan; etc.

1.3 Fees

As consideration for the provision of the Services by the Interior Decorator, the fees for the provision of the Services ("Fees") is *[insert fees here].*

EXAMPLE:

Package (# or name)	$_____
Initial consultation	Free
Second client consultation (including preparing design board and drawing plans)	$150.00
Subsequent consultations	$_____/hour

Arranging contractors $75.00/contractor

Shopping for products/furnishings, etc. $_____/hour

Total: $_____

1.4 Payment

The Client agrees to pay the Fees to the Interior Decorator on the following dates: *[insert details here]*.

EXAMPLE:

$150.00 for preparation of decorating plan due: ___/___/___

25% deposit on decorating project total due: ___/___/___

50% of outstanding balance due: ___/___/___

Remainder of outstanding balance due: ___/___/___

Reimbursement of expenses for products paid for by Interior Decorator due within seven days of purchase

Any charges payable under this Agreement are exclusive of any applicable taxes, duties, or other fees charged by a government body and such shall be payable by the Client to the Interior Decorator in addition to all other charges payable hereunder.

1.5 Warranty and Limitation of Liability

The Interior Decorator represents and warrants that [she/it] will perform the Services with reasonable skill and care.

Subject to the Client's obligation to pay the Fees to the Interior Decorator, either Party's liability arising directly out of its obligations under this Agreement and every applicable part of it shall be limited in aggregate to the Fees. The Interior Decorator assumes no liability due to the quality of items or services purchased for the Client.

1.6 Term and Termination

This Agreement shall be effective on the date hereof and shall continue until the completion date stated in section 1.2 unless terminated sooner. If the Client terminates this agreement for any reason before the scheduled completion date, the Client will reimburse the Interior Decorator for all outstanding fees and out-of-pocket expenses.

1.7 Miscellaneous

Neither Party will disclose any information of the other which comes into their possession under or in relation to this Agreement and which is of a confidential nature.

The failure of either Party to enforce its rights under this Agreement at any time for any period shall not be construed as a waiver of such rights.

If any part, term or provision of this Agreement is held to be illegal or unenforceable neither the validity or enforceability of the remainder of this Agreement shall be affected.

This Agreement constitutes the entire understanding between the Parties and supersedes all prior representations, negotiations or understandings.

Neither Party shall be liable for failure to perform any obligation under this Agreement if the failure is caused by any circumstances beyond its reasonable control, including but not limited to acts of god, war, or industrial dispute.

This Agreement shall be governed by the laws of the jurisdiction in which the Interior Decorator is located.

Agreed by the Parties hereto:

SIGNED by: _____

on behalf of: _____
                [the Client]

SIGNED by: _____

on behalf of: _____
                [the Interior Decorator]

6.6   Meeting to Present the Decorating Plan

At your follow-up meeting with your client, your purpose will be to: (1) present the decorating plan; (2) get approval for the plan; (3) get approval of the project budget; (4) discuss the suggested work schedule; and (5) finalize contract and payment arrangements.

However, don't forget to continue to build rapport with your client. After all, the better your relationship is with your client, the more likely they will be open with you and the more likely they will be happy with the end result (which may help to get repeat business). The items you should bring to this follow-up meeting are:

- Floor Plan(s)

- Design Board(s)

- Written Proposal(s)

- Suggested Work Schedule

- Project Budget

- Contract (2 originals)

After you have prepared the decorating plan, budget and contract, put the room plan(s), written proposal(s) and budget into an attractive two-pocket folder, along with your business card, a brief cover letter, a suggested work schedule, and two original copies of your contract for your client to sign.

Present the Decorating Plan

At this meeting, you should start by reviewing the decorating plan. Have some additional ideas in mind in case your client is looking for a less expensive option or different ideas for decorating. As mentioned previously, when you present the plan, it is ideal to have a written description of what you propose to do and also a draft or preliminary drawing (a floor plan) of what you propose together with a design board to help your client "visualize" the proposed plan even better.

If you have drawn up two alternative plans, you can discuss the various pros and cons of each option and let your client know that either option is open to variance as well. At this stage, your client might decide to go with a plan you have proposed or may decide to go with part of one plan and part of another and throw in some of their own ideas.

Get Approval for the Decorating Plan

Ideally, it would be best to get approval of one plan so that you can start the decorating process. However, if the plan you have proposed is not exactly what your client wants, take the written proposal and cross off any items that your client doesn't want and insert any additional items and/or changes and then have your client initial this (the reason to do this is to "formalize" the plan).

Get Approval for the Project Budget

At this meeting, you will also want to present your client with the project budget and have them review it to ensure that both of you are on the same wavelength. It might be necessary to revise some items and you may find that your client decides that the old sofa they had and were planning on giving away, ends up staying as part of the plan so that they have additional funds for other items.

Once again, take the budget you have prepared and cross off anything that will not be included and add any additional items or revise amounts until you come up with a budget that will work for your client. After the meeting with your client, type up any changes to the budget and then provide a revised copy to your client the next time you see them.

Discuss Suggested Work Schedule

The next item of business to discuss with your client is the suggested work schedule. You will want to do this for a couple of reasons. First, you will want to make sure the timing is acceptable to your client. Second you will want to have a schedule that you can work from to keep you organized with contractors, furniture companies (for deliveries), etc. A work schedule may look something like the following:

Monday, July 7   Contractor in to repair crack in ceiling

Wednesday, July 9   Painter in to prime family room

Thursday, July 10	Painter in to paint family room (1st coat)
Friday, July 11	Painter in to paint family room (2nd coat)
Saturday, July 12	Crown moldings installed
Monday, July 14	Crown moldings touched up/painted
Tuesday, July 15	New light fixture installed in family room
Wednesday, July 16	Carpet installed in family room
Friday, July 18	Area rug delivered and placed
Monday, July 21	New furniture delivered and placed
Tuesday, July 22	Lamps and accessories placed
Wednesday, July 23	Artwork and mirrors hung
Thursday, July 24	Open date to finalize any decorating

Once you have made a decorating plan and your client has agreed to it, you will need to know where to start and have a systematic approach in place so that your client's home is not turned upside down and is still livable throughout the decorating process. The approach may be to decorate one room at a time until it is complete. There should also be a budget in place for each particular room (this can be broken down from the master budget provided earlier).

Most likely your client will have determined which room they want decorated first and which room is to be decorated second and so on. However, if your client needs some assistance with prioritizing the work to be completed, you can ask them a few basic questions to help them set their priorities. Some of the questions you could ask are:

- Is there an immediate need for a transformation in any of the rooms to be decorated? For example, are you expecting company in the next little while and need one of the current rooms transformed into a guestroom? Or, have you decided to run a business from home and need a home based office set up?

- Are there any cracks or leaks or problems and/or other repairs that need to be done sooner than later?

- Which room do you spend most of your waking hours living in?

- Is there a particular room that you want to have decorated first that will include your most precious belongings?

- If you could only decorate one room, which one would you choose to decorate?

After you get some answers to the above questions, you will be in a better position to help your client set priorities and determine where to begin.

Finalize Contract and Payment Arrangements

At this follow-up meeting, this is an ideal time to present your full contract for signature by your client and to collect a retainer for anticipated services to be performed. For example, your client may choose to go with one plan drawn up that you propose will take up to 40 hours of your time to complete.

If you decide to charge a per hour fee of $50.00 for an anticipated total fee of up to $2,000 (not including any disbursements), you may decide to collect 25 percent of this up front (or $500) and another $500 after 15 hours of work has been completed, and so on, to ensure that you do indeed get paid for your time and services.

Additionally, if any new furniture or accessories are being purchased, you will need to clarify how these will be paid for. For example, will these items be paid for by the client directly – possibly with you in attendance so that the client can get a discounted price for such items – or will you be expected to pay for these up front with your client to reimburse you as you go along? These are important points that need to be discussed up front and having a contract in place (with these points covered) is vital to ensure that there are no misunderstandings as to fees, expectations and also to ensure that your legal rights are protected.

As mentioned previously, you should have two originals of your contract and you and your client should sign both originals and one original should be left with your client for their records and you should keep one original for your records.

After finalizing the above plans with your client, you can now start decorating. Refer to Chapter 3 of this guide for step-by-step decorating instructions. As you get into decorating each room, you may find that the plan needs to be revised slightly or that the budget may need some adjusting (for example, if you can't find the "right" area rug for the room in the price budgeted). If this is the case, you will need to keep your client informed of any changes and obtain their approval to continue on with the revised plan and budget.

7. Conclusion

You have almost reached the end of the *FabJob Guide to Become an Interior Decorator*. Hopefully, you are just as excited about this career as you were before reading this guide—but now you have the tools and resources you need to get started and succeed at this fabulous job.

On the next page you will find some words of inspiration from Debbie Travis to keep in mind as you embark on your new career.

Debbie's Advice for New Decorators

Debbie Travis has helped millions of people create more beautiful homes. Her popular TV show, *Debbie Travis' Painted House*, is seen in over 50 countries by several million viewers a week. Her books include *Debbie Travis' Painted House, Debbie Travis' Decorating Solutions, Debbie Travis' Weekend Projects*, and *Debbie Travis' Painted House Living and Dining Rooms*. Her website, located at **www.painted-house.com**, is one of the busiest in the country.

"Interior decorating is a fab job because you are being creative and making people happy. Someone's going to be living around what you've created for a long time. As an interior decorator you also have to be a marriage counselor and a psychiatrist.

Sometimes what people like is not what they say they like. An interior decorator's job is to understand what someone really wants. Bring loads of magazines when you meet with a client. If someone says they like Modern, but keeps showing you pictures of Country, maybe they want a combination of the two styles.

There are so many ways to find inspiration – magazines, books, websites – a homeowner doesn't have time to wade through all the information. Your job is to help them whittle down the choices. There are many decisions, right down to the light switch. Your job is to make it easier.

Learn as much as you can. Watch shows, read magazines and books, take night courses in interior design, go everywhere they have design shows.

Get as much experience as you can. Offer your services – even if free – to friends, family, anyone who'll have you in their home! If someone's asking you about a new color scheme, try it on your own bathroom. The more you do, the better you'll get. And more than any other career, you'll learn from your mistakes.

A passionate person will always do better than someone who's just doing a job."

More Guides to Build Your Business

Increase your income by offering additional services. Here are some recommended FabJob guides to help you build your business:

Get Paid to Stage Homes for Sale!

Imagine having a creative, high-paying career that lets you use your flair for decorating to help people sell home. In the **FabJob Guide to Become a Home Stager** you will discover:

- The most effective home staging techniques to help sell a home more quickly or sell for a higher price (includes tips for every room)

- Potential trouble spots that can keep a home from selling, plus low-cost quick fixes for flaws

- How to create 'curb appeal' with attractive home exteriors

- How to start a home staging business, price your services, and attract clients

Get Paid to Organize!

Imagine having a rewarding career using your creativity to help people, homes and offices get organized. The **FabJob Guide to Become a Professional Organizer** shows you:

- A room-by-room guide to home organizing and reducing clutter (with proven systems to decide if something is treasure, toy, tool or trash)

- How to organize businesses including managing workflow, filing systems, and space planning

- Personal organization and time management tips for yourself and your clients

- How to start a professional organizing business, set your prices, and attract customers

Visit www.FabJob.com to order guides today!

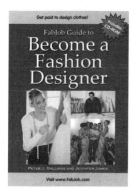